The Dynamics
of Performance Management

Public Management and Change Series

Beryl A. Radin, Series Editor

Editorial Board

Titles in the Series

Challenging the Performance Movement: Accountability, Complexity, and Democratic Values
BERYL A. RADIN

Charitable Choice at Work: Evaluating Faith-Based Job Programs in the States
SHEILA SUESS KENNEDY AND WOLFGANG BIELEFELD

The Dynamics of Performance Management: Constructing Information and Reform
DONALD P. MOYNIHAN

The Greening of the U.S. Military: Environmental Policy, National Security, and Organizational Change
ROBERT F. DURANT

How Management Matters: Street-Level Bureaucrats and Welfare Reform
NORMA M. RICCUCCI

Managing within Networks: Adding Value to Public Organizations
ROBERT AGRANOFF

Measuring the Performance of the Hollow State
DAVID G. FREDERICKSON AND H. GEORGE FREDERICKSON

Public Values and Public Interest: Counterbalancing Economic Individualism
BARRY BOZEMAN

Revisiting Waldo's Administrative State: Constancy and Change in Public Administration
DAVID H. ROSENBLOOM AND HOWARD E. MCCURDY

The Dynamics of Performance Management

Constructing Information and Reform

DONALD P. MOYNIHAN

Georgetown University Press / Washington, D.C.

HF
5549
.M69
2008

Georgetown University Press, Washington, D.C.
www.press.georgetown.edu
© 2008 by Georgetown University Press. All rights reserved. No part of this book
may be reproduced or utilized in any form or by any means, electronic or mechanical,
including photocopying and recording, or by any information storage and retrieval
system, without permission in writing from the publisher.

Library of Congress Cataloging-in-Publication Data

Moynihan, Donald P.
    The dynamics of performance management : constructing information and reform
/ Donald P. Moynihan.
        p. cm. — (Public management and change series)
    Includes bibliographical references and index.
    ISBN 978-1-58901-194-6 (alk. paper)
    1. Performance—Management.   2. Organizational effectiveness.   3. Administrative
agencies—United States—Management.   I. Title.
    HF5549.M69 2008
    352.6'6—dc22

                                                                    2007020696

♾ This book is printed on acid-free paper meeting the requirements of the American
National Standard for Permanence in Paper for Printed Library Materials.

15 14 13 12 11 10   9 8 7 6 5 4 3 2
Second Printing

Printed in the United States of America

Dedicated to my parents,

Donie and Joan Moynihan

Contents

List of Illustrations   ix
Acknowledgments   xi
Acronyms   xiii

Introduction   1

1   An Era of Governance by Performance Management   3

2   Performance Management as Doctrine   26

3   The Partial Adoption of Performance Management Reforms in State Government   39

4   Explaining the Partial Adoption of Performance Management Reforms   58

5   Explaining the Implementation of Performance Management Reforms   75

6   The Interactive Dialogue Model of Performance Information Use   95

7   Performance Management under George W. Bush   118

8   PART and the Interactive Dialogue Model   139

9   Dialogue Routines and Learning Forums   163

10   Rethinking Performance Management   189

Appendix A: Interview Protocol for State Interviews   211
Appendix B: State Backgrounds—Political Culture, Budgeting Practices, Performance Management History, and Corrections Policies   214
Appendix C: Program Assessment Rating Tool   221
Bibliography   225
Index   241

Illustrations

TABLES

1.1 Government Performance Grades for Managing for Results and Information Category · 13

1.2 Data Sources · 21

2.1 The Doctrinal Benefits Claimed by Performance Management · 36

3.1 Performance Management Legislation in the States · 40

3.2 Focus on Performance Information: Range of Documented Performance Data · 41

3.3 Degree of Managerial Control of Specific HR Functions · 44

3.4 Promised Benefits of Performance Management Compared with Case Findings · 53

5.1 Unexpected Instrumental Benefits of Performance Management · 81

7.1 Aligning Strategic Goals with Resources — NASA's FY06 Budget Request · 121

9.1 Case Characteristics and Outcomes · 169

BOXES

2.1 Government Performance and Results Act, Section 2 · 28

3.1 Agency Discretion in Procurement/Contracting in Fifty States · 43

7.1 Congressional Reactions to OMB's Budget and Performance Integration Efforts · 123

8.1 Arguing about Performance Information: Rationales Used in Disagreeing with PART · 153

9.1 Elements of Learning Forums · 179

10.1 Ten Ways to Rethink Performance Management · 190

10.2 Characteristics More Important Than Performance Management · 202

FIGURES

1.1 Integrating Planning, Measurement, and Decision Venues · 6

2.1 How Managerial Authority and Focus on Results Create Different Management Systems · 33

Acknowledgments

The ideas behind this book have evolved over the last ten years, from when I began to work on performance management issues as a graduate student at the Maxwell School of Citizenship and Public Affairs at Syracuse University. Throughout this period I owe the greatest debt to Patricia Ingraham. She pushed my attention to performance management and provided exceptionally insightful advice as my work developed. She has proven a kind and sage mentor. More broadly, I owe a debt to other Maxwell School faculty willing to advise me on my studies of performance management as a graduate student, especially Alasdair Roberts, Stu Bretschneider, Jeff Straussman, Allan Mazur, Scott Allard, and Jodi Sandfort.

I have been fortunate to have worked with some excellent graduate students at the Bush School at Texas A&M and the La Follette School of Public Affairs at the University of Wisconsin-Madison. Their lively debates about the meaning of performance measures helped me to understand the socially constructed nature of performance information. I am also grateful to the many public servants I interviewed at the state and federal level in researching this book. While many of them defined performance in different terms, I was impressed by their desire to succeed, often despite a context of limited resources and difficult tasks.

I would like to thank Bob Durant and other members of the selection committee of the American Political Science Association's Paul A. Volcker Endowment. The endowment supports the work of young public administration scholars and provided funding to support my research on the use of performance information by federal government officials.

My intellectual debts are too numerous to mention and demonstrated by an extensive reference list. I owe a great deal to my fellow PhD students at the Maxwell School and colleagues at Texas A&M and the University of Wisconsin-Madison for providing a lively intellectual atmosphere and for helping my understanding of performance management to develop (though they may not have realized it at the time). I have been lucky to have had excellent research and administrative support from Steve Murello, Sara Pearce, and Nick Sayen in the preparation of this book.

Gail Grella, acquisitions editor for Georgetown University Press, has been a model of patient and steady support for this book. Beryl Radin's expertise in performance management made her the ideal series editor for this topic. Both with this book and with my previous work, she has always pushed me to make a clear contribution to the literature of performance management. Along with two anonymous reviewers, Beryl offered a series of insightful comments that immeasurably helped me develop my manuscript. Others have been willing to generously give their time to read chapters or discuss my ideas. In particular, I thank Roy Meyers, Phil Joyce, John Halligan, H. George Frederickson, Jonathan Bruel, Kathe Callahan, and Clint Brass.

The help of many people was essential in writing this book, but any errors are the responsibility of the author. Finally, I would like to thank my wife, Pamela Herd, for her unwavering support and encouragement.

Acronyms

DOC	Department of Corrections
GAO	Government Accountability Office
GPP	Government Performance Project
GPRA	Government Performance and Results Act
HR	Human Resource
NASA	National Aeronautics and Space Administration
NPM	New Public Management
OLM	Organizational Learning Mechanisms
OMB	Office of Management and Budget
PARA	Program Assessment and Results Act
PART	Program Assessment Rating Tool
PMA	President's Management Agenda
SES	Senior Executive Services
ZBB	Zero-Based Budgeting

Introduction

When the National Collegiate Athletic Association selects teams for the annual NCAA men's basketball tournament, some teams automatically qualify for the "dance" if they win their regular season conference tournament, but more than half of the sixty-four-team field depend on invitations from a ten-person committee assigned to evaluate their performances. In 2007 Syracuse University did not make the cut. The decision, at least for Syracuse alumni such as myself, came as something of a shock. The Syracuse coach suggested that the head of the selection committee was crazy. After all, Syracuse had won more than twenty games, usually the basis for an invite to the tournament, and the team was ranked fifth in the Big East conference, which had six teams invited. These seemingly important and straightforward measures of performance, however, were not enough. The selection committee gave greater weight to a statistic that showed that Syracuse had played too many weak teams in their nonconference schedule, although the head of the selection committee conceded that "if you torture the numbers long enough, you can get them to confess to anything."

Another sports example: Political scientists Brian Sala, John Scott, and James F. Spriggs have investigated bias in Olympic figure skating judging between 1948 and 2002. The judges, who represent national sporting bodies, are expected to provide impartial assessments and can be removed if their judgment comes into question. Nevertheless, Sala, Scott, and Spriggs found distinct patterns of bias. Perhaps not surprisingly, judges consistently awarded higher marks to skaters from their own countries relative to other judges. More interestingly, the pattern of bias suggests that judgment was shaped by cold war politics. Judges from NATO and Warsaw Pact nations tended to mark down skaters from countries perceived as enemies. These biases largely disappeared in the post–cold war era, suggesting something of the fluidity of political identity.

The final example is less whimsical in substance. An article by Karen DeYoung in the *Washington Post*, "Iraq War's Statistics Prove Fleeting," notes that performance data on the Iraq war have been repeatedly invoked when it suits the Bush administration but dismissed as misleading or irrelevant on other occasions. For example, the Department of Defense has made a policy of not counting casualties inflicted by American military except when it wishes to emphasize the number of terrorists killed. The report also describes the ways that performance measures, such as the number of trained Iraqi forces, have changed dramatically depending on how the data was created and how individuals were categorized—as "currently operating," "currently training," "on duty," or "on hand."

What do these three examples have to do with rethinking performance management? Cumulatively, they illustrate a central point of this book, which is that performance information is ambiguous and used in ways consistent with the roles of actors. This insight forms the core of what I refer to as an interactive dialogue model of performance information use (see chapter 6) and this approach could be fairly characterized as a social constructivist perspective. This book challenges what appears to be the almost inherent belief we hold in the objectivity of numbers. My arguments derive from having spent the last decade studying how performance information is created, selected, interpreted, and used. Consistent with the proverb about the man with the hammer seeing nails everywhere, once I settled on a social constructivist approach to performance information, I began to see evidence of it all around me. Each of the three examples cited were ones I came across in a single workday, coming, respectively, from the ESPN website, the lead article in the March 2007 issue of *Perspective on Politics,* and my morning perusal of the *Washington Post.*

While the first half of this book narrates the development of performance information systems in the U.S. state and federal governments, the second half deals with the question of how such performance information is used. This book argues that the creation, selection, interpretation, and presentation of performance information is not an automatic or objective process but is influenced by the roles that actors in the political process occupy. The three examples illustrate this point in slightly different ways. The Syracuse case demonstrates that there are multiple pieces of information that tell us something about college basketball performance and that individuals can place more or less weight on this data. In government, there are often many performance measures that tell different stories about whether a program is successful; one piece of performance data is chosen over another depending on the perspective of the user. In this figure skating example, judges are not evaluating different pieces of information—they all see the same performance and then must quantify this performance on the same scale, but they still construct the information consistent with the roles they have adopted. The Iraq war example shows public officials suggesting how data should be interpreted while repeatedly moving the goalposts on what data was worth reporting and how it was created.

The examples also reflect the ubiquity of performance information in modern life, in government, and elsewhere. This book does not suggest dismantling performance information systems, or that performance information can never be used fruitfully, but it does suggest that we can best move forward by understanding the dynamics of performance information use.

1

An Era of Governance
by Performance Management

The beginning of the twenty-first century finds us in an era of governance by performance management. Frederick Mosher charted the history of government in the United States via the management characteristics of each era, portraying the twentieth century as dominated by two phases: government by the efficient (1906–37) and government by managers (the post-1937 era).[1] In recent decades, the concept of performance has become central to public management reform, reflecting a fusion between the key values of both management and efficiency, now more broadly redefined to include effectiveness.[2]

In this era, public managers are asked to justify their actions not just in terms of efficiency but also by the outcomes they produce. They meet performance-reporting mandates, are asked to do more with less, and must explain the performance of their programs. The public sector is expected to be able to demonstrate its value and to constantly seek new ways that foster performance. The most frequent and widely adopted reforms of the past three decades are tied to the concept of performance. Reforms that have incorporated pay-for-performance, total quality management, strategic planning, performance measurement, benchmarking, contracting out, increased managerial flexibility, and decentralization have consistently claimed improved performance as their ultimate goal. The assumption of these reforms is that changes in management systems could and should be made in a way that enhances performance.

The popularity of performance management is reflected in its semantic fertility. In earlier times, progressive reformers spoke simply of performance measurement. Business executives have recommended strategic planning and management-by-objective. State governments have attempted variants of performance budgeting for decades. In addition to these previous monikers, we hear about managing for results, results-based reforms, and entrepreneurial budgeting. The logic common to each approach is that government agencies should produce performance information and use this information to inform decision making. There will doubtless be additional variations that arise, adding a new luster to a core idea that has, at best, a mixed record of success.

This book is about the era of governance by performance management. It describes why and how performance management systems are constructed and examines the assumption that performance information is used to improve public decisions. In doing so, it argues that we need to rethink the purposes and expectations of performance management.

Performance management reform has enjoyed ardent champions who have laid out a doctrine of how this reform shall save government. But it has also had critics who insist that it is, as Radin puts it, a "hydra-headed monster" that reemerges every few years despite a record of dismal failure.[3] This book seeks to rethink performance management by acknowledging its weaknesses and its potential. The overarching theme of this book is that performance management has not worked as expected, but in some cases it has had positive impacts. Knowledge of the environment of agency-level actors and the nature of performance information dialogue is the key to understanding when performance management can succeed. In practice, performance management reform in the United States has been a messy affair. The implementation of performance management reforms has not strictly followed the recipe of reform proponents and has not led to the benefits predicted by reformers. Despite problematic adoption, we still see benefits from performance management, largely occurring within agencies rather than among decisions made by political officials. The book introduces an interactive dialogue model to understand performance information use. This model points to the ambiguity inherent in performance information. As actors with specific roles and interests communicate with one another, performance information will be used to serve those interests. The interactive dialogue model therefore predicts that cross-institutional dialogues will see performance information used for advocacy purposes. In intra-institutional dialogues, however, interests and beliefs are more homogenous, and it is more likely that information engenders learning and problem-solving rather than advocacy and conflict.

The current era of governance by performance management coincides with a period of antibureaucratic impulses. Proponents of performance management say that it is important not just because of improved effectiveness but also because it is necessary for the credibility of public action. Such claims are overstated because public distrust in government is fed in part by scandals and failures that are often political in nature, and controls to prevent such failures may run at odds with a performance approach that liberates managers. However, in a time of public distrust of government, the rhetoric of reform becomes more potent, and the language of results becomes a rare public currency that citizens view as legitimate.

How important are these performance management reforms to the actual management of government? It is only a slight exaggeration to say that we are betting the future of governance on the use of performance information. The current era is also characterized by a willingness to adopt new structural forms of government and controls, such as networks or outsourcing, or to simply provide greater freedom to managers. New structural forms and modes of control raise difficult questions. How do we coordinate? How do we manage? How do we control? How do we exert accountability? How do we improve? How do we engage citizens? Performance information is frequently cited as the answer. We are told that performance information will allow elected officials and policymakers to set goals. It will provide the basis for accountability. It will be tied to incentives. It will allow innovations to be identified and diffused. It will improve the allocation of scarce public resources. It will allow citizens to give feedback on services. The one constant in visions of future government is the availability and smart use of performance information. If performance information does not prove to be the linchpin for the future of governance, we will have to return to the basic questions listed above and find some alternative answers.

Despite the importance of performance information to the future of governance, we have a weak understanding of how and why it is used in practice. Governments have never been so awash in performance data, mostly because bureaucrats are required to collect and report it. The wealth of performance data contrasts with the poverty of the theoretical and empirical justifications for performance-reporting requirements. We have poor theories of performance information use, largely informed by a combination of common sense, some deeply felt assumptions about how government should operate, and a handful of success stories. The operating theory of performance management reform appears to hold that it is an unambiguous benefit to governance, it should be adopted, and it will foster smarter decisions that lead to better governance. The current theory of performance information use might be characterized as "if you build it, they will come." It assumes that the availability and quality of performance data is not just a necessary condition for use but also a sufficient one.

A Reform in Search of a Theory? Defining Performance Management and Performance Budgeting

Given the range of guises that the performance management idea has appeared in, it is helpful to start by explaining how performance management and performance budgeting are defined in this book. I define performance management as a system that generates performance information through strategic planning and performance measurement routines and that connects this information to decision venues, where, ideally, the information influences a range of possible decisions. Figure 1.1

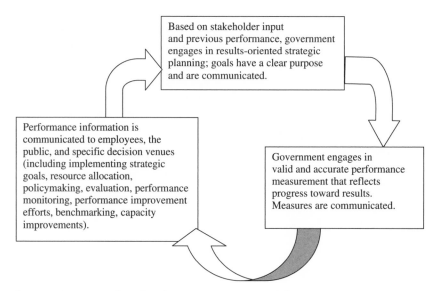

Based on stakeholder input and previous performance, government engages in results-oriented strategic planning; goals have a clear purpose and are communicated.

Performance information is communicated to employees, the public, and specific decision venues (including implementing strategic goals, resource allocation, policymaking, evaluation, performance monitoring, performance improvement efforts, benchmarking, capacity improvements).

Government engages in valid and accurate performance measurement that reflects progress toward results. Measures are communicated.

Figure 1.1   Integrating planning, measurement, and decision venues
Source: Adapted from Ingraham and Moynihan, "Beyond Measurement: Managing for Results in State Government."

represents a simple model of how a performance management system improves governmental decision making and performance.

In this model performance information lifts the focus of managers from inputs and processes to results. Performance management, through its production and dissemination of high-level performance information, promises governmental actors common goals to pursue and an understanding of how present management structures could be adjusted to pursue these goals, improving the ability to make informed decisions about capacity. Performance information is the lifeblood of the performance management model portrayed in figure 1.1. Performance management systems are designed to take information from the environment, through consultation with the public, stakeholders, public representatives, and analyses of the external environment in the strategic planning phase. Because the external environment is so large, public officials need some criterion of relevance to make sense of it.[4] Performance management systems provide a means by which public officials engage in coding—interpreting and refining information from the external environment and internal stakeholders into a series of information categories such as strategic goals, objectives, performance measures, and targets. After this coding takes place, performance information can then be presented to decision makers.[5] Performance information also provides a language for communicating with the external environment, transmitting strategic goals and performance measures via public documentation, speeches, websites, and other means.

Figure 1.1 also points to the linkage between strategic planning and performance measurement, suggesting that effective performance management implies the integrated use of both.[6] Without the linkage, the potential for goal conflict, confusion, and inaccurate measurement arises.[7] Strategic planning without performance measurement fails to link goals to actions or identify implementation issues, failures that generate a lack of credibility among stakeholders.[8] Performance measurement without broader strategic guidance fosters measurement without a sense of overall purpose; a technical exercise undertaken out of habit or administrative compliance, with little practical relevance for decision makers.

What is the purpose of all this activity? One justification for results-based reform is the accountability to the external environment and elected officials.[9] However, public managers report that the more immediate rationale for results-based reform is improved internal decision making and improved public performance.[10] High-quality information, and the ability to communicate it to the right decision-making venue in a useful and timely way, are as necessary to these interim objectives as to the broader accountability purposes.[11] The communication of performance information is intended to act primarily as a stimulus to the decision-making process—provoking, informing, and improving the quality of decisions.[12]

The budget process is perhaps the most visible and important decision venue where performance information can be used. A strict definition of a performance budget is "a budget that explicitly links each increment in resources to an increment in outputs or other results."[13] This strict definition suggests an equally simple theory of how performance budgeting should work. Once politicians decide what level of performance they want and are willing to pay for, they fund accordingly. Programs that fail to perform will lose support relative to the superior claims of higher-performing programs. The budgeting process, in effect, mimics the free market. Agencies compete for resources and chase incentives to increase performance.

This theory of performance budgeting is beguiling in its simplicity and distant from reality. Legislators are loath to link the budget decisions so tightly with any one factor, since it reduces their discretion and would ignore other relevant aspects of public programs. Paul Posner of the Government Accountability Office (GAO) makes this point:

> Performance budgeting is not about a mechanical link between performance trends and budget decisions. If the program does poorly and it is a high priority, it doesn't necessarily mean you are going to reduce funding. In fact, you might find cause to increase funding. If the drug abuse deaths go up, you might need to increase funding. This information needs to inform the agenda, the

questions you ask. It doesn't necessarily tell you the answers on a budget decision because there are lots of other factors that are involved.[14]

If the strict definition of performance budgeting is undesirable and unrealistic, then what about another definition? In practice, performance budgeting is usually defined to suggest a loose connection between performance information and resource allocation without detailing how decision makers should use this information. An example from Schick: "A performance budget is any budget that represents information on what agencies have done or expect to do with the money provided to them."[15] Such a definition is little different from the definition of performance management supplied above, but markedly different from the strict definition of performance budgeting.

Rethinking Performance Management

To rethink something means to challenge a dominant paradigm or set of assumptions and to look at it in a new light. Talbot, in reviewing the study of performance management, writes: "As with many administrative arguments, for every doctrine and its justification there are often counter-arguments and it is important to record these. Perhaps surprisingly the academic critique of the 'performance' movement has been relatively muted."[16] The sheer ubiquity of performance management reforms calls for a careful challenge to beliefs about performance management.

Some have started to make this challenge. An increasing literature has documented the potential for performance measures to create perverse behavior, including goal displacement and gaming.[17] This book is the third in a series that Georgetown University Press has published on performance management. In 2006 Radin published *Challenging the Performance Movement,* and David Frederickson and H. George Frederickson published *Measuring the Performance of the Hollow State.*[18] Each book has turned a critical eye on performance management, contributing to what Radin calls "a new discussion about performance management that integrates the issues of complexity."[19] Each book has its own perspective. Radin draws from democratic theory to point to a basic tension between political values and the values of performance management reforms, most notably the tension between the separation of powers designed into the U.S. political system and the assumption of a single central actor that characterizes performance management. Focusing on the federal level, she argues that performance management techniques fail to incorporate concerns about equity and constitute a top-down approach that excludes and demeans the professionals we rely on to implement our public programs. Frederickson and Frederickson have mapped the complexities of using performance regimes to govern the hollow state. At a time when more and more government work is being performed by third parties, federal managers are increasingly being held accountable to performance standards that are difficult to exert on third parties.

This book joins the debate on the complexities of performance management, but it does so in a number of ways that are different. I focus on understanding why performance management reforms are adopted and how the nature of adoption affects implementation. Radin has argued that performance management reforms can become a "one-size-fits-all" approach, failing to reflect differences between programs. Some functions are simply easier to measure and more suited to the demands of performance management. I also argue that performance management is more likely to succeed in some conditions than in others, focusing on other agency-level variables such as leadership and resources to explain why.

To a greater extent than other treatments of performance management, I am interested in how people interpret and use performance information. The main conceptual contribution of the book is to propose an interactive dialogue model of performance information use. The model examines how performance information is socially constructed. Talbot points out that a social constructionist perspective has been largely absent in the literature of performance management. The social constructionist view could lead to "the conclusion that such approaches should be rejected out of hand or, more constructively, that this should lead to an approach to performance based on dialogue."[20] This book pursues the latter approach, consistent with recent literature that has emphasized the role of dialogue in the policy process.[21] While performance measures suggest the irreducible objectivity of numbers, they are in fact ambiguous: selected, interpreted, and used by actors in different ways consistent with their institutional interests. This model suggests that a dialogue about performance across institutional interests will be more likely to be marked by conflicting interpretations and disagreement than a dialogue within an institution.

In this book I examine recent performance management reform at the federal level and the state level. While most analyses of performance management tend to focus on one level of government, the similarities between the state and federal levels suggest the benefit of considering both when examining how performance management works. Both levels of government have the same basic political institutions. In addition, both levels of government have embraced performance management in very similar ways. Every state government has its own version of the Government Performance and Results Act (GPRA), requiring that agency staff collect and report performance information to a central budget office, usually as part of the budget process. There is an active and ongoing interchange of reform ideas between the state and federal levels, and innovation at the federal level in the form of the PART program may become the next wave of reforms at the state level. The key findings of the book—the reasons performance management is adopted and used; the ambiguity and subjectivity of performance information; and the potential for learning—do not depend on factors unique to the state or federal level.

Given the focus of the book on U.S. federal and state governments, the application of findings to the local level or to other countries should be made carefully. The adoption of performance management routines has been enthusiastically embraced by cities and countries around the world. Some of the basic theories proposed here—such as why performance management is popular and how performance information may be used—are not conditioned on any particular political institutions or tendencies. So why might performance management be different at the local level? One reason is the shorter distance between political officials, managers, and the actual services delivered. While federal and even state governments deal with a broad array of services and deliver few services directly, political leaders and managers at the local level have a much easier time connecting performance information to the activities of frontline employees, and their services are generally more visible to the public. This context makes it more likely that performance management practices have a greater impact at the local level, and research from the local level provides some support for this view.[22]

When comparing to other countries, differences in political institutions and the nature of political-bureaucratic relations will create variation in the adoption and use of performance management routines. One key difference is that the decentralized nature of U.S. political institutions limits the ability of any single actor to establish its own blueprint for a performance management model, define the meaning of performance information, or determine how performance information is used. Another difference is that the deep tradition of politicization of the bureaucracy in the form of political appointments seems to have discouraged U.S. governments from dismantling civil service systems to the same degree as other countries that have pursued performance management (see chapter 3). On the whole, compared with the benchmark adopters of New Public Management (NPM) reforms, the U.S. approach to performance management has not been especially loyal to any particular prescriptive theory in adoption or as rigorous in seeking to link performance information to decisions in the implementation phase.

The dominant paradigm of performance management, what I refer to as *performance management doctrine,* is explored in chapter 2. Performance management doctrine is based on the logic that the creation, diffusion, and use of performance information will foster better decision making in government, leading to dividends in terms of political and public accountability, efficiency, and budget decisions. Performance management doctrine also argues that liberating managers from traditional controls complements the creation of performance information.

Performance management doctrine promises to change the nature of accountability. For the public, performance information provides a transparent explanation of how well the government is doing. For elected officials, performance information provides a basis to reduce information asymmetry and exert oversight, while goal-setting routines provide an additional basis to exert policy control.[23] Case findings question the extent to which performance management is really used for such accountability purposes.

In exchange for holding managers to higher standards of results-based accountability, performance doctrine promises to give them greater freedoms to achieve goals. In short, performance management doctrine calls for both a focus on results and greater managerial flexibility. The doctrine does not anticipate that performance information might remain unused or used in ways that run contrary to an ideal of objective decision making. As becomes apparent in later chapters, this means that many of the predicted benefits of performance management doctrine do not materialize.

In contrast to the performance management doctrine, a more critical literature points to problems with performance management and suggests it is destined to fail. This critical perspective highlights the troubled history of performance management efforts, especially efforts that sought to reorganize the budget process, such as planning programming and budget systems in the 1960s and zero-based budgeting in the 1970s. There are a number of logical reasons for these failures. One basic problem is the issue of information overload. Wildavsky pointed out that performance information systems produce mounds of information that no one particularly cares about and that collectively is beyond the cognitive abilities of any individual to process.[24] Another criticism is that politics makes performance information irrelevant. Strong political preferences make performance information unnecessary. Relative to partisan goals, ideological biases, stakeholder pressure, and constituent needs, performance data is not especially influential. In addition, performance information does not help elected officials by making political decisions simpler—indeed, it is an additional layer of information to incorporate.

Performance management reforms, frequently borrowed from the private sector or parliamentary systems, have been critiqued as incompatible with the separated powers of the U.S. political institutions.[25] Such reforms assume that the executive branch is the critical decision maker in government. Legislators are unlikely to accept any model of performance management that reduces their discretionary power over goal setting and resource allocation.

Another criticism made of public management reforms in general is that they are adopted for symbolic purposes that have little to do with actual performance. Reforms have isomorphic tendencies and communicate political values but do little else.[26] This explains the repeated tendency to adopt similar reforms that have not contributed much in the past.[27] An extension of this argument is that because of the symbolic value of reform, little thought will be given to making implementation of the reform possible. As public managers realize the passing and symbolic nature of reforms, they respond with compliance and occasionally gaming of performance regimes.[28]

Overall, this literature makes criticisms that remain valid. Evidence presented in this book suggests that elected officials are rarely interested in performance information use. Performance management reforms are used as symbolic tools to express frustration with bureaucracy. Legislatures tend to regard performance initiatives from the executive branch with suspicion, and public employees can become cynical about the latest version of performance management.

Despite all these problems, I argue that performance management reforms can change managerial behavior, and performance information will be used. This more positive assessment is simply a function of looking for success in different places. Joyce and Tompkins warn that many of the negative assessments of performance reforms have come because of a focus on elected officials and on the budgeting process.[29] Most of the benefits of performance management reform that I observed occurred at the agency levels, away from resource allocation decisions.

The Outline of the Book

The balance of this chapter provides a summary outline of the chapters that follow and gives a sense of how performance management is reconsidered. Chapter 2 explains the claims of performance management doctrine in greater detail. The success of the performance management doctrine is reflected in its widespread adoption, which is examined in chapter 3. All state governments and the federal government in the United States have devoted significant time, energy, and resources to adopting performance management systems since the 1990s. In effect, this has meant that governments have created reporting requirements for agencies to produce performance information—which includes mission statements, strategic goals, performance targets, and actual measurements of achievement. The Government Performance Project (GPP) graded these efforts in 1999 and 2001, and in 2005 it graded both performance management efforts and aspects of information technology in a revised category called information. The grades were based on how consistently state governments met explicit and widely accepted public management criteria. Information was collected via a detailed survey completed by state government officials, content analysis of public documentation, and interviews of state officials undertaken by journalists from *Governing* magazine. For some aspects of the GPP, quantitative scales were developed based on survey re-

Table 1.1 Government performance grades for managing for results and information category

State	1999 MFR grade	2001 MFR grade	2005 info. grade	State	1999 MFR grade	2001 MFR grade	2005 info. grade
Alabama	F	D+	C	Montana	C	C	C
Alaska	C-	C-	C	Nebraska	B-	B-	C+
Arizona	B-	C+	B-	Nevada	C	C	B-
Arkansas	D	C-	C+	New Hampshire	D+	D	C-
California	C-	C-	C	New Jersey	B-	B-	C
Colorado	C	C+	C+	New Mexico	D+	C	B
Connecticut	D+	C-	C-	New York	D+	C-	C+
Delaware	B	B	B	North Carolina	B-	B	C+
Florida	B	C+	B	North Dakota	D	C-	C
Georgia	C+	B-	B-	Ohio	C+	B	C+
Hawaii	C-	C	D	Oklahoma	D+	D	C
Idaho	C-	C-	C+	Oregon	B+	B	B
Illinois	C	B-	C+	Pennsylvania	B-	B	B
Indiana	C	B-	C	Rhode Island	C	C	C+
Iowa	B+	A-	B	South Carolina	B-	B	B
Kansas	C	C+	B-	South Dakota	D	D	D
Kentucky	B	B+	B	Tennessee	C	B-	C+
Louisiana	B	B+	A-	Texas	B+	A-	B
Maine	C	C+	C+	Utah	B+	B+	A-
Maryland	B-	B	C+	Vermont	B-	B	B-
Massachusetts	C	C	C+	Virginia	A-	A-	A-
Michigan	B	B+	B+	Washington	B+	A-	A-
Minnesota	B	B	B+	West Virginia	C	C	C+
Mississippi	C	D+	C+	Wisconsin	C	C	B-
Missouri	A-	A-	A-	Wyoming	C	C+	C

Source: Government Performance Project

sponses and content analysis that informed the creation of grades, but the final grade assessments represented a judgment of both quantitative and qualitative evidence by the journalists and academics involved in the project.[30] Table 1.1 provides these grades.

The data presented in chapter 3 offers a cross-state snapshot of what state governments are doing. Evidence from content analysis finds that state governments have actively established performance information systems by requiring agencies to create and report on strategic goals and performance measures on a frequent basis. While all state governments appear to produce some form of performance information, the detail, nature, and availability of this information vary a good deal. States have adopted reporting requirements without giving much attention to the part of performance management doctrine that argues that a new focus on performance should be accompanied with a relaxation of the traditional controls that restrict managerial uses of human and financial resources. In effect, state governments have adopted performance information systems proposed by performance management doctrine, but they have neglected the managerial freedom aspects. These cross-state findings give rise to a number of questions: Why are performance management reforms so popular? Why are they being adopted in the manner that they are, focusing on performance information systems but not managerial autonomy? How is performance information used?

Answering these questions, or at least beginning to answer these questions, is crucial to understanding how performance management initiatives work and their prospects for success. To help rethink performance management, I employ existing theoretical approaches (the policymaking and implementation literatures) not frequently used in the performance management literature and develop a new theory on how performance information is used, a theory that I call the interactive dialogue model of performance information use.

Why Are Performance Management Reforms Adopted? Why Are They Adopted in the Way that They Are?

Using theories from the policymaking literature, chapter 4 argues that the adoption of formal performance management reforms is a function of the role of central agencies in defining the reform and the motivation of elected officials selecting the reform. The instrumental costs and benefits of reforms guide elected officials. The adoption of performance management reforms is due to its symbolic value to elected officials and professional value to central agency actors.

Performance management is attractive because it communicates to the public that elected officials share their frustration with inefficient bureaucracies and are holding them accountable, saving taxpayer money, and fostering better performance. These symbolic benefits are useful on the campaign trail, especially for challengers who promise to reform government. Once officials are elected, performance management reforms are a logical policy option, providing at least the appearance of satisfying campaign promises. Reforms can also be used to try to convince the public that the government is being run efficiently and competently, making incumbents deserving of reelection and the public purse deserving of taxpayer monies. Elected officials might also perceive potential benefits in terms of policy control by using performance information as a means of specifying goals and holding bureaucrats accountable, but the case evidence offers few examples of elected officials using performance management in this way.

Elected officials seek to minimize the costs of performance management doctrine. In practice, this means that governments have adopted performance-reporting requirements for agencies, but they have ignored doctrinal arguments for reducing traditional managerial controls. Reporting requirements impose few costs for elected officials. They require little additional funds, and the burden falls chiefly on the agency bureaucrats who collect and disseminate information. Eliminating traditional management controls over financial and human resources has real costs. These traditional controls on bureaucracy are still valued, especially by the legislature but also by public service unions concerned about the potential loss of benefits to their members and possible abuses of power. Central agency actors, who shape public management policy ideas, approve of additional reporting mechanisms that fit with the budget process, but they are wary of loosening controls they have historically been tasked with enforcing.

How Are Performance Management Reforms Used?

Consistent with previous criticisms of performance reforms, the case evidence suggests the symbolic aspects of reform. However, the case evidence also suggests that such reforms do not stop after adoption and that the symbolic nature of reforms is not necessarily inconsistent with practical benefits. Even though U.S. governments adopted reforms in a way inconsistent with performance management doctrine, agency managers often have found ways to make these reforms generate positive benefits, although not always in the ways predicted by performance management doctrine.

Once the adopters of reforms have created an official reporting requirement, it is up to agency managers to do something with it. Chapter 5 uses implementation theory to understand what happens next. Agency options range from passive compliance with the letter of requirements to active use of performance management to bring about organizational changes. The use of performance management reforms at the agency level is a function of the formal reform adopted, agency leadership motivation, managerial authority, and resources.

Given the symbolic motivations behind the adoption of reforms, we might expect that agency managers would be cynical about performance management. There is cynicism, but agency leaders in the state governments I examined saw performance management reforms as an opportunity to add value to their organizations in a variety of ways. Some of these benefits were consistent with performance management doctrine—creating strategic clarity and improving managerial processes. More frequently, benefits were not those specified by performance management doctrine—such as developing alternative strategic goals that essentially rewrote policy, shaping the organizational culture, improving internal and external communication, and fostering leadership development. Leaders pursued these benefits trying to not only improve organizational performance, but also to improve the capacity of the organization. Agency officials, like elected officials, consider the costs and benefits of reforms, but they are more concerned about the instrumental benefits to be leveraged from performance management. In doing so, each leader has an agenda he or she wishes to pursue, informed and constrained by the organizational environment.

Leaders of the state agencies appeared to be the most important factor in the implementation of performance management, but their ability to use reforms has been shaped by their managerial authority. While these leaders gained no additional discretion with performance management reforms, they found ways to use performance management within existing constraints. Resources are another important factor for implementation. Here, the case evidence points to the necessity of adequate resources to enable performance management to work. The absence of resources makes it difficult to provide the personnel to carefully collect, disseminate, and consider data. Poorer agencies are also more likely to be reactive rather than systematically fulfill a plan. Where managers are constantly battling with unexpected crises that can be cured only by resources rather than strategic thinking, performance management is little more than a distraction.

How Is Performance Information Used?

Performance management reforms rest on the assumption that once performance information is made available, it will be widely used and result in better decisions because it will foster consensus and make decision making more objective. But the limited evidence of use does not match that model. Instead, it is consistent with an interactive dialogue model of performance information use.

The interactive dialogue model argues that performance information is not objective and is selected and presented by advocates seeking to persuade others. Performance information is presented and considered in written and oral texts—reports, meetings, presentations, memos, appropriations bills, etc. These texts represent the goals of their authors and their efforts to use performance information to bring others to their cause. How individuals perceive performance data will depend on their individual background and beliefs and the institutional role they fill. Different actors can look at the performance information on the same program and disagree on what the information means. This dissonance may simply be because they select different data to talk about, consistent with their interests. It is also because of the inherent ambiguity of most data, meaning that the same data can hold multiple meanings. Performance information tells us nothing about context and implementation, factors that shape how we interpret whether a program is effective. Performance information does not necessarily result in clearer decisions if the actors involved cannot agree on what it tells them about current performance, changing budgets, or management. As roles motivate the actors involved to understand performance information differently, the inherent ambiguity in performance information will be exploited.

Chapters 6 through 9 develop the interactive dialogue model and offer examples in different settings. Chapter 6 lays out the basic logic behind the interactive dialogue model and points to illustrative examples at the state level. In budget forums, state agencies tend to select performance data that reflects a narrative they are seeking to develop. The narrative generally argues that they are doing well with existing resources and points to current and future needs. This is a familiar story in the budget process, but now agency officials can use performance information in a way consistent with this narrative. There are variations on the standard narrative. Agencies strapped for resources are likely to point to the operational problems created by a lack of cash. Agencies seeking to prompt policy changes will offer evidence of the benefits of new programs versus old ones. The various actors involved in the policy process can be expected to use performance information consistent with their interests. Agency actors will contribute to the dialogue in ways that protect agency preferences and budgets. Central agency officials will seek to assess the persuasiveness of different claims and emphasize performance data that reflects the interests of the leader of the executive branch. Legislative committees will favor information that helps their oversight of agencies and is useful in determining budget allocations.

Some of the distinctions I draw from the critical perspective derive from the interactive dialogue model of performance information use. This perspective suggests that actors do not suffer from information overload because they do not try to process all information but select information that they find useful. At an agency level, information overload is less of a problem because actors deal with a limited number of programs. Agency managers select information that they can use to advocate to the external policy environment or to use for internal management improvements. The interactive dialogue perspective acknowledges that political preferences will dominate decisions, but that does not mean that performance data is not used. Even among actors with strong preexisting preferences, performance information can be used to justify choices made and to convince others of those choices. Advocacy does not fit into the performance management doctrine ideal of performance information use, but it is still a use.

The Office of Management and Budget (OMB) under George W. Bush has aimed to change the frequency and nature of performance dialogue at the federal level. Chapter 7 presents recent performance management reform from the perspective of the OMB. Since the late 1990s federal agencies have faced the same performance-reporting requirements as state agencies in the form of the Government Performance and Results Act (GPRA). The Bush administration has argued that GPRA is a failure, or at best, only the beginning of a coherent performance management strategy. To this end, the OMB has required that agencies build their congressional budget submissions around their annual performance plan. In addition, the OMB has started to assess program performance data using an evaluation mechanism called the Program Assessment Rating Tool (PART), publishing summary assessments of program effectiveness alongside budget recommendations.

The changes pursued by the Bush administration aim to alter the performance dialogue in a number of ways, explored in chapter 8. The OMB hopes that members of Congress will become more comfortable in using performance data. Thus far, many congressional appropriations subcommittees have complained that information on inputs and workload that they consider valuable is being lost in favor of performance information they have little role in selecting and are not interested in. The reaction to PART assessments has also been guarded. The interactive dialogue model points to the role of power in structuring dialogue; the PART experience illustrates the risk of such using power to dominate a dialogue. While the OMB sees PART as transparent and systematic, others view it as subjective, reflecting the perspective of the OMB, the White House, and the Republican Party.

However, the PART process has forced a dialogue within the executive branch, even if agencies have been suspicious of the process. PART provides a third-party review of programs that offers a simple and clear summary opinion on whether the program is effective. It increases the level of discussion about program performance and forces agencies to meet a basic standard of evidence to show that their programs are working. The assessments occur on a regular basis and generate management recommendations that the OMB expects agencies to implement.

PART is also affecting budget discussions. The relationship between PART assessment and budget recommendations is not strongly systematic, but thus far it appears to suggest that programs deemed ineffective or unable to demonstrate results will have lower proposed budgets (which Congress could then choose to ignore). The relationship between performance information and budget recommendations is not systematic because of the additional information that must be considered and because of the ambiguity of performance information itself. For many programs political preferences will override the assessments. The nature of the use of performance information in public budgeting, therefore, does not resemble a rational one-best-way approach to decision making, where performance information fosters consensus. Rather, it more closely resembles an interactive dialogue, where different actors seek to persuade the others by using information that supports their own arguments and by proposing alternate perspectives on the same information.

Even if two actors can agree on what performance means, performance information does not tell us what to do next. The simplest example is a situation in which a program performs poorly. One individual may read the information as suggesting that the program is a failure, a waste of public money, and should be eliminated. Another might look at the program and argue that it provides a valuable public service and would be more successful if given more resources. A third individual might say that the program needs to be reorganized for better management before any funding decisions can be made. Each option offers a logical interpretation of the same piece of data.

Conflicting interpretations increase when a more diverse group of actors are involved, but varying interpretations can occur even within an institution of homogenous individuals. Despite the best efforts of the OMB, budget examiners have been found to interpret performance data differently and apply different standards for what constitutes acceptable evidence of effectiveness. Chapter 8 presents the results of an experiment that further illustrates how ambiguity leads to multiple interpretations. Graduate students in two public affairs programs served as subjects in an experiment where they reanalyzed PART assessments and used logical warrants to disagree with OMB evaluation and funding decisions. The subjects were not motivated by a particular institutional role; they arrived at different conclusions due to the ambiguity of the performance data.

A dialogue about performance can also occur within agencies. Because agency actors are more homogenous and share a focus on implementation, there is greater potential for generating agreement on the meaning of performance data and for building a shared narrative that becomes part of the organizational culture. In this setting politics is less likely to disrupt the use or splinter the meaning of performance information. Dialogue about performance can also foster learning opportunities, which are examined in chapter 9. This learning can come in a variety of forms, whether it is learning to change existing organizational processes for the purposes of performance improvement, learning ways to improve organizational capacity, or challenging the basic underlying goals of the organization. The prospects for dialogue to foster learning improve when organizations create learning forums. Learning forums are routines that encourage actors to closely examine information, consider its significance, and decide how it will affect future action. Learning also improves when these forums include a variety of perspectives, dialogue is based on an equal footing among participants, and different types of knowledge are employed. These conditions challenge some basic practices within hierarchies—managers are not used to stopping to examine performance information, nor are they used to setting aside status differences and treating views from different parts of the organization with equal respect. However, the simple supply of performance data does not create its own demand for use, and the most critical challenge facing agencies is to find ways to encourage managers to examine performance information and then use their collective knowledge to improve how they run agencies.

Chapter 10 concludes the book by summarizing some lessons that emerge from rethinking performance management. In doing so, it is hard not to conclude that our expectations of performance management are at a turning point. Across state governments and at the federal level, there exists an unprecedented machinery to create and disseminate performance information. The creation of this machinery was based on lofty expectations and unrealistic assumptions about the ease of changing existing patterns of decision making. Governments can offer anecdotal evidence that they occasionally use performance data, but few are willing to say that it is used systematically. As the shortcomings of performance management doctrine become apparent, a reevaluation is necessary. Examined alongside the promises of performance management doctrine, actual achievement appears relatively modest.

Rethinking performance management means acknowledging this shortfall, as well as acknowledging that inflated expectations set the reform up for failure. A better understanding of why these reforms are adopted, and what incentives agency managers have to implement reform, is a good starting point. A more credible understanding of how performance information shapes decision making, as offered by the interactive dialogue model, is crucial. These theoretical advances suggest the need for a more modest set of expectations about the contribution of performance management reforms to management and budgeting. Using these standards, even if performance data does enter the dialogue that public managers engage in, it must compete with other factors that influence the decision and will be used according to the interests and interpretations of the different actors involved in a decision. It will not make decision making any easier. Since performance information is ambiguous, it will be one additional piece of contested information that enters the policy process.

This understanding of performance management is a far cry from the model presented in performance management doctrine, which suggests that performance information is the key to unlocking government accountability and effectiveness. But this book also challenges a negative view that suggests performance information is never used, that it is incidental to decisions, and that the management of that information is entirely symbolic. Performance information may not dominate decisions, but it is increasingly present in the dialogue that leads to decisions. While there is certainly a symbolic aspect in how performance management reforms are adopted, the implementation of these reforms and the use of performance information are driven by instrumental concerns.

Data Collection

Assessing the era of governance by performance management requires in-depth analysis of how the political and managerial processes relevant to performance management work and interact and are strengthened if done on a comparative

Table 1.2   Data Sources

Data source	Use in chapter
Government Performance Project 2000 cross-state surveys of performance management, financial management, and human resource systems.	2, 3
Cross-state content analysis of state strategic plans, state performance reports, budget documents, and agency strategic plans and performance reports.	3
Case study analysis of Alabama, Vermont, and Virginia, based on document and interview analysis. Interviews of state budget officials and Department of Corrections senior and line managers. All interviews transcribed. Interview transcripts and state documents coded using qualitative software.	4, 5, 6, 9
Case study of the development and application of the Program Assessment Rating Tool at the federal level. Based on document analysis and interviews of officials in the Office of Management and Budget and the Government Accountability Office.	7, 8, 9
Content analysis of legislative discussion of performance at the federal level.	7
Experiment with graduate students in public affairs to examine the ambiguity of performance information.	8

basis. It is therefore worth briefly discussing the data collected for this book. The book rests on a multimethod effort to understand the creation and use of performance management reforms. Data was collected using close-ended and open-ended surveys, interviews, experiments, and content analysis. These methods and their applications in the book are highlighted in table 1.2.

The data collected was designed to help answer the questions central to the book: Did the adoption of performance management reform in state government actually follow the recommendations of performance management doctrine? What are the motivations behind performance management adoption? How and why are performance management reforms actually implemented at the agency level? How do public actors use performance information? Table 1.2 summarizes each data source and where it is used in the book.

To understand whether actual performance management adoption followed the recommendations of performance management doctrine, I drew data from the first two rounds of the Government Performance Project undertaken at the Maxwell School at Syracuse University. State governments provided in-depth descriptions of performance management systems and their uses, and GPP staff examined public documentation to verify these claims. In particular, the GPP undertook content analysis of strategic plans, budgets, and performance reports to assess the range of performance information available and created measures of state-by-state managerial autonomy based on survey responses. This information is reported in chapter 3.

The cross-state picture shows how performance management reforms were adopted, and this information naturally leads to the questions of why they were adopted in the way that they were and how they were implemented. I sought to answer these questions using in-depth case studies of performance management efforts in three states (Alabama, Virginia, and Vermont) and from current efforts at the federal level. Seeking to maximize theoretical replication and avoid the tendency of best-practice research to generalize from high performers, states were selected for study according to their fit with high (Virginia), medium (Vermont), and low (Alabama) categories of experience and competence in performance management.[31] The selection was consistent with the GPP grades that each state has received for its performance management activities.

The state government evidence on adoption is featured in chapter 4. State government evidence on performance management implementation is featured in chapters 5 and 9. To examine implementation, I controlled for function by focusing on the corrections system in all three states, a large but understudied function in public management.[32] Corrections incorporates a wide range of services—incarceration, education, creating behavioral change, custodial care, the production of goods and services—and is therefore representative of different agency types.[33] I visited each state to undertake in-depth interviews of the key participants in the performance management process: (a) operational managers in correctional institutions, (b) senior managers at the Department of Corrections (DOC), and (c) managers in the state management and budget office. This sampling technique is useful in discovering variation in the views of members of different parts of the same organization.[34] In addition, to gain the views of political and career officials, my interview pool included a mix of appointees and career staff at both the statewide and agency level. I developed a key informant in each pool of interviewees and used a snowball method of sampling the additional interviewees, some of whom were interviewed multiple times. Interviews were semistructured, based on a standard interview protocol and probes (see appendix A for the interview protocol).[35]

In addition to the cross-state data and the three state case studies, I also examined the status of performance management at the federal level, focusing on the Bush administration initiative to evaluate the performance of all federal programs and to make agency budget submissions more performance oriented. These efforts provide a fascinating case study of the creation of a performance management reform, illustrating the difficulties involved when a budget office seeks to develop a performance-focused budget process and a centralized mechanism to assess agency performance. I studied these changes by interviewing federal officials, particularly those in the OMB who were involved in creating and implementing these reforms and legislative actors overseeing the reform.[36] The discussion of the adoption and early experience of these reforms is examined in chapters 7 and 8.

The final key question I pursued is how people interpret and use performance information. To examine this question I relied on a variety of approaches. I had asked my state and federal interviewees how and when they used information, and I looked for examples of use. I also wanted to understand how legislators used performance information in public decision venues. I therefore undertook a content analysis of congressional discussion of performance in appropriations bills and hearings. This data is presented in chapter 7. Much of the evidence on the use of performance information pointed to the influence of institutional perspectives. I wanted to understand if actors would still disagree about performance information even without institutional affiliation. Using graduate students from two public affairs programs, I undertook an experiment to examine the degree of ambiguity associated with performance information. This data is presented in chapter 8.

As with any empirical evidence, generalizations should be made with caution. The state research focused primarily on corrections, and it is also important to note that each state has its own particular history and culture that affect governance outcomes. I describe such basic state differences in appendix B.

Conclusion

This book offers some new perspectives on performance management. While not claiming to be a complete account, it challenges existing thinking and points to ways to gain a more complete understanding of whether performance management has been worthwhile.

Performance management is not (and cannot possibly become) the solution to governmental problems that its advocates promise, but it has benefits that offer clues to how a more effective version of performance management might work. If decades of results-based reform have not lived up to expectations, this is partly because the expectations were unrealistically high: Elected officials and senior bureaucrats would have to change how they make decisions, citizens would have to become avid consumers of performance data, and public managers would have to run public organizations differently. These changes require a different system of governance, not just management changes.

This book focuses primarily on public managers because these are the most likely users of performance information and the best hope for the performance management movement. In most respects, public managers are not driven by performance data in the ways predicted by performance management doctrine, but managers will occasionally use results-based reforms to add value to their organizations. The following chapters identify the logic behind this limited use of performance management as a basis for rethinking how results-based reforms might be implemented in the future, focusing in particular on how performance information changes the dialogue of governance.

Notes

1. Mosher, *Democracy and the Public* Service.

2. Ingraham and Moynihan, "Evolving Dimensions of Performance."

3. Radin, "The Government Performance and Results Act (GPRA): Hydra-Headed Monster or Flexible Management Tool?"

4. Gawthrop, *Public Sector Management: Systems and Ethics,* 45.

5. Katz and Kahn, *The Social Psychology of Organizations.*

6. On the risks of a separation between planning and management, see Ansoff, Declerck, and Hayes, eds., *From Strategic Planning to Strategic Management;* Toft, "Synoptic (One Best Way) Approaches to Strategic Management."

7. Heinrich, "Do Government Bureaucrats Make Effective Use of Performance Management Information?"

8. Wildavsky, "If Planning Is Everything, Maybe It's Nothing."

9. Gormley and Weimer, *Organizational Report Cards.*

10. Melkers and Willoughby, "Budgeters' Views of State Performance-Budgeting Systems."

11. Macintosh, *Management Accounting and Control Systems.*

12. Scott, "Organization Theory: An Overview and an Appraisal."

13. Schick, "The Performing State," 101.

14. Subcommittee on Government Efficiency and Financial Management, *Should We PART Ways with GPRA,* 66.

15. Schick, "The Performing State."

16. Talbot, "Performance Management," 502.

17. Talbot, "Executive Agencies"; Hood, "Gaming in Targetworld"; van Thiel and Leeuw, "The Performance Paradox."

18. Radin, *Challenging the Performance Movement*; Frederickson and Frederickson, *Measuring the Performance of the Hollow State.*

19. Radin, *Challenging the Performance Movement,* 10.

20. Talbot, "Performance Management," 510.

21. For example, see Fischer and Forrester, eds., *The Argumentative Turn in Policy Analysis and Planning;* Majone, *Evidence, Argument, and Persuasion in the Policy Process.*

22. Ammons, "Raising the Performance Bar Locally"; Andrews and Moynihan, "Why Reforms Don't Always Have to Work to Succeed"; deHaven-Smith and Jenne, "Management by Inquiry"; Edwards and Thomas, "Developing a Municipal Performance-Measurement System"; Melkers and Willoughby, "Models of Performance-Measurement Use in Local Governments"; Poister and Streib, "Elements of Strategic Planning and Management in Municipal Govern-

ment"; Tat-Kei Ho, "Accounting for the Value of Performance Measurement"; Wang, "Performance Measurement in Budgeting."

23. It should be noted that the understanding of accountability in performance management doctrine is relatively limited since it largely overlooks the positive aspects of rules-based accountability and neglects other approaches, such as political, legal, or professional norms. See Romzek and Dubnick, "Accountability in the Public Sector."

24. Wildavsky, *Budgeting: A Comparative Theory of Budgeting Processes.*

25. Radin, "The Government Performance and Results Act and the Tradition of Federal Management Reform."

26. On the symbolic nature of public sector reform in general, see DiMaggio and Powell, "The Iron Cage Revisited," and March and Olsen, "Organizing Political Life." On performance management in particular, see Roy and Seguin, "The Institutionalization of Efficiency-Oriented Approaches," and Carlin and Guthrie, "Accrual Output—Based Budgeting Systems in Australia."

27. Downs and Larkey, *The Search for Government Efficiency.*

28. Van Thiel and Leeuw, "The Performance Paradox."

29. Joyce and Tompkins, "Using Performance Information for Budgeting."

30. More detail on the GPP criteria, the information collected by the project, and the process of grade allocation can be found in Ingraham (ed.), *In Pursuit of Performance.*

31. On theoretical replication, see Yin, *Case Study Research,* 2nd ed. On best practice research, see Overman and Boyd, "Best Practice Research."

32. DiIulio, *Governing Prisons.*

33. Wilson, *Bureaucracy.*

34. Ban, *How Do Public Managers Manage?*

35. Responses were recorded, transcribed, and stored in QSR NUDIST, a software program designed for qualitative research. QSR NUDIST allows analysis of data using a hierarchical coding system. The software is flexible enough to allow both inductive and deductive coding and modification of the coding structure to facilitate the interplay of ideas and evidence. As codes are established, the definition of each code may be attached, as well as memos on the emerging trends that are associated with a particular code. The software is therefore ideal for the type of research undertaken here, allowing the creation of broad codes that facilitate descriptive case information, deductive codes based on predicted benefits of performance management, and inductive codes emerging from case evidence.

36. I interviewed ten staff members at the OMB. Interviewees were a mixture of political appointees and career officials. The group included those who had worked directly on the Program Evaluation Team that designed and modified the original PART questionnaire, managers with responsibility for overseeing the implementation of PART, and budget examiners who have used the tool. In addition, I interviewed seven members of the GAO and Congressional Research Service who oversee federal budgeting and performance management issues for Congress. The interviews were largely conducted in person in May of 2005, although a couple of interviews took place via phone at a later date.

2

Performance Management as Doctrine

What does performance management actually mean, and what does it hope to achieve? This chapter examines the basic claims made in performance management doctrine. These claims serve as a theoretical standard against which evidence on the actual implementation of performance management and alternative theories can be compared. The key claim that applies to government organizations is that two mutually dependent reforms should be adopted: Managers should be given more flexibility in human resources and budgeting matters but held accountable by quantitative performance standards.

One of the defining tensions of the intellectual development of public administration is between the field as a social science and as a professional activity undertaken in a highly politicized environment. Frequently, decisions on running public organizations are made on the basis of what Hood and Jackson have described as "administrative arguments" or "doctrines."[1] Such doctrines are ideally suited to policy choices in a political context. Doctrines are a theoretical explanation of cause and effect, often presented as factual and widely applicable. Doctrines are designed to prompt actions consistent with this explanation. Proponents of public administration based on social science have exposed such doctrines as contradictory.[2] Yet this style of argumentation persists, and the history of public administration is replete with examples of management doctrines, often of a very similar nature.[3] As these doctrinal arguments find supporters, they become movements that seek to reform government. This persistence is due, in part, to the demand-driven nature of public sector reform. Practitioners and elected officials constantly seek suggestions on improving public organizations, and they rarely differentiate between knowledge derived from social science and plausible argument.[4]

Performance management closely fits the categorization of management doctrine, employing many of the rhetorical tools of administrative argument.[5] Performance management doctrine gives a sense of symmetry by offering generic solutions to the perceived weaknesses of traditional public organizations. This doctrine also offers a prescriptive theory of cause and effect for how public organizations should be run, resulting in a series of policy options that demand implementation. Traditional public organizations are portrayed as inefficient and ineffective, focused on maximizing inputs and rendering compliance. Existing management systems are to blame for the undesirable state of public organizations. The doctrine promises a more efficient, effective, results-driven public sector.

The credibility of doctrinal claims relies on the credibility of the warrants that underlie these claims.[6] The doctrine of performance management draws from a number of schools of thought, most notably New Public Management (NPM), but also strategic management and management accounting and control. Performance management doctrine is also closely intertwined with political rhetoric on the state of government and the underlying assumption that the public sector can be made more efficient and effective.

The Doctrine of Performance Management

Some basic assumptions are associated with the doctrine of performance management:

- Government is inefficient.
- Government can transform itself to become more efficient.
- The poor performance of government is of major consequence in terms of fiscal health and public trust in government.
- Government can and should make more rational decisions.
- Performance information will improve decisions and can be used to foster accountability.

Explicitly or implicitly these assumptions underlie every speech a politician gives calling for results-oriented government and every proposal that reformers design to the same end. Setting aside the question of whether such broad assumptions are accurate for all, or even most public agencies, these assumptions are entrenched and widely accepted by those who seek to reform government. For instance, let us look at the Findings and Purposes section (see box 2.1) of the federal Government Performance and Results Act (GPRA), which enjoyed bipartisan support and became the model of performance management for state governments.

Like many of our attitudes about governments, the assumptions reflected in the text of GPRA are tenaciously held, though uninformed by a systematic assessment of evidence. They operate at the level of faith or belief, rather than knowledge or

Box 2.1   Government Performance and Results Act, section 2

(a) Findings. —The Congress finds that —
   (1) waste and inefficiency in Federal programs undermine the confidence of the American people in the Government and reduces the Federal Government's ability to address adequately vital public needs;
   (2) Federal managers are seriously disadvantaged in their efforts to improve program efficiency and effectiveness, because of insufficient articulation of program goals and inadequate information on program performance; and
   (3) congressional policymaking, spending decisions and program oversight are seriously handicapped by insufficient attention to program performance and results.
(b) Purposes. — The purposes of this Act are to —
   (1) improve the confidence of the American people in the capability of the Federal Government, by systematically holding Federal agencies accountable for achieving program results;
   (2) initiate program performance reform with a series of pilot projects in setting program goals, measuring program performance against those goals, and reporting publicly on their progress;
   (3) improve Federal program effectiveness and public accountability by promoting a new focus on results, service quality, and customer satisfaction;
   (4) help Federal managers improve service delivery, by requiring that they plan for meeting program objectives and by providing them with information about program results and service quality;
   (5) improve congressional decisionmaking by providing more objective information on achieving statutory objectives, and on the relative effectiveness and efficiency of Federal programs and spending; and
   (6) improve internal management of the Federal Government.

Source: Congressional Record

understanding. This makes them all the more powerful since they are difficult to refute on the basis of evidence. The reformist ethic that emerges from these beliefs is almost immune to evidence that reform efforts consistently fail, therefore encouraging round after round of performance management reforms.[7]

That such assumptions have the status of belief does not mean they are disconnected from ideas or theories. Scholarship and practitioner claims on performance management make a series of claims that allow us to better understand the performance management doctrine. These claims offer a simplified narrative about the problems associated with traditional public organizations, the remedies needed, and what these remedies will bring about. Depending on the source domains of these claims, there is some variation between the doctrine presented but not a great deal. We will examine these claims in turn.

Claims about Traditional Public Management Organizations

The doctrinal claims about traditional public organizations might be summarized as follows. Traditional public management systems provide only certain types of information that act to discourage efficiency. Managers have weak incentives to focus on performance, and they lack the basic goals and data that would focus their attention there. Instead, managers are provided with a list of inputs—budgeted appropriations—that they are obliged to spend on. Financial controls are centered on controlling these inputs, ensuring that money is spent for the purpose for which it is allocated. Managers lack the discretion to reallocate the money they have been allocated, even if it could mean more effective and efficient achievement of goals. Personnel controls reinforce financial controls, restricting the ability of the manager to make decisions about human resources.

Public managers are essentially inwardly focused, concerned with rule compliance rather than goal compliance and short-term issues.[8] Koteen links this nonfocus on results to the rigidity of existing public management systems: "Government and other nonprofit processes too often focus on observing proper and uniform procedure rather than achieving results . . . the focus is on input, not output."[9]

In any case there are no personal or organizational incentives to deviate from existing controls toward more efficient performance. Instead, disincentives exist. Savings made because of efficient budget execution will not be retained by the agency, but reappropriated to the entire government. In making budget proposals, agency administrators are likely to seek more than they need to cover costs and then spend down what money remains before the end of the budget cycle to avoid losing unspent appropriations and receiving lower allocations in the future. The definition of accountability underpinning these control systems is legal compliance, probity, and error avoidance, not goal achievement, technical efficiency, or program effectiveness.[10] Informal systems, reflected in organizational cultural artifacts of language and symbols, reinforce these values.[11] In short, the public sector seeks management expertise but curbs the use of discretion through both formal management controls and the informal culture that develops around those controls.

Claims about Changes Required: Building Performance Information Systems

Given the critiques of the traditional management systems, what does performance management doctrine tell us about changing these systems? Moving from an administrative culture of compliance, error avoidance, and presumed inefficiency to a more efficient and effective public service requires multiple changes to existing formal systems. The first is to create a performance information system. The creation of performance information is not a new innovation, with performance measurement in U.S. public management at least a century old.[12] From this perspective, what makes performance management conceptually distinct from simple performance measurement is the effort to link measurement with strategic planning into a single connected system, illustrated in figure 1.1. Administrative goals should be specified through some sort of formal strategic planning. Short-term strategic goals are intended to be consistent with longer-term strategic plans for the organization. These short-term goals form the basis of a performance contract agreement between elected officials and senior administrators. Goals are defined in measurable terms, with ex-post performance compared with ex-ante targets. Administrators face responsibility for achieving performance goals and are rewarded accordingly. Applying strategic planning will direct attention to results, the external environment, and the needs of stakeholders. Resource allocation will become more strategic and made on a longer-time planning horizon. Strategic goals provide standards for excellence and a basis for control and evaluation.

Figure 1.1 represents a simple model of how a performance management system improves governmental decision making and performance. Evidence from American state governments suggests wide acceptance (if not always actual implementation) of this model. In reporting to the Government Performance Project, states repeatedly emphasized strategic planning and performance measurement as related activities intended to feed into multiple decision venues and improved quality of decisions. Virginia, for example, described its Performance Management System as "comprised of four, linked processes: strategic planning, performance measurement, program evaluation, and performance budgeting . . . these processes are designed to work together to manage the performance of state government." Florida explained its Performance Accountability System as the "framework to ensure the critical link is maintained between the strategic plan, budget, and performance measures." Louisiana's management processes move from "planning to budgeting to implementation to evaluation (or accountability), back to planning and so on. All processes are linked; each builds upon the one that precedes it and contributes to the one that follows. No matter where you enter the circle, you will eventually move through all the processes." Texas described its system as "an integrated comprehensive system of statewide and agency strategic planning, performance measurement, performance-based budgeting, and performance reporting, assessment, evaluation and auditing."

States with more limited experience in performance management do not seem any less in pursuit of the model illustrated in figure 1.1, simply less far along the road to implementing it. For example, Alabama described its system in ways similar to other states. Its Strategic Plan and Performance Measurement System "connects the strategic goals to specific actions and performance measures by the agencies" and "communicates strategic objectives clearly, links objectives to annual budgets, provides a common methodology and framework for all agency performance efforts." The state of Washington illustrates the desire to link performance data with decision venues: "What we are trying to achieve in Washington is a system whereby all types of decisions are routinely informed by performance and planning information, in addition to traditional factors, such as competing priorities, organizational capacity, financial reality, and stakeholder and public opinion."

Claims about Changes Required: Managerial Authority

If the first recommendation of performance management doctrine is to build a performance information system, the second is to encourage its use through expanding the zone of managerial authority. This second aspect of the performance management doctrine is frequently absent from older treatments of performance management, such as calls for performance budgeting in the 1949 Hoover Commission, more technical treatments of how to foster performance management, or private sector treatments of performance management that assume private sector levels of managerial discretion.[13] But this claim is present in more recent treatments of public management, particularly the NPM.[14] The essential underlying logic of this claim is that the constraints imposed by traditional public organizations have limited the ability of managers to make positive changes. Even if they have perfect information about their operations and have a strong desire to bring about performance improvement, their ability to reorganize human and fiscal resources is limited by traditional managerial controls. Should such controls on inputs be relaxed in favor of controls on outputs, managers will be more likely to perform better.

Financial management and human resource systems in the NPM benchmark countries—the United Kingdom, New Zealand, and Australia—were significantly decentralized to achieve this increase in managerial authority.[15] In line with the contractual approach, administrative motivation was based on clear responsibility and linking achievement of goals to monetary incentives and job security. This tactic required the elimination of centralized civil service rules regarding tenure, promotion, and pay. Managers were given similar employer authority as private sector counterparts. Appropriations, the price tag for the services agreed upon in the performance contract, were aggregated. The main limitation on management use of resources was therefore the size of the appropriation, not specific line items. Managers were also allowed to maintain unspent funds to eliminate the incentive for end-of-year spending.

Schick's summary of NPM ideas illustrates the central focus of reform ideas on performance improvement, which is assumed to occur when

- managers have clear goals, with results measured against these goals.
- managers are given flexibility in using resources.

- operational authority is devolved from central agencies and agency HQ to operating levels and units.
- government decisions and controls focus on outputs and outcomes rather than on inputs and procedures.
- managers are held accountable for the use of resources and the results produced.[16]

Schick's characterization of NPM ideas is interactive, illustrating how NPM ideas depend on one another to work and are not simply a menu of independent prescriptions. Flexibility and operational authority are increased in return for an accountability based on results.

These NPM arguments are inherent to performance management doctrine. Performance management doctrine views managerial authority and the existence of performance information that provides a focus on results as the two key variables that shape management systems. The different configurations of these two variables are illustrated in figure 2.1. Performance management doctrine interprets the history of public management as a gradual and logical transition from prebureaucratic spoils systems (box 1) to bureaucratic systems (box 2) to performance-oriented systems (box 3). Box 4 represents a constrained performance system, where managers have limited authority but are expected to produce results. Chapter 3 will argue that this configuration is closest to the reality that public managers in the United States face. For the moment, however, we will focus on the other boxes in figure 2.1, since they represent the logic of performance management doctrine.

Prebureaucratic systems are represented in box 1 of figure 2.1. In this configuration, the combination of high levels of managerial authority with lack of a focus on results creates the potential for public officials to usurp the power of public organizations for noneffective goals such as maintaining political power; rewarding political supporters, friends, and relatives, or personal enrichment. The spoils system in U.S. government exemplified such characteristics. The spoils system was responded to by the introduction of rules that limited how public officials could use their human and financial resources. By limiting managerial authority, governments created traditional bureaucracies, as represented by box 2 of figure 2.1.

According to performance management doctrine, two shortcomings of the bureaucratic model are that managers still lack a focus on effectiveness and lack the authority to improve service provision. Therefore, performance management doctrine argues that the next stage is to replace controls over inputs or process with managerial authority while developing performance information systems that can be used to hold managers accountable for results. This performance management ideal-type is represented by box 3 of figure 2.1. In such a system, the part of the organization with primary responsibility for a goal is identified.[17] This identifica-

	Low focus on results	High focus on results
High managerial authority	**Box 1: Prebureaucratic systems** Focus on goals other than performance or rule probity (political spoils, personal enrichment).	**Box 3: Performance management ideal-type** Managers have clear goals and authority to achieve goals. This should lead to program effectiveness, higher technical efficiency, and results-based accountability.
Low managerial authority	**Box 2: Bureaucratic systems** High focus on inputs and little incentive or authority to increase technical efficiency.	**Box 4: Constrained performance system** Demand for results, but managers lack authority to engineer change, limiting performance improvement and results-based accountability.

Figure 2.1   How managerial authority and focus on results create different management systems

tion helps match incentives to authority and program knowledge to responsibility. Diagnostic control systems capable of measuring results and ensuring goal congruence between different levels of goals become critical. These systems leave it up to employees to figure out how to juggle inputs and processes to achieve the outputs the system requires.[18] Thompson argues that the major difference between the private sector benchmark organizations promoted by the NPM and public organizations is the nature of the control system.[19] Control systems of successful private organizations are primarily built to facilitate the achievement of results. Avoidance of error or malfeasance is of secondary consideration. The opposite is true in the public sector. A comparison of budgets is illustrative:

> Operational budgets in the federal government are highly detailed spending or resources-acquisition plans that must be scrupulously executed just as they were approved. In contrast, operating budgets in benchmark organizations are remarkably sparing of detail, often consisting of not more than a handful of quantitative performance standards. This difference reflects the efforts made by the benchmark organizations to delegate authority and responsibility down into the organization. Delegation of authority means giving departmental managers the maximum feasible authority needed to make their units productive or, in the alternative, subjecting them to a minimum of constraints.[20]

The goal for benchmark organizations is to make operational budgeting into a form of responsibility budgeting, where a manager is responsible for achieving a certain performance standard or standards. In contrast, public budgeting emphasizes the use of inputs rather than the achievement of results: In other words, operating managers have no authority to acquire or use assets. But without authority, they cannot properly be held responsible for the performance of the administrative units they nominally head.[21]

NPM ideas were sometimes repackaged by U.S. public management writers, most commonly as "reinvention" or as reforms to the budgeting process but with the same recommendations for performance management. For instance, Osborne and Gaebler's widely read manifesto for government reform, *Reinventing Government*, employs NPM principles:

- Steering Rather Than Rowing: This claim suggests that the public actors who set goals (elected officials or those who work most closely with them, political appointees, or central agency actors) should not be the ones implementing these goals. Critical to this claim is the assumption that government priorities should and can be set in terms of strategic goals, with measures of those goals sufficiently clear that they can be used to manage other actors implementing goals. This assumption is also clear in other reinvention prescriptions such as the call to inject competition into service delivery, even within quasi-market settings where public organizations are competing with the private sector or each other.
- Transforming Rule-Driven Organizations: Osborne and Gaebler see public organizations as traditionally focused on compliance with rules and on the amount of resources they receive. They call for organizations and employees to be guided by organizational mission and goals rather than rules or budgets, requiring an increase in managerial flexibility and discretion to align mission with actions, elimination of rules that prevent alignment of mission and behavior, and the use of mission and strategic goals to motivate employees rather than rule compliance.
- Funding Outcomes, Not Inputs: To encourage a focus on the goals of an organization, budgeting and other systems of monetary reward, including pay or bonuses, should be linked to performance.
- From Hierarchy to Participation and Teamwork: Traditional bureaucracies are too hierarchical, removing decision-making power from those with a close knowledge of management problems and processes. Decision making needs to be decentralized in a way that provides substantially more discretion in the hands of managers.[22]

Clearly, the above principles call for strategic planning and performance measurement, which act as a means by which to set organizational goals, as well as motivate, judge, and reward performance. The need for increased managerial authority is reflected in the calls for employee flexibility, more decentralized decision making, and less reliance on formal rules. The benefits claimed of this increased authority will be improved performance as employees make better-informed decisions and reengineer existing management processes.

The Promise of Performance Management: Claims about Improvement

If governments adopt the recommended reforms of performance management doctrine, what benefits are they promised? Performance management doctrine claims a variety of positive benefits, including improved resource allocation, improved responsiveness of bureaucrats to elected officials, enhanced accountability to the public, and improved efficiency.[23] This section describes those claims, which are summarized in table 2.1. Chapters 3 and 5 return to these claims to see how well they have been achieved in practice.

Allocative efficiency is "the capacity of government to distribute resources on the basis of the effectiveness of public programs in meeting strategic objectives."[24] It essentially refers to the pursuit of better decisions in allocating resources and therefore applies particularly to budgeteers and elected officials. Performance management doctrine proposes to increase allocative efficiency by providing a process whereby information on goals is generated through strategic planning and levels of performance through performance measurement. Greater knowledge about the performance of programs and process allows more informed allocation decisions. Budgeteers and elected officials, less concerned with tracking how money is spent, have more time to focus on providing allocations according to strategic goals, observing whether these goals are achieved, and holding managers accountable for results.[25]

Performance management doctrine claims it can facilitate a new approach to accountability in the public sector, one based on the achievement of measurable results. The prospect of result-based accountability is one of the most frequently mentioned positive benefits of performance management, but it is often left unexplored. There are two main ways to consider how performance management might change accountability. *External accountability of the government to the public* changes accountability because the public now has greater information available on the level of performance of the government the people fund. Performance management also provides the opportunity for the public to influence public goals through citizen participation in strategic planning or assessment of services.

The second type of accountability is *internal accountability of bureaucrats to elected officials*. Without performance information, bureaucrats can exploit their information advantage over elected officials in a number of ways, including lack of responsiveness, work shirking, and budget maximization. Performance information systems allow elected officials to specify the goals they wish to achieve and

Table 2.1 The doctrinal benefits claimed by performance management

Benefit claimed	How benefit will occur
Allocative efficiency	• Budgeteers will incorporate performance information in making better budget decisions, reflected by greater allocative efficiency in the distribution of resources.
Accountability of government to the public	• Performance information available for use. • Public better informed about performance of public institutions. • Potential for public involvement in setting goals and evaluating performance.
Accountability of bureaucrats to elected officials	• The policy goals of elected officials are translated into lower level goals that direct the actions of agency-level employees. • Performance information makes the performance of programs become transparent. • When bureaucrats are given control over goals, the introduction of performance information allows elected officials to hold them responsible for performance.
Technical efficiency	• Performance information provides transparency of productivity, making shirking more difficult and facilitating a top-down pressure to perform. • Decision makers have greater knowledge about the performance of programs and processes. Such single-loop learning informs decisions about process reengineering. • As managers are granted increased authority, they can employ their functional knowledge with single-loop learning for a greater number of process reengineering and performance improvement opportunities.

makes transparent the success or failure of public organizations over time. Elected officials gain an improved ability to direct public services, ascertain bureaucratic performance, and make decisions as a result.

Internal accountability may simply mean the availability of performance information, enabling elected officials to keep a performance scorecard and fostering oversight accountability. Another type of internal accountability is the ability of elected officials to direct, through setting of strategic goals, the policies and activities of bureaucrats or exert policy control. Performance information facilitates the achievement of this benefit by creating a goal-setting process that is transparent and can be controlled by senior officials. Policy control essentially assumes a top-down relationship between elected officials and appointees and bureaucrats. The justification for such a top-down relationship is based on the normative dimension of democratic control and is particularly present in economic theories of public organizations, which emphasize elected officials reasserting control over bureaucrats by focusing on performance goals rather than inputs.

Results-based internal accountability can be taken a step further, to imply answerability for performance. *Responsibility accountability* means holding agencies or individual managers responsible for achievement. If responsibility accountability is dependent on having requisite authority, it logically requires matching levels of authority over resources with responsibility.

Improved technical efficiency targets the actions of managers. By offering a set of ex-ante objectives, managers will have clear direction as to what they are trying to achieve. Performance information provides transparency of productivity, making shirking more difficult and facilitating a top-down pressure to perform. Managers, stifled by traditional management controls, can improve productivity once they are given greater authority in managing assets and employees. By reducing input-based controls in favor of a focus on results, managers will have the flexibility, combined with their expertise and judgment, to spend the money more effectively than can be mandated by central budgeteers or the legislature. Greater managerial knowledge about the performance of programs and processes allows informed management decisions. Decisions that exploit knowledge and improve productivity through reengineering are more likely to occur where managers have authority to undertake change. Increasing managerial authority is, therefore, linked to greater use of performance information to improve productivity.

Performance management doctrine calls for removing existing disincentives and creating positive incentives for improved technical efficiency. Allowing carryovers of unspent money gives agencies an incentive to be more efficient with resources.[26] Some performance management systems use explicit rewards tied to the achievement of specific goals, but such experimentation has primarily occurred among contracting relationships, and pay-for-performance systems have had a mixed record within traditional government bureaucracies.[27]

Conclusion

This chapter has summarized the claims of performance management doctrine. This doctrine promises that by following its prescriptions, public organizations can reorganize themselves to move from an inefficient past to a results-driven future. The following chapters examine just how realistic this vision is.

Notes

1. Hood and Jackson, *Administrative Argument.*
2. Simon, *Administrative Behavior.*

3. Downs and Larkey, *The Search for Government Efficiency.*

4. Forrester and Adams, "Budgetary Reform through Organizational Learning."

5. Hood and Jackson, "Key for Locks in Administrative Argument."

6. Barzelay, "How to Argue about the New Public Management."

7. Downs and Larkey, *The Search for Government Efficiency.*

8. Moore, *Creating Public Value.*

9. Koteen, *Strategic Management in Public and Nonprofit Organizations,* 15.

10. Stewart, "The Role of Information in Public Accountability."

11. Miller, Rabin, and Hilldreth, "Strategy, Values, and Productivity."

12. Williams, "Measuring Government in the Early Twentieth Century."

13. Bouckaert, "Measurement and Meaningful Management"; Hatry, *Performance Measurement.*

14. See, for example, Cothran, "Entrepreneurial Budgeting"; Gruening, "Origin and Theoretical Basis of New Public Management"; Keating and Holmes, "Australia's Budgetary and Financial Management Reforms"; Osborne and Gaebler, *Reinventing Government*; Thompson, "Mission-Driven, Results-Oriented Budgeting"; Schick, "Opportunity, Strategy, and Tactics in Reforming Public Management."

15. Barzelay, *The New Public Management.*

16. Schick, "Opportunity, Strategy, and Tactics."

17. Hongren, Sundem, and Stratton, *Introduction to Management Accounting,* 10th ed.

18. Simons, *Levers of Control,* 165.

19. Thompson, "Mission-Driven, Results-Oriented Budgeting."

20. Ibid., 94.

21. Ibid., 95.

22. Osborne and Gaebler, *Reinventing Government.*

23. Aristigueta, *Managing for Results in State Government;* Poister and Streib, "Strategic Management in the Public Sector."

24. Schick, *A Contemporary Approach to Public Expenditure Management,* 89.

25. Grizzle, "Linking Performance to Decisions."

26. Cothran, "Entrepreneurial Budgeting."

27. About rewards tied to achievement, see Heinrich, "Organizational Form and Performance." On the subject of pay-for-performance systems, see the following: Ingraham, "Of Pigs in Pokes and Policy Diffusion"; Kellough and Lu, "The Paradox of Merit Pay in the Public Sector"; VanLandingham, Wellman, and Andrews, "Useful, But Not a Panacea."

3

The Partial Adoption of Performance
Management Reforms in State Government

This chapter reviews current knowledge on performance management implementation at the state government level.[1] From one perspective it looks optimistic. A number of surveys show that state governments have been busy creating performance management systems. State governments have mandated that agencies create and disseminate performance reporting requirements, but they have not provided the type of personnel and budgeting flexibility that performance management doctrine suggests is needed. Therefore, we see only a partial adoption of performance management doctrine. In addition, there is little evidence that this information is being used among decision makers in the governor's office or in the legislature. I illustrate this point with case evidence from my research on the use of performance management in Vermont, Virginia, and Alabama.

The Rise of Performance Information Systems

At the federal level agencies have been producing strategic plans in accordance with GPRA since 1997, performance goals since 1999, and performance results since 2000. At the state level, the 1990s saw a period of adoption of similar types of performance reporting requirements. Surveys have found a high level of adoption of performance information systems that create strategic goals and performance data, based on measurements of formal requirements for performance reporting or surveys of budgeteers or administrators.[2] By the late 1990s, thirty-one states had legislative requirements creating performance information systems, and sixteen states had similar administrative requirements. By 2004, the level of adoption grew to include all states. Thirty-three states had a performance management statute on the books (listed in table 3.1), and the remaining seventeen states had an administrative requirement.

Table 3.1 Performance management legislation in the states

State	Legislation	Year Passed
Alabama	State Code 41–19-11	1995
Alaska	State Code 37.07.010	2002
Arizona	State Code 35–113-115.5	1997
Arkansas	Act 1463 of 2003	2003
Colorado	State Code 2–3-207	2001
Connecticut	Sec. 4–7(b) CGS	1985–86
Delaware	State Code 70 Ch. 492 and Title 29 Part V Ch. 60B	1996
Florida	State Code Ch. 216	1996
Georgia	State Code 45–121	1993
Hawaii	State Code 101 Sec. 26.8	1970
Idaho	State Code 67–19	1994
Iowa	State Code Ch. 8.22	2001
Kentucky	HB 502 Part 3 Section 35	2002
Louisiana	State Code 39–87.2	2003
Maine	State Code Title 5 Ch.151-C, Sec. 17.10K-Q	1999
Minnesota	State Code Ch. 16A.10	2003
Mississippi	State Code 27–103-153 through 27–103-159	1996
Missouri	Revised Statutes, Chapter 33.210	2003
Montana	State Code 17–7-111	1999
Nevada	State Code 353.205	1996
New Mexico	MNSA 6–3A-1	2001
Oklahoma	State Code 74–9.11	1975
Oregon	Oregon State Code 285a.150	1993
Rhode Island	State Code 35–3-24, Section 16 Article 1	1996
South Carolina	State Code 1–1-820	1995
South Dakota	State Code 4–71972	amended 1985; 4–7-35–38 enacted 1994; repealed 1999
Tennessee	Chapter 874 of Public Acts	2002
Texas	State Code 322.011 under General Government	1993
Utah	State Code Title 36 and Title 62A	1997
Vermont	State Code Title 32, 307c	1993
Virginia	State Code 2.2–5510 and 2.2–1501, -1509, -1511	2003
Wisconsin	Act 27 91561997	1997
Wyoming	Code Title 28, Section 28 115–116	1995

Source: Melkers and Willoughby, *Staying the Course: The Use of Performance Measurement in State Government.*

Evidence collected as part of the GPP confirmed the widespread adoption of performance management policies and offered an additional insight. By using content analyses of performance management documents across the states rather than measuring requirements for performance management, or relying on self-reporting, it was possible to verify the actual existence of performance information in state documentation and to demonstrate wide variation among states in terms of the range

Table 3.2   Focus on performance information: Range of documented performance data

State	Range of performance information	State	Range of performance information
Alabama	13.00	Montana	45.00
Alaska	10.00	Nebraska	71.00
Arizona	101.00	Nevada	43.00
Arkansas	.00	New Hampshire	0.00
California	33.00	New Jersey	44.00
Colorado	41.00	New Mexico	57.00
Connecticut	38.00	New York	21.00
Delaware	82.00	North Carolina	33.00
Florida	69.00	North Dakota	50.00
Georgia	68.00	Ohio	48.00
Hawaii	63.00	Oklahoma	22.00
Idaho	66.00	Oregon	63.00
Illinois	53.00	Pennsylvania	55.00
Indiana	36.00	Rhode Island	56.00
Iowa	77.00	South Carolina	44.00
Kansas	19.00	South Dakota	24.00
Kentucky	52.00	Tennessee	59.00
Louisiana	98.00	Texas	89.00
Maine	69.00	Utah	52.00
Maryland	55.00	Vermont	47.00
Massachusetts	14.00	Virginia	79.00
Michigan	27.00	Washington	61.00
Minnesota	72.00	West Virginia	21.00
Mississippi	20.00	Wisconsin	16.00
Missouri	81.00	Wyoming	47.00
State average			48.08

Source: Moynihan, "Managing for Results in State Government: Evaluating a Decade of Reform."

of performance information produced.[3] Table 3.2 provides the result of content analyses of budget, strategic planning, and performance reports. States with higher numerical scores in table 3.2 have built better performance information systems. States increase their standing on the scale if they feature a range of performance information such as quantitative measures/targets and qualitative mission/vision statements and goals, link responsibility for achievement of goals to specific actors, have clear goals and specific measures, show consistency between goals and measures, track performance measures across time and against preset targets, and maintain consistency of goals across different policy documents.

While all states say they have some type of performance management system in place, and most states require agencies to produce strategic plans and/or performance reports, the availability and quality of the resulting information can look very different from state to state. Even with this caveat in mind, the fact that all state governments have willingly accepted one of the basic recommendations of performance management doctrine—to build a performance information system—is indicative of the success of at least this part of the doctrine. However, states have been much more reluctant to embrace the second recommendation of this doctrine, that is, to foster managerial flexibility.

Managerial Flexibility: Financial Controls

Many states claim to have loosened managerial authority with financial tools. However, either central executive branch agencies or the legislative branch remains involved in the use of these tools, eliminating any real increase in discretion at the agency or operational level. Levels of centralization on financial controls that constrain process change—procurement, contracting, and the use of resources—are reported here, based on 2001 GPP survey responses from state financial management officers. The potential to carry over cost savings across years, a means to encourage efficiency in operations, is also discussed.

In the area of procurement and contracting, agencies have a fixed dollar sum under which they have discretion (see box 3.1). These sums are relatively low, with an average of $18,300 for procurement and $24,567 for contracting. Above such levels a formal bidding process will be required, over which agencies rarely have discretion without central approval. While the agency may be involved in the process, the governor and/or the executive budget office usually makes the final decision. In only seven states do agencies have complete discretion in formal procurement bids, and only four states for contracting.

A similar pattern exists for discretion in resource allocation. Efforts to switch money between programs, object classifications, and line items may be prohibited or subject to ex-ante approval by the Office of the Governor, the finance department, or the legislature. In only seven states is there limited discretionary power for agencies to switch money among programs, and this discretion is unlimited in only one state. Controls become more decentralized for smaller resource categories, such as object classifications and line items. Thirteen states claim limited discretionary power for agencies to switch between object classifications, and thirteen other states claim unlimited discretion. Eleven states claim limited discretionary power for agencies to switch between line items, and nineteen states claim unlimited discretion. In some cases the discretion applies to some but not all agencies. Another frequent and significant limit on resource discretion is the explicit prohibition to affect wages or salaries, protecting the largest departmental operating ex-

Box 3.1   Agency discretion in procurement/contracting in fifty states

Agency discretion in nonformal contracts	Yes = 80%
Limit before formal contract required	$24,567.69 (average)
Agency discretion for formal contracting	Yes = 8%
Agency discretion in nonformal bidding process	Yes = 90%
Limit before formal bidding process required	$18,300 (average)
Agency discretion for formal bidding process	Yes = 14%
External oversight of procurement process	Yes = 96%

Source: Moynihan, "Managing for Results in State Government: Evaluating a Decade of Reform."

penses from change and reinforcing human resource (HR) controls. A final form of financial control is the requirement to return unspent appropriations rather than allow carryovers, denying a possible incentive for greater efficiency in spending resources. While twelve states allow the possibility of carryovers, it is usually subject to uncertain ex-ante central permission. Only two states claim to offer agencies unlimited discretion in carrying over unspent funds.

Human Resource Management Controls

Recent analyses of HR trends in state governments note increased decentralization, most significantly in personnel classifications.[4] However, this decentralization is relative, largely reflecting a shift in control of personnel functions from state-level HR offices to agency-level central HR offices.[5] Central agencies at the statewide and agency level clearly define the framework within which managers can work, usually guided by some form of civil service legislation. GPP survey data find that managers have high levels of autonomy in establishing performance expectations and are largely responsible for administering performance appraisals. However, they are closely guided by centralized performance-appraisal instruments and scoring systems, and they have little control in determining compensation to reflect performance. Similarly, classification systems that detail the duties and status of employees are largely centralized at the state level, beyond the control of individual managers. In terms of hiring, managers are usually involved in approval to fill a position, interviewing candidates, recommending appointments, and making appointment decisions. However, a mixture of the agency and statewide HR agencies first establish

Table 3.3 Degree of managerial control of specific HR functions

HR function	Average
Recommending appointments	5.40
Establishing performance expectations	5.34
Making appointments	5.26
Administering performance appraisal	4.86
Determining promotions	4.80
Interviewing	4.76
Approval to fill position	3.76
Determining appraisal grading/scoring systems	2.77
Screening candidates	2.59
Ranking candidates	2.55
Developing performance appraisal instruments	2.18
Establishing candidate list	2.12
Developing tests	2.04
Administering tests	2.04
Scoring tests	2.02
Determining compensation	2.00
Developing classification	1.24
Conducting classification	1.94

Note: Managerial authority on a 1 to 6 scale, where 6 is complete managerial control and 1 is complete control by statewide central agency actor.
Source: Moynihan, "Managing for Results in State Government: Evaluating a Decade of Reform."

the screening, ranking, and selection of a candidate pool. Table 3.3 illustrates these findings, providing average state score on HR discretion, where a six represents managerial control and a one represents central statewide agency control.[6]

Survey evidence supports the picture painted of statewide performance management systems. Melkers and Willoughby's survey of executive and legislative budgeteers caution that actual implementation of performance management is still a work in progress, partly due to diverging expectations for use and success among different actors.[7] Surveys of senior administrators reported by Brudney, Hebert, and Wright find that the most intensively adopted reforms of the 1990s were related to creating performance information systems, while the least intensively adopted reforms were the reduction of HR and financial management controls.[8] Later work by Burke, Cho, Brudney, and Wright supported this earlier research, finding that factor analysis confirmed the division of 1990s state government reforms into two distinct categories relating to managerial authority and results, and that the managerial authority category lagged behind the results category in terms of adoption.[9]

Perhaps most telling is the survey results of Anders, who surveyed administrators and central budget officers in 1996 and again in 2004. The results show that most public managers see the arrival of performance information systems as having added an administrative burden but not an increase in discretion. These negative perceptions of performance information systems are hardening over time. In both periods a vast majority agreed that performance information systems increased the number of rules and instructions they had to comply with (72 percent in 1996 and 73 percent in 2004) and increased the resources needed to comply with them (61 percent in 1996 and 68 percent in 2004). In 1996, 66 percent of respondents disagreed that the introduction of performance information systems had reduced the number of rules involved in budget execution, increasing to 79 percent by 2004. In 2004, only 14 percent agreed that the new performance information systems were accompanied with legislative grants of discretion in budget execution, down from 26 percent in 1996.[10]

Managers have a variety of different types of discretion, of which discretion over HR and financial matters is only one. Indeed, chapter 5 shows the ability of managers to use performance management reforms even without any increases in management discretion. The point, therefore, is not that managers have no authority to use performance information, but that among U.S. states, the increasing emphasis on performance data has not been accompanied by increases in managerial authority, contrary to the premise of performance management doctrine.

The Partial Adoption of Performance Management Doctrine

States have embraced the creation of performance information systems, but they have been reluctant to increase managerial authority. This suggests a partial adoption of performance management doctrine. HR authority remains largely shared between statewide and agency-level specialists, and there have not been significant increases in authority for operational managers. Evidence suggests that deregulation of key controls largely implied shifting more authority to agency-level personnel specialists, not to managers themselves.[11] In short, increases in managerial authority did occur, but not to the degree called for by performance management doctrine.

On the other hand, there has been a good deal of activity in focusing on performance information systems in recent years. GPP surveys also found state governments emphasizing performance management as a new wave of reform, and previous reviews suggest limited state government interest in performance management prior to the 1990s, followed by a renewed interest in the topic in implementation of performance information systems during the 1990s.[12] Table 3.2 suggests that some states have advanced more quickly than others in producing a wide range of performance information.

If states were pursuing a complete performance management doctrine, we would expect to see a significant positive correlation between the focus on results scale indicated in table 3.2 and different measures of managerial authority. We find a positive but far from significant correlation in each state's focus on performance information and the overall measure of HR authority (a summary of the data used in table 3.3) of 0.073.[13] The relationship between financial management authority and focus on performance information is stronger but still less than implied by performance management doctrine. An overall weighted measure of financial authority that includes program reallocation powers and carryover power has a 0.265 correlation with focus on results, not significant at 5 percent in a two-tailed test.[14] The individual measures of financial authority provide a mixed picture. There are significant or near-significant positive correlations between the limited discretion over object classifications and line items and the focus on performance information measure. However, there is no relationship between the more substantive program measure of reallocation discretion and focus on performance information. Furthermore, there is only a weak positive relationship between the ability to carry over funds and focus on performance information. It appears that states that adopt create a wide range of performance information are more likely to provide a narrow range of increased financial discretion, but not broad increases in either financial or personnel authority. Even the modest indicators on financial authority are overstated, since low personnel authority severely limits financial discretion. The most prominent limitation on the use of resources is that any changes cannot affect personnel, where most public organizations spend the majority of their budget. Even if managers gain new financial authority, this limitation means that they can redirect only at the margins of their operating budget.

This evidence undercuts the proposition that performance management reform is being implemented in stages and that managerial authority simply lags the implementation of performance information systems. States that have led the way in focusing on results have not taken on significant parallel reforms of authority and have not viewed the two aspects of performance management as closely connected. Such a connection may be realized in the future as the limitations of the current approach to performance management become evident, but it does not appear to be the current blueprint for reform.

The evidence presented thus far focuses on the states. But what about the federal level? Here, the evidence is not as clear-cut but nonetheless suggests a similar pattern. As other chapters will discuss, the federal government has adopted successive rounds of performance management reforms, first with the Government Performance and Results Act and later in the form of the Program Assessment Rating Tool. At the same time, there has not been an overhaul of governmentwide federal personnel laws, despite multiple efforts by both the Clinton and George W. Bush administrations. Under President Bill Clinton and Vice President Al Gore, efforts to reform personnel rules were met with opposition from both public sector unions and Republicans in the legislature.[15] The White House tried to find alternative ways to provide flexibility to innovators, but without a statutory basis, the effect of such efforts was limited. One exception was the area of procurement, where legislative change did have an impact. But overall, as Rubin and Kelly note, "throughout the 1990s the U.S. attempted, but largely failed, to introduce an expenditure management system with fewer input controls in exchange for performance contracts."[16]

The Bush White House also proposed expanding managerial discretion and struggled with these efforts until the aftermath of September 11 allowed them to push such management reforms in the Department of Homeland Security and the Department of Defense.[17] The pattern follows a more piecemeal approach to HR reform, where specific agencies have won varying degrees of exception from the standard personnel system, to the point that it is difficult to say that a single personnel system still operates. However, this patchwork model of personnel has not, as yet, evolved into anything resembling the performance management ideal model identified in figure 2.1 or seen among NPM benchmark countries. Indeed, focus groups of federal managers reported concerns similar to those expressed by state government counterparts in Anders's survey: They perceive that they have no greater discretion than before, even as they are being held to more explicit performance expectations.[18] A survey of federal managers provides a similar finding: 57 percent of non–Senior Executive Service (SES) managers and 61 percent of SES managers felt they were being held accountable for outcomes, but significantly less—38 percent and 40 percent, respectively—felt that they had the authority to achieve these results.[19]

High Results Focus and Restricted Authority:
Implications for Public Management

Performance management doctrines did indeed exert an influence in the United States, leading to a new configuration of governmental systems. This finding is in itself significant, but what is more interesting is that the outcome did not mirror the performance management ideal-type called for in performance management doctrine and pursued by NPM benchmark countries. Instead, U.S. state governments shifted toward a configuration characterized by a high focus on results but constrained managerial authority, illustrated by box 4 in figure 2.1.

What are the implications of this constrained performance system as a new configuration for governance? The performance management ideal-type portrays the potential for improved efficiency and results-based accountability, but performance management doctrine also emphasizes that efficiency gains through process improvement are inherently limited by constraints on managerial authority. Likewise, results-based accountability will not occur when managers lack authority over processes and, ultimately, outputs. Whether performance management has any positive benefit at the managerial level depends largely on the willingness of agency leaders and managers to search for ways to utilize performance management within existing constraints.

Ultimately, therefore, the potential for performance systems where managers seek to improve performance and are formally held accountable to results is undermined by the continued existence of financial and personnel control systems that emphasize compliance and error avoidance. The existence of performance information has not replaced these systems as the fundamental way in which state governments attempt to control managerial behavior. The ability of public managers to achieve high-level outcomes is already stretched by factors beyond governmental control, but internal management controls further restrict the ability to direct and improve more modest organizational outputs. There are many valid arguments to be made for such controls, in terms of the need for probity and avoidance of improper use of public power. However, state governments have lurched headlong into the pursuit of results-based government hoping for improved efficiency and results-based accountability, while only partially implementing the reforms necessary to achieve these goals and maintaining control systems contradictory to them.

A performance information system ensures that data is available to decision makers. But the availability of performance information does little to improve the capacity or incentives for decision makers to use this information, and their existence tells us little about how decisions are actually made. Providing performance information is a necessary, but not sufficient condition to ensure its actual use. Ultimately, the most telling standard for performance management is not whether performance information exists, but whether it is used in various decision-making venues in government, from day-to-day management of programs to high-level resource allocation decisions. It is by incorporating performance data into decisions that governments move from simply measuring results to managing them.

Ascertaining whether and to what degree performance data was actually used in decision processes is difficult. Self-reported surveys tend to be more positive on whether information is being used than evidence from case research. In responding to surveys such as the GPP or those undertaken by the GAO or the Governmental Accounting Standards Board, state officials are usually able to give examples of how performance data influenced specific decisions but cannot show any systematic use of performance data.[20] At the same time, legislators complain of information overload and poor data quality, expressing mistrust toward the performance data given to them.[21]

This book relies primarily on case study evidence to try to ascertain if performance information is being used and if it matches the doctrinal claims laid out in chapter 2, including expected uses in the areas of resource allocation, accountability, and technical efficiency. The following chapters examine whether these claims have been satisfied and try to explain factors that lead to their occurrence or not. Chapter 4 discusses the potential for political oversight and policy control using performance management benefits of reform, and chapter 5 includes a discussion of responsibility accountability. Chapter 6 deals with the case evidence on resource allocation, and both chapters 5 and 9 examine managerial uses of performance information in greater detail. The balance of this chapter introduces the three cases and previews case findings to illustrate how the partial adoption of performance management systems affected the doctrinal claims of performance management in Alabama, Virginia, and Vermont.

Performance Management Adoption in Alabama

Performance management in Alabama lacks a glorious past, although it has made some progress. In the 1999 assessment of performance management practices in state government, the GPP issued the state an F grade, finding little evidence of any sort of strategic planning or performance reporting. Such practices had been introduced in previous administrations, but faded away once these governors left office. The only vestiges of previous efforts were a pronounced sense of cynicism among long-term employees toward results-based reform and a barely implemented legislative requirement for performance management. Under legislation, performance reporting occurs in conjunction with the biennial budget cycle: The governor is required to develop a statewide strategic plan, and agencies are required to produce goals, objectives, and plans for implementation and performance measures. These requirements, passed under Governor Folsom (1993–95), were largely ignored or led to pro forma completion when he failed to win the following election. Subsequent governors did not create strategic plans. Some agencies reported a handful of performance measures or nothing at all. In instances when performance information was reported, it was widely acknowledged that such information had little impact on either resource allocation or management, and neither have more recent reform efforts. Performance measures were no longer included as part of the printed budget by 1999, eliminated, says a budget official, because "it just wasn't worth what it was costing to print extra pages."

Governor Siegelman (1999–2003) tried to reignite performance management in Alabama. A statewide strategic plan, *Achieve: Achieving Accountability for Alabama,* was created by the governor, policy staff, and officials from the Department of Finance in 1999 and 2000. *Achieve* and subsequent agency planning adopted a balanced scorecard approach, a technique suggested by the consultants hired by the state. *Achieve* itself explicitly mentions many of the performance management doctrinal benefits identified in chapter 2: improved accountability, efficiency, aligning individual actions with overall state expectations and strategies, communicating strategic objectives clearly, and linking objectives to resource allocation.[22] Following the development of *Achieve*, Governor Siegelman required five pilot agencies, including the Alabama DOC, to undertake performance management.

The creation of a statewide strategic plan was seen as the first step in building what was called a Strategic Plan and Performance Measurement System that "aligns individual actions with overall state expectations and strategies."[23] The main linking mechanism to provide goal congruence between statewide goals and individual action was the creation of agency-level plans. A logical order is presented in the selection of goals, suggesting that choices are first made at a governmentwide level and become increasingly specific. According to *Achieve,* the Strategic Plan and Performance Measurement System is patterned on the following chronological order of actions:

- Create a mission statement for Alabama.
- Determine strategic issues areas, called "focal areas of great importance."
- Determine strategic objectives that provide direction for activities occurring at the agency level.
- Establish the long-term goals Alabama would like to achieve.
- Identify performance measures that match the strategic objectives and will help determine levels of success, prioritize allocation of resources, and create needed accountability.
- Create agency action plans to implement goals.
- Results, which are intended to be reviewed and to feed back into every element of the process for future adjustment of the system.

While this research focuses largely on the Siegelman reforms, it is notable that Alabama has continued to search for new modes of performance management after Siegelman lost his reelection bid in 2002. Siegelman's successor, Governor Bob Riley, abandoned *Achieve* and has introduced another attempt at performance budgeting, in the form of SMART, which is short for Specific, Measurable, Accountable, Responsible, and Transparent.

Performance Management Adoption in Virginia

Virginia is arguably the foremost exponent of performance management among U.S. state governments, pursuing results-based government in one form or another since the 1970s. Central agencies contain experienced specialists on performance management, and the state has consistently received an A- grade for its performance management efforts across three GPP surveys, the only state to do so. The GAO, the National Performance Review, and others have pointed to Virginia as an exemplar that the federal government could learn from.

By the time Virginia legislated performance management in House Bill 1065 in 2000, it was, unlike Alabama or Vermont, codifying existing practices of performance reporting rather than seeking to initiate new policies. H.B. 1065 does not describe the nature of the reporting requirements for agencies, but it gives discretion to the Department of Planning and Budget to determine what performance information is to be reported with the budget. The Department of Planning and Budget has been fulfilling this role since 1995, at various times requiring issue analysis, environmental scanning, discussion of customer service needs, linkage of performance targets to budget requests, and activity-based costing. H.B.1065 was followed by more comprehensive legislation in 2003, H.B. 2097, known as the Virginia Government Performance and Results Act, which further formalized the process by mandating that each agency develop a strategic plan that included goals and objectives on a three-year basis. Governor Gilmore (1998–2002) also developed a statewide strategic plan intended to provide guiding principles for agency goal-setting and operations. This was followed by Governor Warner's (2002–6) *Roadmap for Virginia's Future.*

Virginia has developed a performance management system that claims to link strategic planning, performance measurement, evaluation, and performance budgeting. Budget analysts are called on to assess performance information in terms of resource allocation, management decision making, and program improvement. Publicly available performance information is everywhere: in the budget, the governor's statewide plans, annual statewide performance reports, agency strategic plans, and in the case of the Virginia DOC, subagency strategic plans. The Department of Planning and Budget has developed a web-based central database for such information, whose information has been assessed and audited by one or more of three central agencies with oversight for performance management.

Performance Management Adoption in Vermont

The state of Vermont did not have a performance management system as comprehensive as Virginia, but it did have greater experience than Alabama. At the statewide level, legislators in 1994 adjusted the appropriations process to require that budget submissions contain a strategic plan for each state agency and department, including a statement of mission and goals, a description of indicators used to measure outputs and outcomes, identification of the groups of people served by programs, and the strategies for meeting the needs of the agency or program.

Unlike the other states surveyed, there was no single statewide strategic plan in Vermont. Governor Howard Dean (1991–2003) was not a strong supporter of formal statewide planning, preferring to promote policy goals through his policy staff and weekly cabinet meetings, and his successor Jim Douglas proved little different. The most formal statement of the governor's goals appeared in the budget. The main vehicle for producing performance information came from the five overarching agencies and subordinate departments through their statutory reporting requirements as part of the budget, although the legislation did not lead to systematic use of performance information in resource allocation. Staff at the Department of Finance and Management were all too aware of the political nature of decision making, even at department-level budget preparation decisions, where budgeteers allocate resources based on their expectations of the reactions of other budgeteers at Finance and Management and the legislative branch. However, the Department of Finance and Management pursued performance management anyway. According to one department official, this was "because it makes sense," it was how resources should be allocated, and the Department of Finance and Management had a responsibility to make that aspiration as close to a reality as possible.

The Department of Finance and Management has also emphasized the possibility of using performance information for managerial decisions, with performance information becoming part of the decision-making culture of agencies. However, efforts to prompt agency-level managerial uses have been limited. The main vehicle for trying to ingrain performance information into departmental culture and management decisions remains the statutory requirement to report such information in budget submissions. It is not surprising, according to one Department of Finance and Management employee, that many departments "don't treat it as a management tool. They treat it as an exercise they do once a year in their budget."

Matching the Promise of Doctrine with Reality

Chapter 2 identified the promise of performance management, including specific claims about resource allocation, accountability, and performance improvement. This section briefly describes whether performance management reforms met these goals, summarized in table 3.4.

For resource allocation, the findings suggest that the use of performance data is episodic, especially by legislators. In the states examined, performance information was discussed in some instances, but usually prompted by an advocate using information to support a preestablished position, rather than a careful consideration by unbiased actors on what the data meant. This case evidence is supported by other research. For instance, Joyce and Tompkins find some limited evidence of use

Table 3.4 Promised benefits of performance management compared with case findings

Benefit	Description
Resource allocation	Performance information available and occasionally discussed in budget process in each state, but not used in a systematic way.
External accountability	Performance information available to public in all states; range, quality, and accessibility of data better in Vermont and especially Virginia. Little evidence of public use of this information, with exception of Vermont DOC, where some members of public could participate in goal-setting.
Internal accountability	Availability of performance information provides opportunity for elected officials to exert greater oversight and control, but there is little evidence that they use performance information to the degree necessary to achieve such control. No evidence of management systems or actions consistent with goal of responsibility accountability.
Performance improvement	Some evidence that agency staff used performance data for operational improvement, but its use was not systematic.

among budgeteers in the executive branch but almost negligible use among legislators.[24] Melkers and Willoughby found implementation of performance management proceeding slowly. They also found that performance information had not, thus far, affected budget decision outcomes, noting that "while governments continue to strongly emphasize integrating budgeting with performance assessment, there is little recognition of how performance measurement applies to budget balancing."[25] Indeed, the most significant problem in the application of performance measurement as cited by state budgeteers was lack of regular use by top management and elected officials and the low priority assigned to performance measures in the budget process.[26] The GAO found that even in states with exceptional performance, budgets use data to inform but not to determine budget allocations.[27] Anders found that 22 percent of administrators and central budget officers surveyed in 2004 believed that performance information had an influence on political decision makers, down from 25 percent in 1996.[28] Other in-depth case studies of performance management efforts have found little evidence that statewide actors use performance information.[29]

The case findings on agency-level performance improvement are similar. All three DOCs had strategic goals and matching performance targets, and they reported actual performance on a regular basis. However, there was little evidence that organizations systematically evaluated this knowledge in the search for improved alternative organizational processes. There were some uses of performance information by managers, explored in chapter 9, but there was little evidence of managers changing processes for the purposes of performance improvement.

For external accountability, the case evidence suggests that, while performance information is indeed provided in often impressive detail, it is uncertain whether the general public has been really demanding it or knows what to do with it. Another and somewhat higher standard of external accountability would be that the public was involved in setting goals, a standard largely unmet by the states studied.

For internal accountability, performance information provides improved capacity for elected officials to exert both oversight and policy control. However, elected officials have largely shown a disinclination to actually use performance management for these purposes. In part, this is because they are unlikely to be a willing audience for performance data for any purposes, and performance information is not always of a quality to provide useful oversight. The process of selecting goals provides an opportunity for elected officials to exert explicit policy control by requiring agencies to ensure that their strategic plans are consistent with their goals. Central agencies usually review these plans, but direct intervention is the exception rather than the rule. There are few goals critical to the governor, and the agency is likely to already have made an effort to reflect this. In any case, broad gubernatorial goals can usually be easily satisfied with the existing policy objectives of agencies.

Performance management doctrine also suggests the possibility of responsibility accountability, where bureaucrats would be directly held to account for performance. The doctrinal claim is that improvement comes when the bureaucrat has clear goals to achieve, with a set amount of resources, and is deemed responsible for the achievement of these goals, which may be tied to financial incentives. The motivated bureaucrat figures out more efficient means of delivering these goals. This model of responsibility accountability has clearly not been implemented in U.S. state governments. Senior managers in agencies have performance goals to achieve, but there is not an expectation that ex-post performance will be carefully examined and have an impact on their tenure or finances. In part, this is because strategic goals are not treated as a contractual promise, and performance results do not bring about benefits or punishments. Indeed, it is hard to imagine how this might work in the U.S. system, where strategic goals are established prior to legislative resource allocation and not renegotiated after budgeting decisions are made.

Conclusion

Evidence on the adoption of performance management offers a number of insights. States have been creating performance information systems, although the range and quality of the information that results varies a great deal. States have been less active in adopting recommendations to provide managers with more authority, suggesting a partial adoption of performance management doctrine. On the critical issue of use, evidence from the three cases suggests that performance information was not widely used, and as a result, the predicted benefits of performance management were largely unfulfilled. Later chapters expand on this point, but they also suggest that there are additional uses of performance information that are positive, though largely unanticipated by performance management doctrine.

State governments have not begun to identify and respond to the weaknesses of the current approach to performance management. The 2005 GPP survey found that aspects of performance management that can be converted into standard procedures are spreading. Aspects of performance management that require behavioral change on the part of users remain weak, in particular the issue of performance information use. More states are creating performance information than ever before. But in some cases, they are failing to build off past efforts. Instead, a new model of results-based government is presented by successive governors. For instance, the most recent round of GPP analysis credits Governor Bob Riley's efforts to introduce performance budgeting in Alabama. But this effort is the third such performance budgeting reform in the last decade. The previous efforts of Governor Siegelman and Governor Folsom were introduced with fanfare, but they never seemed to affect agency decision making and died quietly.

A skeptical viewpoint suggests that such an episodic approach to performance management is doomed to a familiar cycle of failure. Lots of time and energy is devoted to creating a performance information system that fails to be used by agency officials, who assume it will disappear over time and who are proved correct when it is abandoned by a new governor anxious to put his or her own mark on government reform. While Alabama may be an outlier in terms of repeated failures, the 2005 GPP reports that many states are in the same position: starting to embrace performance management; in the process of planning, building, or improving a performance information system; optimistic about the future of results-based government; and in some cases able to offer examples of how performance information has made a difference. The 2005 GPP report offers numerous examples. Alaska has "positive momentum"; Wyoming's "recent adoption of a results-based accountability model are promising developments"; "although Arkansas does not currently have a statewide strategic plan, there is momentum in the state due to the Governor's new performance-based budgeting system"; in Georgia "the agency strategic planning system appears somewhat fragmented, but new requirements just passed may add value to the process"; planning in Illinois and Kansas are both described as "a work in progress"; "Maryland became in engaged in strategic planning in 1997, but has yet to fully implement the process."[30]

For many states, the promise of performance management looms large, and the major gains and benefits of performance management appear just a couple of years away. But at this stage in the development of performance management systems in state government, it is reasonable to expect that states would have progressed beyond this point.

Notes

1. Some of the cross-state comparative analysis in this chapter previously appeared in Moynihan, "Managing for Results in State Government."

2. Anders, "Performance Measures as Strategic Management Tools"; Brudney, Hebert, and Wright, "Reinventing Government in the American States"; Melkers and Willoughby, "The State of the States"; Melkers and Willoughby, *Staying the Course;* Office of Program Policy Analysis and Government Accountability, *A Report on Performance-Based Program Budgeting.*

3. For more detail on how the measures were constructed to track performance information systems, human resource authority decentralization, and financial control, see Moynihan, "Managing for Results in State Government." The data drew from public documentation and GPP survey responses, and the content analyses of public documents employed multiple coders for each documenting, with intercoder reliability of 0.83.

4. Selden, Ingraham, and Jacobson, "Human Resources Practices in State Government."

5. Moynihan, "Managing for Results in State Government."

6. Details of how these measures were developed can be found in Moynihan, "Managing for Results in State Government."

7. Melkers and Willoughby, "Budgeters' Views of State Performance-Budgeting Systems."

8. Brudney, Hebert, and Wright, "Reinventing Government in the American States."

9. Burke et al., "No 'One Best Way' to Manage Change."

10. Anders, "Performance Measures as Strategic Management Tools."

11. Selden, Ingraham, and Jacobson, "Human Resources Practices in State Governments."

12. Denhardt, "Strategic Planning in State and Local Government," 174–79. Other support for this claim comes from table 3.1, where of the thirty-three states listed, all but two saw the legislative changes occur during the 1990s or since 2000. Brudney, Hebert, and Wright, "Reinventing Government in the American States"; Snell and Grooters, *Governing-for-Results: Legislation in the States;* Seong, "Adoption of Innovation."

13. Georgia did not offer responses to the questions upon which the HR data was based. The state has significantly decentralized its personnel system, essentially eliminating its civil service system. It could be argued that Georgia most closely resembles Texas in this regard, and if we were to give Georgia a Texas score of 4.83, then the correlation rises to 0.148.

14. A simple average of the four measures of financial authority (program reallocation powers, objection classification reallocation, line-item reallocation, and carryover power) has a 0.308 correlation with focus on results, significant at 5 percent in a two-tailed test. However, the use of a simple average as an overall measure would be misleading, incorrectly implying that the four

measures are of equivalent importance, e.g., that the ability to move around resources among line items is equivalent to the power to move resources among programs. The weighted measure reflects differences between the measures. Details on how this measure was created can be found in Moynihan, "Managing for Results in State Government."

15. Moynihan, "Public Management Policy Change in the United States 1993–2001."

16. Rubin and Kelly, "Budget and Accounting Reforms," 576.

17. Moynihan, "Protection versus Flexibility."

18. Anders, "Performance Measures as Strategic Management Tools"; Dull, *The Politics of Results.*

19. U.S. General Accounting Office, *Observations on the Use of OMB's Program Assessment Rating Tool,* 23; Frederickson and Frederickson, *Measuring the Performance of the Hollow State.*

20. U.S. Government Accountability Office, *Performance Budgeting: States' Experiences Can Inform Federal Efforts.*

21. Joyce and Tompkins, "Using Performance Information for Budgeting."

22. Siegelman, *Achieve,* 3, 5.

23. Ibid., 5.

24. Joyce and Tompkins, "Using Performance Information for Budgeting."

25. Melkers and Willoughby, *Staying the Course,* 17.

26. Ibid., 26.

27. U.S. GAO, *Performance Budgeting: States' Experiences Can Inform Federal Efforts.*

28. Anders, "Performance Measures as Strategic Management Tools."

29. Aristigueta, *Managing for Results in State Government;* Franklin, "An Examination of Bureaucratic Reactions to Institutional Controls."

30. Quotes taken from state reports prepared by Barrett et al., "Grading the States '05."

4

Explaining the Partial Adoption of Performance Management Reforms

The previous chapter presents two puzzles. First of all, why do elected officials advocate for the creation of performance information that they rarely use? A related puzzle is why performance management reforms were adopted in the manner that they were. Performance management doctrine argues for an increased focus on results while providing managers greater authority over their fiscal and human resources. Chapter 3 demonstrates rapid advances on the focus-on-results half of the reform equation—through strategic planning, performance measurement, and customer service assessment—but a neglect of managerial flexibility. Why was there a partial adoption of performance management doctrine?

I return to the three state governments of Alabama, Vermont, and Virginia and to the literature on policymaking and political reform of the bureaucracy to develop an explanation.[1] In each of the three states, the legislature, supplemented by central agency guidance, required agencies to produce performance information, but did not significantly increase managerial authority during the same period. As we saw in the last chapter, this pattern of adoption of performance management is typical of state governments.

Explaining Performance Management Adoption

So why did these three states, mirroring all other states, decide to adopt requirements that created performance information systems? In framing the discussion of the policy-adoption phase, I utilize concepts from the policymaking literature.[2] This literature points to the malleability of reform ideas in the policy stream and the artful process of linking problems with a solution. All three states shared the issue image of poor governmental performance, with performance management reforms portrayed as the solution. Performance management doctrine, whether cast in the context of NPM or reinvention, provided the underlying reform ideas.[3]

A summary of this theory of adoption is as follows:

> The adoption of formal performance management reforms is a function of the role of central agencies in defining the reform and the motivation of elected officials selecting the reform. The costs and benefits of reforms guide elected officials. The failure of elected officials to pursue the instrumental benefits of performance management suggests that they are primarily attracted to performance management for symbolic benefits.

This theory is at odds with the doctrinal argument that performance management reform is driven by actual government inefficiency and deficits that create the need for savings through better performance and cutting ineffective programs. Empirical evidence suggests the opposite is true, that performance budgeting or strategic planning requirements are more likely to be passed in times of fiscal health than in difficulty and that agencies with resources are more likely to be adopters.[4] However, the widespread perception of government inefficiency is important in setting the stage for which public management policy ideas are deemed appropriate and in motivating elected officials to adopt them.

The Role of Central Agencies in Defining Policy Ideas

A key concept in the policy-adoption literature is that of the policy subsystem. Budget and management central agencies tend to be key players in public management subsystems, given their expertise, continuity, and power. The common pattern in performance management adoption has been for elected officials to rely on central agencies to design and oversee reforms, and states with influential budget offices tend to be the most enthusiastic adopters of performance management systems.[5] Central agency officials are therefore in a strong position to select and shape policy ideas to match their preferences. In each state the main promoters of performance management were central agencies, primarily the finance department, and to a lesser extent the statewide personnel office and legislative auditors. Together, this group of actors made up the main formal source of public management reform expertise within government, although states with less internal capacity (Alabama and, to a lesser extent, Vermont) relied proportionately more on consultants.

Central agency staff may not be familiar with the underlying claims of performance management doctrine, but they are familiar with popular representations of these claims that propose reinventing government by making it more focused on achieving results and enhanced flexibility. The claims are buttressed by success stories. Case studies of successful performance management in the public sector tend to be repeated over and over. The story of how Indianapolis used benchmarking, activity-based costing, and managed competition to spur public performance has become the modern equivalent of the corporate legend of how Xerox first used benchmarking to improve performance.[6]

Financial and personnel specialists are receptive to success stories and the ideas they represent. They are also aware of the adoption of performance management in other states, particularly the states perceived as "leaders." Virginia is considered one such state. The Virginia Department of Planning and Budget actively diffuses its experience to other states through professional conferences and other forums. More than in other states, the Department of Planning and Budget has pushed performance management ideas. To a large degree, this is because governors cannot succeed themselves in Virginia, and the weakness of gubernatorial powers is compensated for by strong central agencies and an emphasis on administrative professionalism in general (see appendix B for more detail on Virginia's political culture). In Vermont, a commission was established to report on performance management experiences in other states, and consultants in Alabama brought in representatives from "leader" states to make presentations.

Central agency staff are also familiar with the promotion of performance management by professional organizations, including the Governmental Accounting Standards Board, National Academy of Public Administration, the National Council of State Legislatures, and the International City/County Managers Association. These organizations characterize performance information systems as a desirable standard for governments, which is increasingly necessary to receive various types of formal accreditation. Professional standing for these actors is linked to having some reform in place that equates with performance management since, as one official said, "our profession as a whole has recognized that this is a direction that government is going and that we need to be going in also."

Federal program requirements and bond agencies are also important encouragers of performance information systems making such reforms more attractive to central agency officials. Brudney et al. find that agencies who are dependent on federal aid, and therefore have to meet reporting requirements, are the strongest adopters of performance management reforms.[7] According to the GAO: "Many federal grant programs, for example, require states to report on program performance in order to receive funding. Bond rating companies, whose ratings affect a state's ability to finance government projects, include the public reporting of performance information as a criterion for assessment in the rating process."[8]

However, the professional training and work experience of central agency staff also leads them to continue to view themselves as the maintainers of control systems at odds with performance management doctrine. Financial management specialists emphasize probity, spending that matches appropriations and is not used for unspecified purposes. These norms arose from the progressive era and have been adopted as professional standards for financial managers to maintain and legal standards for operational managers to obey. While a greater results orientation is appealing to financial managers, norms of fiscal probity are so ingrained that they do not see a conflict between restrictive financial control systems and a theory of performance improvement that assumes a high degree of managerial authority.[9]

Statewide personnel office staff maintain a set of beliefs similar to their finance counterparts. Since the progressive era, public personnel management has revolved around the goal of preventing abuse of managerial power, resulting in civil service systems that have failed to discriminate between employees for almost any reason, including performance.

These traditional norms of control have not disappeared with the rise of the performance management doctrine; instead they coexist despite clear conflicts. Finance and personnel specialists have tried to align the idea of top-down controls with improved performance by creating highly centralized, formal, pay-for-performance structures that continue to place greater emphasis on equality—and that simply have never worked very well in the U.S. public sector.[10] Central agency staff are aware of the idea that enhanced managerial authority is a means of improving performance, but they have never operationalized it to the degree demanded by performance management doctrine: giving operational managers significant discretion for how they use their money and human resources and using ex-post performance accountability mechanisms. Presenting the idea of managerial authority in such an extreme fashion is at odds with the norms of control that central agencies are trained to protect and continue to value, and that provide them with a source of power over line agencies. To maintain the coexistence of traditional norms of control with the performance management doctrine, central agency officials produce reform ideas that call for a focus on results but not a dramatic increase in managerial authority.

Although consultants are not central players in policy decisions, they do have a role in shaping policy ideas and influencing central agency officials. The interests of consultants, like those of central agency officials and elected officials, are consistent with an understanding of performance management that emphasizes performance information systems but neglects reform of financial and personnel control systems. Consultants have a professional interest in promoting government reform that enables them to sell services to a client. Performance information systems are a good product. They allow consultants to sell information technology products, expertise in designing performance information systems, and training of public employees in how to undertake strategic planning and performance reporting. Increased managerial authority is less amenable to easy translation into a product, unless it prompts a demand for training managers in how to use their authority. In any case, the models that consultants draw upon for understanding performance management fail to recognize managerial authority as an area in need of reform. Alabama provides an example. The consultants there promoted the balanced scorecard approach, a model derived from the private sector. In translating this model to the public sector, the consultants did not adjust for significant differences in managerial authority between the two sectors and the impact this factor has on performance information use. Consultants in Alabama bemoaned the constraints of a "very bureaucratic, difficult system," but at the same time they did not view their role as promoters of performance management reform as advocating increased managerial authority. Another example of consultants' tendency not to recognize the particular terrain of the public sector comes from the Performance Institute, which specializes in providing downsizing and performance management services to government. The institute has pushed for adding private sector–style incentives to the budget process, with high-performing programs maintaining budgets and programs rated as performing poorly being cut or eliminated.[11] As chapter 7 discusses, few actually working in budgeting consider this a realistic or even desirable approach.

Motivation of Elected Officials

In the three cases central agency officials defined performance management as a policy idea, but to some extent this definition was prompted and shaped by an awareness of the demands of elected officials. Elected officials created a demand for performance management reform—which may be as vague as a call for more efficient and effective government—rather than simply reacting to the supply of ideas from others. Without this demand it seems unlikely that the states would have adopted a statewide performance management system. Elected officials are ultimately responsible for deciding what reforms are adopted. In Vermont the legislature led the adoption of performance management reform, but the executive-led reform of Alabama and Virginia are more typical.[12] In all three states the legislature adopted requirements for agency strategic planning and performance reporting.

Examining the motivations of elected officials with regard to performance management helps us understand why they want it in the first place and why they adopt it in the way that they do. This chapter proposes that elected officials develop a rough cost-benefit calculus in deciding whether to support a public management reform and that they adopt reforms that maximize the instrumental and symbolic benefits while minimizing perceived costs.[13] Such a calculation explains why elected officials would adopt performance management in terms of a performance information system while not increasing managerial authority.

Instrumental benefits: Public accountability

The introduction of performance management offers potential instrumental benefits for elected officials, particularly in the form of external accountability to the public and political accountability to elected officials. In each state, performance management reforms required the same basic accountability processes: Agencies created and reported performance information publicly and to the central budget office as part of the budget process. However, the prospect that performance information truly provides enhanced accountability is akin to a mirage. It might motivate the inexperienced public official, but older hands should know better.

In all three states the rhetoric that accompanied performance management emphasized the need to satisfy a vociferous demand for public accountability. For instance, the Virginia guide to performance management preparation says: "The public wants more results-oriented government. No longer are taxpayers willing to blindly accept pleas for added resources and expanded programming. They want to see, concretely, what they are getting for each tax dollar spent."[14]

It is questionable whether such a demand for accountability exists or can be satisfied by the provision of performance reports that are only slightly more interesting than the budgets that they often are a part of. The perception of public employees was that strident public demand has not actually occurred in any direct way in Virginia or elsewhere, where the increase in performance information seems to have been greeted by yawning indifference by members of the public. While citizens at the local level may have a direct interest in and information about services received, at higher levels of government most citizens have little clear idea of what the government does in terms of specific programs and are largely uninterested.[15] One central agency official in Virginia put it this way: "I'll tell you who cares the least about it, is the public. You hear all this public demanding accountability. I don't think so. I really don't. I never have anybody call and say, I'm a citizen and I'm interested in a performance measure. Never. It has never happened. It never will. The public does not care about performance."

Promoters of performance management have begun to realize public indifference. They have reacted in two ways: (1) targeting performance information to specific groups and (2) creating high-level outcomes for all citizens. Specific groups may be interested in a certain type of information, and targeting these groups (as the Vermont DOC did) or making performance highly accessible (as Virginia did with its *Virginia Results* web database) suggests meaningful efforts to provide information to those stakeholders. The alternative to linking performance information with defined group interests is to make it so aggregate that it is of some interest to everyone. Both Vermont and Virginia have developed a series of statewide indicators that track high-level outcomes such as the economy and the environment. While such measures are clearly important, it is difficult to attribute accountability for performance to specific programs, or even government itself. In addition, citizens will be more likely to be interested in such scorecards if they can provide truly local results—down to even the neighborhood level.[16]

The expectation that simply providing information satisfies external accountability suggests a fairly low standard of accountability in the first place, and it is one that all three cases achieved, although Vermont, and especially Virginia, had more performance information, of a better quality, and across a greater period than Alabama. A higher standard of external accountability is public involvement in the setting of goals. Only in the Vermont DOC did performance management lead to the inclusion of the public in goal setting, as Vermont undertook citizen surveys and focus groups with key stakeholders. The willingness to invite public involvement in Vermont is not surprising, as it has been a trademark of state governance (see appendix B). Elsewhere, despite the rhetoric on public accountability, performance management did not foster public inclusion in goal-setting forums among the agencies studied or in any statewide planning efforts.

Instrumental benefits: Political accountability

Elected officials are likely to be more concerned with performance management as a tool of internal accountability, via improved oversight and policy control, since this allows them to reassert control over the runaway bureaucracy sometimes portrayed in political rhetoric and public choice theory. Oversight accountability refers to the ability of elected officials to discern the operations and outputs of public organizations. Economic theories of organizations are particularly concerned with information asymmetry, the ability of bureaucrats to disguise their actual goals and level of productivity. Simply making more information available would appear to solve this problem, and by this standard the introduction of performance management helped foster the potential for internal accountability, most markedly in information-rich Virginia. There is some cross-state evidence to support the idea that performance information for oversight purposes is important to elected officials. States with more decentralized political structures (i.e., with major departments headed by independently elected officials rather than by gubernatorial appointees) are more likely to adopt performance management legislation.[17] The most plausible interpretation of this finding is that in such states the legislature and the governor are motivated to create mechanisms to generate information about public organizations they have limited direct political control over. In states where the governor and legislature can rely on strong traditional modes of accountability, they are less motivated to create performance information.

In recent years, the increased size of corrections and the growing proportion of general fund dollars it swallows have made it the subject of closer oversight. Even with performance information more widely available, overseers from the executive and legislative branches have a difficult time using it. Apart from other claims on the overseer's attention, there is both too much information for a statewide official to sort through and not enough to substitute for function-specific knowledge that can inform good decisions. This is especially true for overseers who are not specialists in a particular function or who lack adequate staff support.[18] Performance information cannot fully reduce information asymmetry, since it fails to produce an understanding of context that enables the statewide official to make sense of performance information. Overseers are for the most part still beholden to the bureaucrat presenting the information for a sense of context to inform judgment or risk making bad decisions. In Vermont, for example, one member of an appropriations committee made extrapolations from the performance information and "came up with some fairly simplistic ideas on how to reform things based on a partial understanding of the numbers he was given," according to a Department of Finance and Management official.

Another reason performance information will not replace information asymmetry with transparency is because the information itself can be used as a way to maintain asymmetry. Large amounts of performance data make contextual knowledge of the program more important in shaping interpretations. In interaction with overseers, the information also allows bureaucrats to direct attention to the performance information that best serves their needs or to divert attention from issues that they do not wish to talk about. A Vermont Department of Finance and Management official observes that providing voluminous amounts of performance information is "a way of protecting yourself from more questions. If you throw a lot of information at people, they cannot ask you the question that you are afraid of." The danger for agency bureaucrats is that if overseers become aware of and frustrated by continued asymmetry, they may seek outside expertise to help them make sense of the performance information. The legislator in Vermont who had been accused of making simplistic judgments convinced fellow members of the appropriations committee to hire an independent firm to do a benchmarking study comparing the performance of Vermont's correctional system with others.

Performance information promised not only to reduce information asymmetry, but also to enhance policy control of the bureaucracy. A formal framework of strategic planning and performance measurement provided elected officials with an opportunity to define what was important for the bureaucracy to pursue. The case studies offer evidence that performance management has changed managerial routines in ways that enhance policy control. Such routines were created and used in all three states, most notably Alabama. Performance management established formal procedures for creating and stating policy goals at the state or agency level (or both). Elected officials or appointees will have some degree of interest in these procedures and will be involved to emphasize policy goals important to them. Statewide plans direct agency staff attention to the governor's policy priorities as they set their own goals and may require some formal process of linking multiple level of goals, for example, agencies in Alabama were required to link their goals to relevant statewide goals from the governor's plan. Another routine to facilitate policy control is the process of central review. As agency strategic plans and performance reports are created, they may be submitted to a central office for review to ensure consistency with the governor's policy priorities, with the possibility of change if goal congruence is not apparent. Direct policy redirection is rare. One exception was Alabama, where the Department of Finance pushed the Alabama DOC to adjust strategic goals to ensure consistency with the governor's priorities.

Elected officials view performance management as a supplementary source of policy control, albeit one less significant than more traditional means of control such as political appointments and the power of the purse. Explicit policy intervention via performance management occurs only when central agencies or the Governor's Office feel that traditional controls have failed and that line agencies must be brought into step with the governor's priorities. More frequently, there is no outward friction, since agencies will anticipate and adjust to the wishes of elected officials in choosing agency goals. This is particularly true since agency-level political appointees dominate the process of strategic planning. This does not mean that performance management is not used as a means of policy control; rather, the process is built to smoothly reflect the existing channels of control. From the agency perspective, governors may have a handful of policy priorities they care about but are largely uninterested in most of the existing organizational goals and will not disagree with them.

The likelihood of major policy redirection through performance management is, therefore, limited. In addition, the policy priorities that elected officials care about are usually so broad that agency officials have little trouble in finding preexisting goals that link to these statewide goals. For example, the frequently stated goal of "public safety" as a policy priority is so vague that a corrections department could argue that almost all its goals contribute in one way or another. The process of integration between statewide and agency priorities is less a matter of agencies first examining the statewide goals and then creating a new set of goals, than of agency staff interpreting statewide goals to facilitate the closest fit with their preexisting goals. For instance, DOC staff in Alabama matched statewide goals of "Keeping our streets safe" with agency-level objectives designed to increase resources, for example, number of correctional officers and inmates, and beds not occupied because of employee vacancies.

If the idea of accountability provides a limited motivation for performance management reform, the benefits of traditional financial and personnel control systems in terms of controlling the bureaucracy give elected officials reason to maintain these systems. Traditional controls serve a purpose—the most public accountability problems come from scandals and failures, which evoke a demand from the media and legislators to find out who made a mistake. To make sure the mistake does not happen again, the legislative branch imposes constraints on the use of inputs, or procedural requirements for the delivery of services. Such forms of control help ensure that bureaucrats behave in ways deemed appropriate for their role, implementing laws as desired by elected officials and doing so in a way that avoids error, failure, or scandal that could damage elected officials more dramatically than possible inefficiency. Another benefit of traditional control systems is that they require attention from elected officials only when they seriously break down. From the perspective of performance management doctrine, these traditional constraints serve a political purpose not equal to their managerial costs. From the perspective of elected officials, these controls provide an instrumental value.

One plausible explanation for why elected officials demand performance information that they rarely use is that this demand is consistent with prevailing modes of legislative control. Rosenbloom has argued that, as governments grow, legislatures will no longer be able to directly oversee all agency actions.[19] Instead, they seek to foster legislative values in the executive branch, such as transparency, participation, and debate. One way to do so is to force agencies to produce public performance data about themselves and to consult with stakeholders, including the legislature, in setting goals. Such an approach appears consistent with what McCubbins and Schwartz refer to as a fire-alarm approach to legislative oversight.[20] Rather than policing all agency activities, the legislature intervenes only when a fire alarm goes off. If an agency's performance is problematic, it will become apparent through performance data and prompt intervention, possibly at the prodding of stakeholders who have a strong incentive to monitor performance information in their particular area.

For fire alarms to work assumes that someone is paying attention to data and that the legislature will occasionally examine the information. Unfortunately, although it appears to be a typical assumption associated with performance management reforms, this remains an uncertain proposition. Many of those involved justify the creation of performance information not because they plan to use it but because they hope someone else might. Elected officials can reassure themselves that other central and agency staff actors will find the data useful for the instrumental benefit of management. Central agency actors, in turn, hope that agency officials and, to a lesser extent, elected officials will use the information. This fits with survey evidence from executive and legislative budgeteers, which finds that even though budgeteers do not generally use the information, they continue to believe the process is important and worth continuing.[21] Optimism that others use the information is lowest among agency staff, who hope to convince budgeteers and politicians to take account of performance data when making budget decisions, but are regularly provided with experiences that demonstrate that this is unlikely.

Symbolic benefits

For elected officials the symbolic benefits of performance management are more important than the instrumental benefits. The symbolic benefits are based on the ability to communicate to a variety of audiences that government is being run in a rational, efficient, and results-oriented manner and that bureaucrats are being held accountable for their performance. As elected officials and appointees convince audiences of these claims, they are more likely to accrue benefits that are important to them: a positive public image in the media, improved chances for reelection, and a greater capacity to implement the policies that they want.

In Vermont the espoused purpose of new performance management reporting requirements was to provide a rational way to make choices about what programs to cut during a budget crunch in the mid-1990s. But performance information did not inform resource reductions or other budget decisions. Even if such information was not required or used, its availability provided a sense of legitimacy to the budgeting process.

In Alabama the image of effective and efficient government was seen as having tremendous potential benefits in terms of revenue-raising. A narrow revenue base had constricted the inflow of taxes to the government, but this tax structure could not be changed without constitutional reform (see appendix B for more detail). There is little electoral incentive in advocating for tax reform when much of the population perceives government as wasteful. A member of Governor Siegelman's office noted: "If you read the letters to the editor almost any day of the week there will be one letter in there saying 'Why are they talking about this stupid tax reform? The government has lots of money, if they just stopped wasting it, it would be enough.' However, if public perceptions could be swayed toward a belief that a more efficient government was in place, then the possibility for tax reform becomes more likely: "The governor has a pretty strongly felt view that Alabamians are really suspicious of state government, of governments generally, state and local governments, and until people are going to be convinced that their money will be well spent they are not about to support tax reform."

There is a historical connection between revenue-raising efforts and performance management in Alabama. A predecessor to Siegelman, Governor Fob James (1979–83), also tried to introduce performance budgeting while seeking to change the revenue system of the state. Similarly, Siegelman's successor, Bob Riley, introduced his performance budgeting initiative to demonstrate to the public the efficiency of public services after his constitutional initiative failed to gain public support (see appendix B for more detail).

Apart from the general public, the audiences for performance management symbols in Alabama are other branches of government. Two of five pilot agencies undertaking performance management (Mental Health and Corrections) were selected at least partially because of their high-profile interactions with the courts. Agencies under court oversight could point to formal goals that they are pursuing to satisfy court orders, reducing the risk of more constrictive court orders. The existence of strategic plans and performance measures help justify to legislators and the public the increased resources required by court mandates. In this way, performance management serves as a symbol for a number of constituencies who are unlikely to ever actually view or use the performance information, representing purposeful, efficient, and prudent spending of public money. As the Alabama strategic plan noted: "Through this plan, we present a direction, we set goals, and we provide measures for accountability and efficiency. This plan, along with performance-based budgeting, means we will give Alabama taxpayers more accountability for how tax dollars are spent, and we will advance Alabama further and faster toward our strategic goals."[22]

Alabama is an extreme example of how popular perceptions of government inefficiency, though largely uninformed by evidence, are tenaciously held.[23] Elected officials believed that the public supported the idea of making government more accountable, results oriented, and efficient. For elected officials the adoption of a reform that appears to satisfy these requirements is an appropriate response, regardless of whether the reform actually has these effects. While the public may be uninterested in the specific performance information generated by performance management, the adoption of such reforms offers symbolic reassurance that there is some effort to make government more accountable, effective, and efficient.[24]

Virginia maintains not only the most comprehensive performance management system of the three states, but also the greatest awareness among employees about the symbolic aspects of performance management, creating a sense of cynicism for some, who call performance management a public relations product for elected officials on the campaign trail. Two officials from Virginia offered the following comments:

> First of all if you introduce the law, you look good. I'm the guy that put accountability in government. So I introduced the law. Score ten points for me. If I co-sponsored, that's probably not ten, but it's probably five or six points. I still look good. So it's really the image, the political power, creating the perception of doing it. Will any of these legislators ever read or look at any of the product of any of this stuff? Maybe one or two. . . . All we're saying is, it is a PR tool. At least internally let's call a spade a spade. We understand calling it that externally is a big problem. That's the risk. It's the social risk of being honest when we say the governor or the emperor has no clothes.
>
> They come in and what incentive do they have to use this? Same incentive we have been saying all along: This looks good. It makes them look good. . . . And you use it for advertising. "You ought to give us power. And one of the

reasons that we can prove to you or to show you as evidence why you ought to support us is because we manage this like a business, rationally, according to top management principles." That's a public relations tool. It doesn't matter whether it fits with reality. . . . It's very functional for public relations. But it's not functional for what the folks who said you ought to have a system like this say it is for, which is quality improvement and service-delivery effectiveness and efficiency. It's not for that. But that's the weird thing about it. When you look at it you have a system . . . yeah, we got a system, absolutely. Nobody asked, Are you using it mostly for service delivery and efficiency and effectiveness, and give me examples, systematic examples of how you actually use it for improving service delivery, efficiency, and effectiveness. . . . The dominant work of the system is to define public policy and implement it. And to do what you can to mobilize the power to make it happen. And managing for results has been molded and bent as a tool for those purpose. . . . Government is politics, and so who is going to win? Managing for results? Or politics, which is what it's all about? Politics is going to win.

Such comments echo claims made by March and Olsen on public sector re-form.[25] Simply promising to reform government is a popular act, communicating a frustration with bureaucracy, and the intent to introduce rationality and efficacy, values widely shared by the public. According to March and Olsen, "Announcing a major reorganization symbolizes the possibility of effective leadership and the be-lief [in] that possibility may be of greater significance than the execution of it. The most important things appear to be statements of intent, an assurance of proper values and a willingness to try."[26] However, incentives do remain for elected offi-cials to adopt some type of reform if elected. Not only can elected officials say that they have kept their promises, but there are also external validations of reforms that allow positive media coverage.

Performance management has been particularly good to the commonwealth of Virginia, providing it with an international reputation for innovative and results-oriented government. Such a reputation may not top the priority list for most vot-ers, but it certainly does not hurt. All of these benefits depend on having a system in place that could plausibly claim to enhance performance. The system does not necessarily have to achieve improved performance since simply convincing exter-nal observers that it could provides most of the benefits.

Reducing costs
A reform that makes government more accountable, results oriented, and efficient is, on the face of it, difficult to oppose, with little apparent downside. The reform

is relatively easy to adopt, unless it confronts status quo interests. In the case of performance management, overturning long-standing statutory financial management and personnel control systems has costs. Deciding how managerial authority would be increased requires difficult choices. How would government avoid excessive abuse of such authority? How would elected officials structure accountability relationships with bureaucrats? Performance information systems are a less difficult choice because no existing systems need to be reformed. A new system simply needs to be added to preexisting systems.

New legislation takes time and effort, which could be devoted to other policies. Legislative action is already difficult in the separation of powers systems of U.S. states.[27] It is even more difficult given the active opposition of key stakeholders to reform in a policy subsystem.[28] In particular, public service unions will oppose changes to personnel systems that jeopardize benefits for members.[29] Vermont officials, who face the most centralized personnel system, pointed to the power of public service unions in the state, which lobbied the legislature to maintain centralized controls to ensure that its members enjoy similar and predictable treatment. As discussed previously, central statewide financial and personnel staff will also act as opponents to reshaping managerial controls. Such opposition does not usually need to be overt since it will already be reflected in the policy options that these actors present to elected officials.

Far-ranging and controversial revisions of existing financial management and civil service statutes are therefore a daunting task. On the other hand, there is no natural constituency that opposes more performance information. It is far easier, therefore, to ignore managerial flexibility and concentrate on the creation of performance information systems.[30] The main costs of implementing (as opposed to adopting) performance information systems are the time and effort expended in creating, tracking, measuring, reporting, and validating performance information. This burden is borne not by elected officials, but by bureaucrats in central and line agencies and by legislative audit staff.

The costs of passing legislation for performance management are consistent with the pattern of other good government proposals. Such proposals often enjoy support that is a "mile wide but an inch deep."[31] Their ability to become a viable possibility for legislation rests on the assumption that they will not meet committed opposition. If stakeholders do resist, supporters have limited incentive to devote time and political capital on policies that have little direct relevance to their constituency.[32] The potential success of performance management reform proposals rests, therefore, on not tying them to eliminating managerial controls that key stakeholders continue to support. This would require a political battle that only the most ardent supporters of performance management would contemplate.

Conclusion

For elected officials, performance management reforms provide a high number of benefits and some manageable costs. The burden of collecting performance information is significant, but it lies chiefly with bureaucrats. One main cost for elected officials is taking on public service unions to eliminate the personnel protections, which would allow for greater managerial flexibility. States generally have shied away from such battles by ignoring this reform prescription. Another main cost imposed on elected officials is changing their decision-making patterns to account for performance; however, use of performance information is purely voluntary, and so this cost may also be avoided.

There are some limited benefits for elected officials to create performance information systems. Greater information means greater capacity for elected officials to exert oversight and control of the bureaucracy, although case evidence suggests that this form of control is rarely used. The chief benefit for elected officials appears to be symbolic. Performance management reforms communicate to the public a shared frustration and a desire for results. If the reforms themselves do not live up to the political rhetoric that spawned them, that is secondary to ensuring that the reforms are adopted in a public fashion. Such a pattern of partial adoption does not set a promising stage for implementation, which is examined in the next chapter.

Notes

1. Portions of this chapter and chapter 5 previously appeared in Moynihan, "Why and How Do State Governments Adopt and Implement 'Managing for Results' Reforms?"

2. Kingdon, *Agenda, Alternatives, and Public Policies;* Baumgartner and Jones, *Agendas and Instability in American Politics.*

3. This literature was popularized most notably by Osborne and Gaebler, *Reinventing Government.* NPM ideas are also to be found in public management professional magazines and journals, including symposiums devoted to NPM in *Governance* 2 (1990), *Public Administration Review* 3 (1999), and *Journal of Public Policy Analysis and Management* 3 (1997).

4. Brudney et al., "Reassessing the Reform Decade"; de Lancer Julnes and Holzer, "Promoting the Utilization of Performance Measures in Public Organizations"; Seong, "Adoption of Innovation"; Berry, "Innovation in Public Management."

5. Brewer and Li, "Implementation of Performance Budgeting in the States."

6. The Xerox experience has been described as "perhaps the most repeated story in benchmarking lore" by Ammons, "A Proper Mentality for Benchmarking," 106. A more detailed description is provided by Camp, *Benchmarking.*

7. Brudney et al., "Reassessing the Reform Decade."

8. U.S. Government Accountability Office, *Performance Budgeting: States' Experiences Can Inform Federal Efforts,* 9.

9. As one interviewee pointed out, part of the problem is that central agency staff are promoting reforms that they do not actually use in their own work and usually have not had experience in actually managing a service. Therefore, the shortcomings of this theory of performance management, including contradictions between control systems and managerial authority, are not apparent. The same observation could be extended to other promoters of performance management, including many consultants, public management academics, and foundations.

10. Ingraham, "Of Pigs in Pokes and Policy Diffusion"; Kellough and Lu, "The Paradox of Merit Pay in the Public Sector."

11. Performance Institute Press Release, "President's Budget Uses Performance Budgeting to Help Make Tough Decisions," February 7, 2005. The Performance Institute describes itself as a "private think tank seeking to improve government performance through the principles of competition, accountability, performance, and transparency. The institute serves as the nation's leading authority and repository on performance-based management practices for government." The institute also illustrates the overlap between politics, money, and management. While describing itself as nonpartisan, the Performance Institute was established by a former Bush campaign adviser in 2000 who is also a senior fellow at the conservative Reason Foundation. The institute has won millions of dollars in contracts from the Bush administration.

12. Research has found that states with stronger gubernatorial powers tend to be more enthusiastic implementers of performance management. Brewer and Li, "Implementation of Performance Budgeting in the States."

13. Given the importance of these terms, it is worth clarifying what is meant by *instrumental* and *symbolic action.* Since we are dealing with public management, instrumentality is defined in terms of government capacity and performance. Actions judged to have a direct positive impact on organizational effectiveness and efficiency, both in the short run and long run, are deemed to produce instrumental benefits. Symbolic actions are those whose main goal is to enable communication to an external audience, rather than actually dealing with the underlying issue the symbol refers to. Symbolic actions are focused on establishing and communicating an image of government, rather than changing government itself. Symbolic actions provide reassurance to the public, espousing a particular set of values, usually in a way that benefits the communicator. See Edelman, *The Symbolic Uses of Politics.* In practice, as discussed in the conclusion of this chapter, such a neat dichotomy is problematic as an action can to varying degrees be both instrumental and symbolic, and both approaches interact to produce reform outcomes. However, in explaining the motivations of different actors engaged in adopting and using performance management it is helpful to categorize the nature of benefits actors hope to enjoy as instrumental or symbolic.

14. Virginia Department of Planning and Budget, *Virginia's Handbook on Planning and Performance for State Agencies and Institutions,* 11–12.

15. Goodsell, *The Case for Bureaucracy;* Delli Carpini and Keeter, *What Americans Know about Politics and Why It Matters.*

16. When the National Performance Review tried to encourage the creation of measures that tracked agency performance for "High Impact Agencies" that had the most interaction with the

public, it drew little public attention. One former member of the National Performance Review that I spoke to suggested that the difficulty they faced is that creating such a connection between citizens and results is more likely to occur at more local levels, as Baltimore has attempted to do with its CitiStat program, which ties results to city maps that are viewable over the Internet. To paraphrase the late Tip O'Neill, all results are local. See Henderson, "The Baltimore CitiStat Program."

17. Seong, "Adoption of Innovation."

18. There is significant variation in the level of professional support across states and especially across state legislatures. At the federal level, professional support is better. The efforts of the OMB to evaluate information through the Program Assessment Rating Tool, examined in chapters 7 and 8, can be seen as an effort of governmentwide officials trying to make sense of agency information. However, this effort has required a small army of functional specialists at the OMB, and the workload demanded has given rise to complaint.

19. Rosenbloom, *Building a Legislative-Centered Public Administration.*

20. McCubbins and Schwartz, "Congressional Oversight Overlooked."

21. Melkers and Willoughby, "Budgeters' Views of State Performance-Budgeting Systems."

22. Siegelman, *Achieve,* 3.

23. Goodsell, *The Case for Bureaucracy.*

24. Edelman, *The Symbolic Uses of Politics.*

25. March and Olsen, "Organizing Political Life."

26. Ibid., 290; see also Brunnson, *The Organization of Hypocrisy,* who argues that reforms tend to remain in the realm of talk and decision and rarely affect action: "Redesigning organizational charts need not disturb organizational activities. Reforms give management a chance to fulfill their intention to generate action" (p. 226).

27. Weaver and Rockman, eds., *Do Institutions Matter?*

28. Baumgartner and Jones, *Agendas and Instability.*

29. The case evidence here is supported by recent cross-state survey evidence of the adoption of personnel reforms in state governments. See Hou et al., "Decentralization of Human Resource Management"; Kellough and Selden, "The Reinvention of Public Personnel Administration."

30. Case studies in Florida, another perceived leader in performance management, have found similar results. Despite promises of exchanging performance for rewards and flexibility, budget controls remain in place, and legislators have been reluctant to provide additional managerial flexibility or budgetary rewards. However, as with the cases studied here, there is evidence that agency managers are finding ways to use performance measures despite the failure to gain new incentives or flexibility; See Berry, Brower, and Flowers, "Implementing Performance Accountability in Florida"; VanLandingham, Wellman, and Andrews, "Useful, But Not a Panacea."

31. Moynihan, "Protection versus Flexibility."

32. Ibid.

5

Explaining the Implementation of Performance Management Reforms

Reforms work in unanticipated ways, sometimes positive, sometimes negative. Research on previous performance management portray pro forma implementation and eventual abandonment.[1] These negative assessments are partly because of how we judge performance management—we tend to look at decision making at the political level and, as the last chapter suggested, there is little evidence of performance information use there.

However, part of the hope for performance management is that lower-level bureaucrats would take the reform to make their organization more strategic and efficient. There is less research on this front. Findings from the three case studies examined in this chapter offer grounds for cautious optimism. Agency managers in Virginia and Vermont were positively disposed toward performance management and believed that it had helped to develop a clearer vision, create more strategic decisions, and improve communication. Agency-level leadership played a key role in taking the formal performance reforms that were passed at the state level and finding ways to make them useful for their agencies, usually ways that were not predicted by performance management doctrine. These leaders were driven by the constraints and opportunities faced by their agency, as well as their own vision for the future. Case evidence from Alabama provides an example of performance management failure—where agencies have no resources to spare and are engaged in a pro forma adoption of the reform purely to satisfy their political masters.

Explaining the Implementation of Performance Management

Despite the unpromising conditions of adoption outlined in the last chapter, there is evidence that results-based reforms have been a success for some state agencies.[2] For instance, Franklin's two-state case study found evidence of use of performance information among agency officials in one state but not in the other. Despite broadly similar patterns of adoption across states, there therefore appears to be variation in the implementation of performance management reforms at the agency level. The puzzle here is what explains this variation. In other words, how do agency successes occur despite the partial adoption of reforms and nonuse by statewide officials?

In answering questions of how agencies implement policies created by statewide officials, we are best served by inviting implementation theory to guide us. Over the two decades, as NPM ideas have gained increased prominence in public management discourse, implementation theory has suffered a decline.[3] The implementation literature points to the difficulty and complexity of making policy work, particularly when multiple actors with different motivations are involved.[4] While the NPM-influenced version of performance management doctrine was not a direct reaction to implementation theory, it did speak to many of the problems implementation scholars had raised. Performance management promised elected officials a chance to reassert control over policymaking: They would set the goals and hold bureaucrats accountable for achieving those goals. The complexity of the policy process portrayed by implementation theory was replaced with the beguiling image of a simple and clear separation between policy and administration. Performance information promised the means to specify goals and hold managers accountable.

Performance management doctrine promised to eliminate the traditional headaches of implementation. This chapter demonstrates that such public management policy reforms must themselves be implemented and are subject to the same problems as other policies that elected officials specify but expect others to achieve. This chapter, therefore, is not just a study of the implementation of a particular policy; it is the study of the implementation of the policy that promised to cure the ills of implementation theory and finds that the cure faces the same challenges as the disease. Great expectations about statewide performance management systems are dashed, and unexpected—frequently positive—outcomes occur at the agency level.

Consistent with implementation theory, the case evidence suggests that as elected officials impose a reform on agency officials, each group acts in a way consistent with their motivations, norms, and interests. As a result, many of the benefits associated with performance management, particularly those that rely on active use of performance information by statewide actors, simply do not occur. Some benefits do occur, however, and tend to have common characteristics: They occur at the agency level, are led by agency management, and are based on agency leadership views about how performance management might further their agenda. The result is, unsurprisingly, a complex picture of reform, one of mixed support for performance management. Positive outcomes occurred, but not quite in the ways expected. The theory to explain these findings is premised on the difference between political and agency perspectives on the utility of performance management found at the state level, and it should be noted that such variation in perspectives is less likely to occur at the local level where elected officials have greater opportunity to deal with management issues and city/county managers must be more keenly aware of political concerns.

If the symbolic benefits of performance management are indeed the most important factor in policy adoption of formal reforms, it becomes easy to think of performance management as solely symbolic, that the reform is a fable, told to conjure images of effective government that reflect well on the central agency or elected official promoting it. However, such a view is simplistic and misleading, since it ignores how managers react to and use performance management reforms. In all three states, performance management had real effects on managerial routines. The most obvious change, detailed in chapter 4, was the creation and tracking of performance information to meet legislative requirements. This chapter details ways in which agencies used performance management to derive instrumental benefits.

The degree and type of positive outcomes varied by state, and my explanation of this variation can be summarized as: *Reform outcomes are a function of the interaction of the formal reform adopted, agency leadership motivation, managerial authority, and resources.*

Formal Reform

The outcome of the policy-adoption phase discussed in the last chapter is a formal reform: a requirement, or enabler, to change managerial routines. For the three case studies, the formal reform was a performance-reporting requirement on the part of line agencies as part of the budget process, with the finance department overseeing the process and collating this information.

The adoption of a formal reform is a cue for change that agency managers must react to in some way, a cue that creates requirements for managers as well as opportunities to use their authority. Managerial controls shape the range of discretion agency managers have to meet the requirements, as do the specificity of these requirements and the degree of compliance enforcement exerted by central agencies and elected officials. However, even with the highly specified and rigorously monitored requirements featured in all three cases, and typical of other states, managers have a high degree of discretion as to how they react to and use the reforms. First, specific reporting requirements can force managers to implement a reform but cannot force them to generate the positive outcomes that the policymakers hope the reform will produce. While legislatures can specify the exact type of performance information to provide, they cannot specify the use of this information in decision making (even if they did specify such an outcome, it would be almost impossible to monitor and enforce). Second, managers have a high degree of discretion in finding unanticipated uses of the reform.

The actions of elected officials have an important role in promoting and using reforms. One of the factors that agency managers will look to is the degree of seriousness elected officials display toward implementation. For example, Bourdeaux has found that states with greater legislative involvement in performance oversight are associated with higher managerial uses of performance information.[5] If elected officials do not send signals that the reform is important to them, this creates a greater likelihood that managers will react with pro forma completion. In Alabama, prior to the Siegelman administration, elected officials had become so indifferent to performance information that it was no longer deemed important enough to be published in the budget, a point not lost on agency officials, who complied with legislative requirements by delivering poor performance information, if any. In all three states, the knowledge that elected officials did not use performance information for resource allocation increased cynicism, reducing the perceived importance of performance management.

If the formal reform is in the form of an administrative requirement by a governor or central agency rather than a legislative requirement, it has a greater battle against skepticism and minimal compliance, since there is a greater potential that it will be overturned in the future. Previous performance management reforms in Alabama and Virginia suffered such fates.

Agency Leadership Motivation

Public officials in each state studied identified agency leadership as the most important factor in explaining reform outcomes: whether agency leaders believed in performance management and whether they saw it as a waste of time or an opportunity to be exploited. Leadership is a difficult concept to deal with, and generalize, in the public sector. The case findings reflect an integrative view of leadership. The integrative approach examines how a cadre of agency leaders use administrative systems such as performance management to add value to their organizations, and it assumes that the interaction between leadership ambitions and vision, and the management reform in question, shape management capacity.[6] In deciding how to use performance management within their zone of discretion, agency leadership will, similar to elected officials, do an approximate cost–benefit analysis of the reform. This calculation will be based on the environmental conditions of their organization, organizational needs, the costs of implementing the reform, and ambitions for how the organization should be run and what it might achieve.[7]

At a very basic level, agency leaders are crucial in determining if a reform is a priority, what resources and administrative energy it receives, and whether it is communicated to staff. One obvious difference between Alabama and the other states studied was that the leadership did not consider the reform significant enough to communicate to wardens and frontline managers who worked in corrections institutions. In Vermont, and especially Virginia, the leaders attempted to communicate to such employees. In such communication, the agency has to explain just why the reform matters to the core tasks the employee performs. This is sometimes difficult. Performance management reforms might appear as abstract distractions relative to the more immediate matter of avoiding major failures under limited resources. Consider the comments of a frontline supervisor in a Virginia corrections institution:

> We kind of have to measure based on, you know we come in at 8:00 and under our own power we're leaving at 4:00, and everybody is going out with us. We're all safe. No inmates died today, and we didn't have any serious assaults. Those are the kinds of things we have to use to evaluate our successes and failures. Sometimes it is measured on the number of mistakes either made or not made. You know you had a zero-mistake day—that's a good day. Those are the correctional industry measurements. That is simply the nature of the business. In corrections, it's: Nobody died today, had no escapes, the public was not jeopardized.

These performance indicators relate to the core value and objective held by virtually all correctional officers: safety. Maintaining routine order among offenders guarantees the safety of inmates, as well as the safety of the staff that guard them and ultimately the public.

The ability to win resources to cover basic needs, and work within a budget that may face midyear reductions, is also a more fundamental concern than performance management. In Virginia, one corrections official considered staying within spending limits as the primary performance target:

> Well, we certainly have budget targets which are set at the beginning of the year and probably change a number of times based on the number of cuts that we receive. That's probably the biggest target that the wardens and other program managers have. They have a budget which is a moving target. It is set at the beginning of the year, but then as the cuts come they have to be focused on what they can do.

Convincing employees that performance management is consistent with the safety ethos and can help to work within tight resources is a challenge, and it will not happen without determined communication.

Instrumental benefits

Agency leaders, in contrast to elected officials, see the symbolic benefits of reform as less important relative to potential instrumental benefits. This perspective has much to do with the different roles of elected officials and agency managers. Agency managers are actually running an operation, and they have the capacity to link managerial reforms to improving service delivery. Agency managers do not (usually) run for election. They must satisfy particular constituencies but are less concerned with using performance management as a symbol for external audiences than for its internal uses to create instrumental value for the agency. How agency leaders view organizational conditions and needs will shape the possible benefits pursued.

For agency leaders in the case studies, performance management requirements acted as top-level cues for change, creating administrative space that gave agency managers opportunity to use the reform. In the case of the DOC in Alabama, this resulted in little more than compliance with requirements. In the other states studied, managers used these reforms to create instrumental benefits for their agencies. These benefits were not those predicted by performance management doctrine. Table 5.1 lists these unexpected benefits, which include organizational learning, leadership development, redefining organizational culture, and internal and external communication.

A good example is the use of performance information to facilitate major policy changes in the Vermont DOC, which is discussed in greater detail in chapter 9. Typically, organizations use performance management to formally state previously accepted goals, not to pursue dramatic changes. In any case, the dialogue of strategic planning is unlikely to be structured to include such fundamental questioning of the organization. The potential to question existing organizational policies is determined by organizational leaders, who shape the agenda and nature of acceptable dialogue in strategic planning. This, in turn, may be prompted by external events or trends, or the obvious failure of existing organizational procedures. In the 1980s and 1990s, such a trend was the increasing size and cost of the corrections population. One Vermont official said:

> What are the outcomes for corrections? What are the outcomes for criminal justice? Nobody ever asked. We just did it. Asking what are the outcomes is a provocative act. We have been doing corrections for 200 years, and we have these outcomes and who cares? Until about 1980 nobody cared about outcomes. By 1990 people are starting to care. By 2000 people are screaming because it costs too much.

It is worth remembering that corrections costs had increased in the other two states as well, yet it did not foster major policy change, so we return to the mediating role of leadership. It is clear that the senior members of the Vermont DOC were

Table 5.1 Unexpected instrumental benefits of performance management

Benefit	Description
Major policy changes (double-loop learning)	Vermont used strategic plans and performance measures as a vehicle to question basic goals and philosophy of program; see pp. 80–81 [122–23 in original] and pp.170–73 [256–60 in original].
Cultural change	Virginia used strategic planning and training in performance management as a way of building an employee-centered, mission-based culture; see pp. 82–83 [123–25 in original], and pp. 168–70 [253–55 in original].
Internal communication and coordination	Virginia used statements of goals and measures as a way of fostering communication and coordination between institutional staff and community programs staff; see p. 84 [127 in original].
Leadership development	Virginia used strategic planning and training in performance management as a way of grooming future leaders, providing them with a better understanding of the goals and policies of the department, along with a chance to shape those goals and policies; see pp. 83–84 [126 in original].
Reshaping the external environment	All states attempted to use performance information to argue for more resources. Vermont was most successful at using goals and strategic planning to attract new stakeholders and at using performance information to change policies and reallocate resources; see pp. 173–75 [261–67 in original].

predisposed to question the efficacy of the previous and existing approaches to corrections. This leadership cadre was not trained in corrections, criminal justice, or even law. They had developed their understanding of corrections from social science analysis of corrections and a knowledge of the history of the function in the United States and elsewhere. This knowledge was helpful in recognizing that the technologies and purposes of corrections had changed dramatically over the last two hundred years. The Vermont DOC leaders therefore did not have a preconceived acceptance toward prevailing approaches to corrections, and they were willing to ask provocative questions. As one Vermont official noted:

"If you are going to do strategic planning, having some concept of what outcome you wish to achieve helps. The problem with corrections is its outcomes are all absurd. . . . Well then, what is the purpose of corrections? And you have to look, if you are going to do strategic planning, at what the essential purposes are.

The positive experience for performance management in the Virginia DOC also had more to do with the actions of its commissioner and senior management than statewide reporting requirements. The Virginia DOC strategic plan gained a life of its own unrelated to these requirements, containing more information and involving greater employee participation than required. The Virginia DOC staff viewed central agencies and reporting requirements as either a bureaucratic nuisance or as irrelevant to what they were trying to achieve: "Relationships are good, but I don't think they [the Virginia Department of Planning and Budget] have any awareness or concern or interest in our strategic plan."

The strategic planning process was prompted, says the Virginia DOC plan, by the need for more effective means of managing corrections, in the context of the abolition of parole and the advent of truth-in-sentencing laws, which had dramatic effects on costs for corrections, as more offenders were incarcerated for longer periods. However, the high-level cue for strategic planning was, in fact, Governor George Allen's (1994–98) 1996 directive to agencies to undertake strategic planning and performance reporting. The DOC commissioner at the time, Ron Angelone, and his executive staff used this cue to kick-start strategic planning. The initial round of planning was devoted to identifying core issues for the Virginia DOC by setting up benchmarking teams to collect information about each issue. The experience resulted in changed practices in critical areas that were regarded as successful, although perhaps the only area where new processes had measurable advantages over existing procedures was with managing inmate medical costs.

Initial strategic planning sessions also drew attention to other organizational issues: an aging leadership cadre and weak communication, especially among different divisions of the DOC. As the performance management process matured, the Virginia DOC connected it with a revised and expanded training program to create a mission-based culture, groom future agency leaders, and improve internal communication and cross-divisional relationships.

The Virginia DOC leadership saw performance management as an opportunity to reshape the agency culture in two key ways: making it mission based and emphasizing the central role that employees played in achieving this mission. A focus on empowerment fit an organizational culture where the central managers tried to portray themselves as supporting field staff rather than in confrontation with them. It is notable that more than half of the organization vision statement that emerged from the 1996 meeting is given to the critical role of employees: "The employees of the Department are the cornerstone of the agency. They share a common purpose and a commitment to the highest level of professional standards and excellence in public service. The Department, through its unwavering commitment to its employees is a satisfying and rewarding place to work and grow professionally."

This is employee-centered performance management, an effort to build a culture characterized simultaneously by a results focus, a sense of organizational unity, employee support, and empowerment. The Virginia DOC leadership believed that in a people-intensive industry like corrections, improved performance depends on the active engagement of its employees and the internalization of organizational goals, an outcome better generated by voluntary rather than coerced actions, and therefore dependent on organizational culture. The focus on culture was partly a reaction to a similar strategic planning effort in the 1980s that resulted in "a nice document that I'm not sure anybody in particular paid attention to" according to one manager.

The Virginia DOC sought to shape culture via symbols, concrete evidence of support, and communication. Symbols included the vision statement listed above, prominently displayed in every correctional facility in the state, along with a mission statement and list of goals. Concrete benefits included an improved retirement system, improved safety through a revised classification system, and more days off by moving to twelve-hour work shifts. Improved communication occurred primarily through training and was the most frequently cited benefit arising from performance management in Virginia. Better communication led to a greater sense of organizational unity, purpose, and especially cross-divisional cooperation. In surveys, employees have largely shown support for the organizational changes. Different staff members made the following comments:

> He [former Commissioner Ron Angelone] has convinced the corrections officers that they're important. He has partnered with them from day one. Those folks know that somebody's looking out for them. Now I call that a major policy of investing in the line people. And that's been dramatic.
>
> They [employees] know that they fit somewhere; that they have expectations placed upon them and they have results-oriented opportunities, that they can make difference. . . . And it's not one giant bureaucracy that overwhelms all of us as individuals. . . . It's a machine, but it has individual parts in which we all have a purpose.

The results-driven training sessions were also expanded for the purpose of creating a next generation of agency leaders to replace an aging cohort of senior staff. The central role of employees was reinforced by offering mid- and lower-level managers the opportunity to participate in strategic planning, and employee training incorporated discussion of organizational goals and the skills to achieve those goals. The senior staff point to leadership development as one of the key successes of performance management. Two officials made the following comments:

> I think we saw in our department a need to bring on upper-management and mid-management people, to get them trained and indoctrinated toward a strategic plan because a lot of us in a short period of time are going to be gone. The deputy director for administration is sixty-four years old. Deputy director for the field operations is sixty, sixty-one. I'm sixty-three. And even the crop below us

are people in their mid- to upper-fifties. People make a career here. We have very little change at the top. But that's going to change. And there was a need to bring on, get people trained and get them to thinking about how to run an organization not by the seat of your pants, but in a very methodical, put-it-on-paper, management-by-objectives approach, and that's how I think we got into it. I think that was the driving force.

Once they [senior managers] recognized how important strategic planning was to them, then the decision was "well we need to go down to the next layer [of] our senior staff and supply for them the same kind of development tool," so that we have the strongest leadership that's actually at the point where implementation begins.

Better communication, especially from agency leaders to the line staff, was central to reshaping culture. But the initial strategic planning meeting also revealed problems in communication between institutional staff and community programs. Differences in task, location, employees, and work environment led to a sense of distance and distrust between the staff of the two divisions, a major problem when both parts of the organization are expected to achieve a common goal and deal with many of the same offender population. Initial training sessions sought to break down these divisions by emphasizing common goals. Later sessions took it a step further by deliberately making members of both divisions interact, which led to a worker exchange program, where members of one division were temporarily assigned to work in the other. This increased interaction fostered stronger working relationships and cooperation on common problems, such as communicating salient characteristics of offenders, and additional institutional preparation for inmate parole. There is now greater information shared between institutions and community staff about prisoners on probation or parole, and procedures for preparing prisoners for release have improved. One manager said:

We forced the mix. And I think the comment we heard initially more than anything was "I didn't believe they had the same problems I had." . . . What they found was that everybody was dealing with similar problems. It's just a different venue. . . . So there was a better understanding about what the operations officer can do when an inmate is released to the community to make a parole officer's work a little easier. So, again the goal for a better understanding of the work environment gets met.

Symbolic benefits
There are symbolic benefits of performance management at the agency level, but unlike the statewide level, the most critical benefits—more resources and operat-

ing discretion—accrue almost entirely to the organization, not to individuals. Agency leaders will seek to use performance management to portray themselves as rational and efficient to other branches of government and to external stakeholders and to appear as progressive professionals among peers. All three DOCs used the existence of the performance management reform and actual performance information as part of their advocacy to elected officials for increased resources for an essentially unpopular function. The existence of strategic plans, like accreditation from professional organizations, can also be used to convince courts that the DOC is purposefully moving toward achieving goals consistent with the court's wishes.[8] Function-specific professional organizations, such as the American Correctional Association, have also prompted the diffusion of standards for evaluating the security of institutions and have moved toward standard benchmarks for corrections professionals to pursue.

In the case of Vermont, performance management was used to convince external stakeholders and even the general public to accept a dramatically new philosophy and set of policies for the Vermont DOC. Convincing stakeholders requires more than simply producing and diffusing performance information to the public, as Virginia and Alabama did to little effect. In Vermont, external communication was persuasive because it built on previous citizen surveys and focus group research into "customer" demand from the system; community involvement in the justice system; and active, targeted marketing of results to the stakeholders. The Vermont DOC was able to convince the governor, legislature, judiciary, and public that the prevailing punitive approach to corrections was expensive and ineffective and that viable alternatives existed.

Symbolic aspects of reforms can also produce instrumental benefits for agencies. Corrections is a field where tangible success is difficult to observe, and the adoption of progressive reforms provides a sense of momentum and professional standing to corrections employees.[9] Similarly, the DOC leadership in Virginia used performance management not only for its immediate instrumental uses, but also as a symbol of organizational purpose, which became a self-fulfilling prophecy toward the instrumental goal of a mission-driven culture.

Reducing costs

Agency leaders also try to implement performance management in a way that limits the potential downside of a reform. One potential cost is that performance information will portray the organization negatively. On the other hand, poor agency performance may lead to increased rather than reduced funding. This potential cost can be mediated by how information is presented, and in all three case studies, the DOCs prepared performance information in a way designed to protect their resource base (see chapter 6 for additional discussion).

Another standard cost is the amount of staff time and effort involved in implementing the reform. If agency leaders see little potential for positive benefits of performance management, but know they need to maintain compliance, they will meet the minimal requirements for compliance, reducing the burden on staff in terms of time and changed managerial routines. Such was the case in Alabama, where a resource-poor DOC determined that the only benefit of performance management was in increasing resources but accepted that this outcome was unrealistic. Possibly the most salient single fact about the Alabama DOC is that it was, by far, the lowest funded in United States. When I visited, the commissioner produced data from the American Correctional Association showing that Alabama budgeted $9,176 per prisoner annually, compared with a national average of $27,114. While part of this disparity was because of the lower-than-average cost of living in the state, it is worth noting that the next lowest state, Louisiana, budgeted $14,185 per prisoner.

Because performance management in Alabama was viewed as a tool for increasing resources rather than as a management tool, there was little willingness to engage in wider organizational change through training or changed work processes. Within the Alabama DOC, performance management changed work routines only for the budget staff that prepared and reported the performance information, not the operations staff. In fact, only a handful of staff knew that an Alabama DOC strategic plan existed, since it was not distributed to managers who worked in prisons.

The need for resources, an atmosphere of crisis, and awareness of the passing nature of executive-led reforms directed attention away from performance management in Alabama, but agency leaders recognized the necessity of complying with the governor's wishes for reform. Staff accepted the governor's authority over the DOC. They even viewed performance management as a good idea on some level, but they simply saw it as inapplicable to corrections in Alabama. Compliance was done knowing that the only immediate cost to the Alabama DOC was the time and effort involved in preparing performance information. Even if the reform would later fade away, it was easier to comply with the governor's wishes than to defy him and risk a negative political reaction.[10]

Managerial Authority

A central argument of performance management doctrine is that the current limited sense of authority over procedures, and in turn, responsibility for goals, reduced the potential for finding improved ways to achieve a preexisting goal, and therefore the potential for performance improvement. Instead, bureaucratic controls encouraged either rule-based observance or entrepreneurial avoidance of the rules. According to this logic, adjusting the focus of control to include performance and not just inputs, and providing an enhanced degree of authority, enable managers to understand and take responsibility for achieving organizational goals.

Performance management doctrine suggests a circular relationship exists between the use of performance information and the authority to initiate change, and the frequent mismatch of these qualities for the purposes of performance improvement. A willingness to use performance information will be influenced by whether managers believe that such learning can be put to good use. The manager who believes that learning from performance information is unlikely to be used because of controls limiting authority is less likely to invest time and effort in using the information for organizational improvement in the first place. Senge notes that "frustrations appear to occur in settings where teams seeking to develop their learning capabilities lack the power to act in the domains about which they are learning."[11]

There were instances of performance data use for process improvement, such as the benchmarking teams in Virginia, but these were rare. Those who have the time, interest, and expertise required to examine information and make well-informed judgments are likely to be lower-level managers, who lack the authority to make the appropriate changes. Senior managers or elected officials with high authority are likely to lack the interest, motivation, and operational expertise to consider and make informed judgments about specific processes. As a result, performance information is likely to remain unused, potential learning opportunities untaken, and ineffective managerial processes unchanged.

However, the implementation perspective employed in this chapter demonstrates just how wide the discretion of agency managers actually is and the ways it can be used in conjunction with a reform. In Virginia and Vermont agency leaders found uses for performance management that were feasible under existing authority, even if they were not directly related to performance improvement. Clearly, some positive change is possible within existing authority if motivated leadership exists.

These benefits occurred despite the failure of the responsibility accountability model to materialize. A general problem with the concept of responsibility accountability is whether the bureaucrat has control over the processes that produce the performance results for which they are being held responsible. This control will be limited by the existence of external factors beyond governmental control that impinge on results, such as the influence of the economy on recidivism rates. For any meaningful outcomes it becomes extremely difficult to figure out causal relationships and the importance of the actions of a public official or program. A central agency official in Virginia said: "You try to tease out causality and attribution. Good luck. The greatest researchers in this planet haven't been able to figure it out. And I don't think Joe Schmo over there in the Department of Planning and Budget or the Governor's Office is going to figure out 'they caused that, they need to be held accountable.'"

For responsibility accountability it is, therefore, more suitable to have an output or intermediate outcome measure over which bureaucrats have a high degree of control and by which their performance may be judged.[12] This runs contrary to demands for more outcome-based management. Linking control and achievement will also be determined by whether the bureaucrat in question has authority to change managerial processes. If not, it becomes unfair to hold that person responsible for goal achievement. In all three states there was little effort to enhance wide-ranging managerial authorities in ways that would allow bureaucrats to achieve goals and subsequently increase their scope of responsibility.

In addition to causality problems, the nature of the U.S. political system, prevalence of traditional modes, and political control all stymie the responsibility accountability model. The separation of powers in the U.S. political system precludes establishing a contractual relationship between resources provided and goals achieved. Senior agency managers in the three states studies had performance goals to achieve, but without expectation that their ex-post performance would be carefully examined or have an impact on their tenure or finances. Performance goals were not used as a contract for performance, where both bureaucrats and elected officials would have agreed to a given level of performance in exchange for a given level of resources and incentives.[13] Strategic plans that emerged from the executive branch operated more as an investment option where achievement of goals was conditional on receiving adequate resources. If the legislature failed to provide the resources requested, then the level of expectation for the achievement of goals is reduced. None of the three states had a process to revise goals after the legislature provided the budget to reestablish the sense of connection between resources and organizational goals. Corrections budgets for all three states were growing, but DOC staff saw them as still inadequate to deal with demands. Where the disconnect between goals and resources is extreme, as it was in Alabama, agency officials see inadequately funded strategic plans as a basis for denying rather than accepting responsibility. Instead of saying, "Here is the list of things we take responsibility for," agencies use performance management to say, "Here is what we can do if you give us the resources, but don't be surprised if we fail when you don't."

Another limitation to responsibility accountability is the system of political appointments. It is unlikely that appointees who win a position based on political loyalty or shared ideology will lose their position for reasons related to performance, unless performance failure is so pronounced it becomes a public issue. This was not a relevant factor among the DOC staff I met, where all commissioners and staff were seasoned professionals, knowledgeable about their function, and cared about their organizations. It was apparent, however, that this had not always been the case. For bureaucrats, civil service systems, with their tenure protections and pay guarantees, offer an equivalent form of protection from being held responsible for all but the worst performance.

Another prerequisite to responsibility accountability absent in the cases was actual use of performance information by elected officials and central agency staff in allocating resources and making tenure or financial punishment/reward decisions on the basis of results. The idea of responsibility accountability is stymied by an unwillingness to move from existing forms of decision making, as traditional control systems remain focused on accounting for probity rather than achievement of goals. Despite creating reforms intended to foster performance-based budgeting, legislators remain more concerned about appropriate use of resources rather than goal achievement.

A corrections officer in Alabama noted:

> The way it was desired, when they passed legislation was, "This is our crime rate, this is your budget, we will give you this to bring down the crime rate. These are the things you're going to try to accomplish, these are your measures, here is the outcome, and this is how much money you have to spend." And we've never really gotten that. We're still at "how much are you spending on pencils? How much are you spending on cars?" People don't want to get away from that.

Resources

A fairly straightforward factor in the implementation of reforms is resource adequacy. Empirical work has shown that the availability of resources is associated with agency adoption of performance reforms and greater use of performance information.[14] While resources do not guarantee the success of reforms, chronic inadequacy guarantees failure.[15] The importance of resources is best illustrated by the Alabama case. Low funding has shaped every aspect of corrections in Alabama and of any management reform that was introduced.

Alabama political culture is conservative, suspicious of government spending, and willing to impose high punishments on criminal behavior (see appendix B for more details). Senator Jack Biddle III, the Republican chair of the legislature's Joint Prison Oversight Committee, summarized the policy conflict that follows: "Everyone wants all the prisoners locked up forever, but they don't want to spend the money for it or have the prisons in their neighborhood. We're just doing the best we can without any money."[16] Lack of resources, combined with a punitive approach to sentencing, has led to chronic overcrowding, warehousing of offenders, and a crisis management or coping approach to running the correctional system.

As more and more prisoners entered the system, there was a failure to hire new staff, and one commissioner in the early 1990s closed down the Alabama DOC's training academy. By 2002 the department had approximately the same number of staff as in 1991—but ten thousand additional prisoners.

By any measure, the Alabama prisons were overcrowded, with approximately twenty-six thousand prisoners in a system originally designed for fourteen thousand. The county jails, themselves overcrowded, were effectively subsidizing the state corrections system by holding additional overflow prisoners, and they had gone to court seeking to force the state to retake the prisoners. The state estimated that it cost $26.00 a day to house prisoners, but the county received only $1.75 per day. The courts agreed with the county jails, but the state delayed accepting the prisoners, leading one court to give the county jails the power to simply drop the state prisoners off at a state prison. On one visit to a state prison, my interviews were cut short and I was asked to leave because local TV news reporters had arrived outside the prison. The previous appearance of reporters had been the only warning of an effort by the counties to return some of the state prisoners. In that instance, the counties brought approximately 150 state prisoners to the prison, handcuffed them to the perimeter fence, and drove off. (Understandably, the sight of TV reporters made the prison staff a little nervous that there would be a repeat incident, although in this case it turned out to be a false alarm.)

Before I left Alabama, another court case (Civil Action No. CV-92–388-SH and CV-92–399-SH) concluded. The judgment gave the Alabama DOC thirty days to transfer all state inmates in county facilities into the state system but prevented the county jails from transferring inmates without first gaining permission from the DOC. Even so, the task of introducing two thousand additional prisoners into the state prison system in a month seemed infeasible if prisoners were to be classified in an orderly fashion and even ad-hoc lodgings found. In its judgment, the court acknowledged overcrowding problems and highlighted the role of elected officials in providing basic resources: "The Courts of this state can only go so far in remedying prison and jail overcrowding. The real solution must come from the executive and legislative branches of state government. They have the capacity to fund and provide for enough prisons and correctional staff to insure the safety and well being of the citizens of this state."

The image that emerges of the Alabama DOC is not one of lean, purposeful efficiency, but rather of a department desperately trying to keep a lid on a steadily degenerating situation. I asked one DOC staff member about whether strategic planning matters in an environment where the department faces an unanticipated event or crisis. The reply: "Basically it doesn't. We don't think, well, we're going to miss our performance indicator." In fact, facing situations such as the drop-off of the 150 prisoners leads staff to cope in ways that compromise even standard operating procedures. For Alabama DOC employees, the environment appears highly uncertain and unstable, even though the majority of technologies involved in safely incarcerating prisoners are straightforward and achievable given adequate resources. If, as Mintzberg claims, planning works best in highly predictable conditions, it is unsurprising that performance management became of marginal interest to members of the Alabama DOC.[17] The factors that most influence their work lives—money and overcrowding—are factors they have had least control over.

The lack of resources in Alabama affected the implementation of performance management reform in two ways. First, and most importantly, the sense of crisis management that pervaded the Alabama DOC meant that organizational focus was on coping with immediate problems created by a lack of resources, rather than on long-term strategic agendas. A sense of crisis was the norm rather than exception. A senior manager noted, "We're pretty much in a constant emergency situation in the Department of Corrections. We are in crisis mode." Adequate resources can remedy much of this basic instability and become the lens through which everything is viewed. The positive aspect of performance management for Alabama DOC staff was that it might help them to justify additional funding (this is discussed in chapter 6). Once it became apparent that this was not going to be the case, then the irrelevance of setting goals and targets based on an assumption of resource adequacy also became clear, invoking cynicism about the possibility of performance management. One senior manager said:

> We can sit here and do a strategic plan for five, six years, but [when] I don't have the funds to accomplish those dreams, it's kind of rough, especially when your hands are tied. . . . They [colleagues] weren't too enthused about it because it's something they've done before. And [if] you're going into the battlefield to fight a war [and] you don't have the resources, you're going to lose that war. . . . So, that was the attitude, you know. Setting goals is fine, but how are we going to accomplish this if we don't have the resources? So naturally they did have a little negative attitude at that time.

The second way in which inadequate resources affects a reform is that insufficient time and administrative attention are allocated to implementing it. The DOCs in Virginia and Vermont had full-time staff focused on collecting and diffusing performance information, while in Alabama the additional duties of performance management were shared between one-off consultant support and already overworked DOC budgeteers. Unsurprisingly, the budget staff in Alabama focused simply on ensuring the required information was reported to the Department of Finance, rather than seeking to find ways that performance information could bring about organizational change. Managers working in prisons were unaware that a strategic plan even existed, and senior departmental management viewed it as a tool and responsibility of budgeteers. The perception of one Alabama

DOC staff member that "about 99 percent of the people in corrections don't know anything about it yet" appeared accurate based on my conversations with staff. I asked if he meant institutional staff or more-senior managers. He said, "I'm talking about everybody. I mean, some of the support directors were interviewed, but really they could care less cause they don't think anything will come from it."

Once performance information was produced, no additional bothersome mechanisms—high employee participation, communication, training, performance reviews, or other learning opportunities—were set up in Alabama to take advantage of the information and to emphasize its part in day-to-day management. The budget staff did not welcome the additional responsibility or view it as a chance to extend their power in the organization. It was viewed simply as an additional onerous task that had to be performed, without additional resources, on top of their existing budget-preparation duties.

Conclusion

Different approaches have been adopted to explain political and administrative behavior. Rational choice is associated with the assumption of self-interested behavior, which for elected officials leads to the conclusion that policy adoption is partially used to improve reelection chances. The sociological approach to the new institutionalism emphasizes professional norms and the search for legitimacy in the diffusion of new ideas. Interestingly, both rational choice and the new sociological institutionalism are consistent in treating reform as having essentially symbolic value that allows its proponents to use it for other ends. Traditional public administration theories have largely eschewed a consideration of the symbolic dimension of reform, debating instead the instrumental benefits. The economic version of the new institutionalism that underlies the NPM and performance management doctrine has adopted rational choice assumptions in a prescriptive, rather than behavioral, framework and also focuses on using reforms to create instrumental benefits.

By studying management reform from an implementation perspective, this research paints a reality of reform that is messier, more interactive, and more interesting than portrayed by any single approach mentioned above but that incorporates different elements of each. To present a theory that seeks to explain both policy adoption and implementation requires understanding reform in both symbolic and instrumental terms, and in recognizing the interaction between these concepts. There are elements of self-interested behavior, particularly in the selection of performance management as a reform by elected officials. The institutional isomorphism of the new sociological institutionalism is also undoubtedly present, diffusing ideas of performance management to government professionals and making performance management a standard of legitimacy for state governments.[18] In this respect performance management is a symbolic reform.

However, the case evidence also makes clear that symbolic actions are not inconsistent with instrumental benefits.[19] Reforms driven by symbolic motivations can be taken and used for real purposes, sometimes in unexpected ways. Such reforms provide managers with administrative space and top-level support to create changes. Where agency leaders actively pursued such change, they were largely motivated to create additional organizational value.

March and Olsen argued that behavior is shaped not by a logic of consequentiality, as rational choice suggests, but by a logic of appropriateness determined by environmental norms, structures, and routines.[20] But a logic of appropriateness does not necessarily exclude a logic of consequentiality. Rather, both logics can operate side by side, within organizations, individuals, and even actions. An action can be both instrumental and highly symbolic. Reforms intended to be instrumental can become normative and symbolic for some actors, as occurred in the policy adoption of performance management. Transfer of reforms also means their transformation, and as reforms such as performance management are adopted, they are changed to suit the needs of the adopting actors and the context of implementation. In the case of U.S. states, performance management reforms were adjusted in the policy adoption phase to deemphasize calls for increased managerial authority. Agency managers, in turn, adapted the reform, searching for ways to implement it within their zone of discretion while being consistent with the organizational context and their goals for the organization.

Notes

1. See, for example, Downs and Larkey, *The Search for Government Efficiency;* Radin, "The Government Performance and Results Act and the Tradition of Federal Management Reform: Square Pegs in Round Holes"; Schick, "The Road to PBB"; Wildavsky, *Budgeting: A Comparative Theory of Budgeting Processes.*

2. Franklin, "An Examination of Bureaucratic Reactions to Institutional Controls"; Liner et al., *Making Results-Based State Government Work;* Governmental Accounting Standards Board, *State and Local Government Case Studies.*

3. DeLeon, "The Missing Link Revisited"; O'Toole, "Research on Policy Implementation."

4. Pressman and Wildavksy, *Implementation;* Mazmanian and Sabatier, *Implementation and Public Policy.*

5. Bourdeaux, *Legislative Influences on Performance-Based Budgeting Reform.*

6. Ingraham, Sowa, and Moynihan, "Public Sector Integrative Leadership."

7. Berry, Brower, and Flowers also identified leadership as important in fostering agency use of performance management techniques, even in the face of a discouraging statewide context. The leaders in their cases also tried to use performance management processes to identify agency

mission and improve agency capacity while managing the agency's external stakeholders. Berry, Brower, and Flowers, "Implementing Performance Accountability in Florida."

8. However, if strategic goals are not consistent with the court's wishes, or are patently unlikely to be implemented, as was the case in Alabama, courts can choose to ignore strategic plans, effectively prioritizing the goals of the court over the goals in the strategic plan.

9. DiIulio, "Managing a Barbed-Wire Bureaucracy."

10. An interesting postscript to the Alabama case came in November 2002 when Governor Siegelman lost his bid to be reelected. Siegelman lost to an opponent who based his campaign largely on a promise to clean up government, accusing Siegelman of running an incompetent and corrupt regime. Siegelman's aides were surprised that the charges stuck—they thought they had the perfect "good government" candidate. At the time, the public and press seemed uninterested in hearing about performance management or other good government initiatives, and an increasingly negative campaign ended in defeat for Siegelman. The outcome illustrates March and Olsen's observation that promising reforms may be a more effective electoral tactic than actually implementing them. From the point of view of bureaucrats, the outcome further reflects the passing nature of executive-led reforms. See March and Olsen, "Organizing Political Life." Things would get worse for Siegelman, who was convicted of conspiracy, bribery, and fraud in June 2006, the second Alabama governor in thirteen years to be convicted of wrongdoing.

11. Senge, *The Fifth Discipline,* xvii.

12. A more detailed version of this argument is made by Frederickson and Frederickson, *Measuring the Performance of the Hollow State.*

13. This difficulty has much to do with the fact that, unlike the parliamentary systems of the benchmark countries, U.S. state systems have a powerful legislative branch. This means you have two sets of principals, the executive and legislative branches, for the single bureaucratic agent, complicating the ability to create a contract-like structure for accountability. Moe, "The New Economics of Organization."

14. Brudney et al., "Reassessing the Reform Decade"; de Lancer Julnes and Holzer, "Promoting the Utilization of Performance Measures."

15. Mazmanian and Sabatier, *Implementation and Public Policy.*

16. Firestone, "Packed Alabama Jail Draws Ire of Court Again."

17. Mintzberg, "The Pitfalls of Strategic Planning."

18. DiMaggio and Powell, "The Iron Cage Revisited."

19. The findings here are of interest because they expand upon some insightful work that has documented the symbolic aspect of results-based reforms. For instance, Roy and Seguin apply the institutional isomorphism argument to such reforms, focusing on the adoption of cost–benefit analysis in the federal government. However, they fail to examine whether cost–benefit analysis offered any instrumental benefit and dismiss it as a solely symbolic reform. The contribution of the research presented in this book is that it considers both the symbolic and instrumental aspects of reform. Roy and Seguin, "The Institutionalization of Efficiency-Oriented Approaches for Public Service Improvement." Another case of the gap between rhetorical claims about reform and actual practice comes from Australia's use of accrual budgets. See Carlin and Guthrie, "Accrual Output Based Budgeting Systems in Australia."

20. March and Olsen, *Rediscovering Institutions.*

6

The Interactive Dialogue Model of Performance Information Use

When we were asked to do a problem in our childhood math classes, numbers offered simplicity. There was one correct answer, which we found or missed. Performance data is given the same reassuring status of clarity and objectivity.[1] But this understanding of performance information is usually overly simplistic and incorrect. Performance data is ambiguous and subject to disagreement. Performance information is not definitive, and interested actors interact in a dialogue to establish its meaning. This insight informs the next three chapters, which develop the interactive dialogue model of performance information use.

Why interactive? Why dialogue? Dialogue works as an alternative to the mechanistic metaphor of decision making in performance management doctrine, and it also captures multiple elements of an alternative theory of performance information. My case findings show that performance information is used, though not systematically. The presentation, exchange, and interpretation involved in a dialogue reflect the fact that this is a theory of information use, not a theory of why information is not used. This use has a clearly interactive component. Managers using performance data have never done so as a solo exercise, creating, interpreting, and acting on a piece of information by themselves. They create or use it at the behest of more senior officials, in conjunction with colleagues as they search for solutions, or to control other actors. The creation and use of performance information is, to use Wildavsky's term, a form of *social interaction.*[2] In contrast to centralized planning by a dominant actor, social interaction models are characterized by actors with discretion, interests, and the capacity to express their perspectives. Actors come to agreement through bargaining rather than arriving at some definitively correct decision.[3] Wildavksy also identified how institutional roles shape behavior, an observation I extend to examine how roles influence the use of performance information.[4]

Interactive dialogue evokes the social aspects of performance information use. Information is exchanged between multiple parties, suggesting the potential for multiple interpretations of information. Information is not static, but is created and presented to have an impact on another actor, who may in turn respond with his or her own interpretation of events. The meaning of information for different actors is established in the exchange. Interactive dialogue therefore implies the ambiguity and subjectivity in the construction of meaning. In the same ways that some interactive dialogues lead to agreement, and some crystallize conflict, the exchange of performance information can sometimes lead to greater agreement and coordinated action between parties and sometimes do little more than reflect the different positions of the actors involved.

A final advantage of the term *interactive dialogue* is that it suggests that performance information is part of a political conversation between actors. Majone points out, "As politicians know only too well but social scientists too often forget, public policy is made of language. Whether in written or oral form, argument is central in all stages of the policy process."[5] Because the dialogue is political, its impact is neither determinative nor easy to predict. The impact depends on the political makeup of the actors involved—the positions they advocate, the roles represented, and the different levels of power and resources possessed. In short, the term *interactive dialogue* clues us to look at what information is being presented, by whom, under what conditions, the meaning it is intended to generate, and the affect on other actors.

One clear implication of the interactive dialogue approach is that actors in the policy process who use information need to know the craft of constructing an argument. A good craftsman does this effectively and competently; a bad one loses credibility because of incompetence.[6]

This chapter begins by looking at how performance information is used in one specific decision forum, the budget process, to understand performance information use more broadly. Drawing on evidence from state governments and previous theories, I develop the basic assumptions of the interactive dialogue model of performance information use.

The Lack of a Performance Budgeting Theory

The concept of performance budgeting is bedeviled with definitional vagueness and a lack of an operational theory. In 1940 Key noted that the basic problem with budgeting was that it lacked a theory that would allow budgeteers to determine "on what basis shall it be decided to allocate x dollars to activity A instead of activity B."[7] The doctrine of performance management suggests that performance information provides the basis for making these choices. Performance data offers us more information, but it is a mistake to assume that performance information resolves Key's quandary. First of all, it is difficult to allocate costs to performance, although governments are improving at this skill. Second, decision makers often disagree on what constitutes an acceptable measure of performance and are especially unlikely to find acceptable units of comparison across different types of programs. Third, even if decision makers can agree on what measures of performance to use, they are still likely to disagree on the relative value of different program performance. For example, for some legislators an increase in spending on education, instead of transportation, is worthwhile if it can prompt a small increase in literacy. For others, the benefits of spending on a new road are obviously superior.

To some extent it is misleading to talk about performance budgeting as distinct from performance management. The budgeting process includes execution, which is really just another name for management. Central budget officials at the state and federal levels argue that one of the key functions of performance information is for management purposes, and they express hope that managers are using it. So how is performance budgeting different than performance management, if at all? If it has any meaning at all, performance budgeting must include budgeteers using performance information to make resource allocation decisions. How should they use it? The failure to resolve this question serves as an impediment to creating a specific and distinct definition of performance budgeting, as we saw in chapter 1. While the concept of linking performance information to resource allocation is widely supported, the extension of this idea to its logical conclusion of a strict model of performance budgeting is not.

If a strict theory of performance budgeting is not acceptable, what are the alternatives? A looser standard for performance budgeting is to hope that it fosters allocative efficiency, tying resources to where the money will be most effectively spent. Greater knowledge about the performance of programs and process allows more informed allocation decisions. Budgeteers and elected officials, less concerned with tracking inputs, have more time to focus on providing allocations according to strategic goals, observing whether these goals are achieved and holding managers accountable for results.[8]

But the concept of allocative efficiency is not a theory of performance budgeting for a number of reasons. First, allocative efficiency is a goal, not a theory of how budgeteers behave or even of how they should behave. Second, the concept is abstract and inherently subjective. Allocating resources is at the heart of the political process and provides a critical power to elected officials. If budgeting is indeed about allocating values, defining what allocative efficiency looks like will be an exercise in subjectivity.

Previous experience with budget reform suggests that a relatively loose link between performance information and resource allocation, with particular emphasis on the budget execution stage, may be as much as we can reasonably expect from performance budgets. The unrealistic ambitions of previous reforms set the stage for dashed expectations.[9] These failures were best explained by incrementalism theory.[10] Incrementalism identified the importance of political values in decision making and the importance of previous decisions or allocations in guiding current decisions. In a political environment, elected officials face pressing claims for their attention and support, including party policy, interest groups, constituent wishes, media views, and competing policy issues. A comprehensive use of performance information is beyond limited human cognitive capacities, leads to information overload, and is a distraction for policy analysts. Instead, moderations of previous agreements serve to simplify problems and limit political conflict. Incrementalism ultimately suggests that performance information does not matter, hence the continuing failure of overly mechanical and rational models of performance budgeting.

The failure of the strict model of performance budgeting to reflect reality has not led to the abandonment of calls for performance information systems. Some simply discount evidence of failure or suggest that it is because the reform has not been fully implemented. One central agency official in Virginia discussed how counterparts in other states deal with what they perceive as their continuing failure to properly implement performance management:

> You know they pretty much have ingested it and are working the party line without really realizing what it means. [They say,] "You know it's a little frustrating sometimes. Yeah, it could be better. We're going to try. We're going to keep working on this. We're going to do the training next year and then we have these new forms that are coming out" . . . They don't think that it's the theoretical construct [that is the problem]. I think they still believe that that's what's supposed to work. Either they're doing something wrong or they haven't had the training. . . . You know, the logic is airtight, so they're going to hang on to it.

If the strict model is unrealistic, perhaps we need to set more achievable goals for performance management, consistent with the idea that it is desirable to have performance information in the decision mix, but that it is unlikely to be determinative. Joyce argues that instead of striving for performance-based budgeting, we should seek to improve models of "performance-informed budgeting."[11] Lauth argues we should not expect that performance information will ever offer a systematic guide to budgeting, and so instead we should ensure that budgets are "friendly" to productivity improvement efforts.[12] Melkers and Willoughby suggest that we should consider communication as an interim or initial goal of performance management, and they find that there is moderate support for this concept in a survey of state budgeteers and agency staff.[13] Chris Wye of the GAO notes:

In no other context would we have the least hope that the use of information would determine the course of decisionmaking. At most, we would expect it to inform the decisionmaking process. Where indicators are concerned, however, we expect a perfect world where truth not only speaks to power but tells it what to do. . . . The true standard should be whether or not performance information is *taken into account* in the decisionmaking context, not whether it is the basis for a given decision (italics in original).[14]

The common element in these observations is that a plausible theory of performance budgeting rests on a realistic expectation that performance data informs dialogue but is not deterministic. Evidence on performance budgeting from state governments is consistent with this view. This evidence also points to the importance of roles and advocacy in the use of performance information, moving us closer to an interactive dialogue model of performance information use.

Evidence from the States

In searching for a theory of performance budgeting, let us return to the state level. In all three states studied, reform advocates described their reforms as performance budgeting, reflecting a deliberate effort to tie the creation and diffusion of performance information to the budgeting process. Evidence suggests that actual use of information lagged the sophistication of performance information systems, was episodic rather than systematic, and largely occurred at the agency level rather than among statewide actors.

This data is consistent with previous research. Aristigueta finds little evidence of use of performance information for resource allocation in the three state governments she examined, which included Virginia.[15] Joyce and Tompkins find that performance information may be used by managers when allocating resources or might enter the legislative budget debate, but has a marginal influence.[16] The GAO studied perceived leaders in performance management in the states and could find instances of where performance information was used, but cautioned that "none of this information, however, led to automatic budget decisions. Instead, it helped to inform budget deliberations by highlighting problems, supporting claims, or enriching the debate."[17] Florida, another perceived leader in performance budgeting, has had organizational and technical problems in its system, and the key benefits appear to have come at the agency level.[18]

The repetitive nature of performance budgeting requirements underlines their lack of success. For instance, in Alabama, Governor Siegelman pursued new performance budgeting requirements even though existing ones were in statute, albeit largely ignored. Florida and Texas have switched from performance budgeting to zero-based budgeting (ZBB). ZBB recalls President Jimmy Carter's efforts to require the federal government to assume it starts with zero resources and to justify all programs. Carter had used the same budget model in Georgia, but closer inspection suggested that it had never really been applied in any significant way in Georgia or at the federal level.[19] ZBB, if actually implemented, abandons the heuristics of incremental budgeting that make the process manageable. ZBB also rejects the premise that performance information is important. If performance budgeting is based on the idea that more information makes for better budget decisions, ZBB takes the opposite approach, assuming that a reliance on information has failed to prompt budgeteers to consider the fundamental question of whether something is worth funding or not. That two states regarded as leaders in performance budgeting have turned their attention to ZBB is not a positive sign for performance budgeting, as budgeteers abandon a seemingly failed reform to reach back to the 1970s for one that defies the basic logics of budgeting.

The absurdity of ZBB was illustrated by the Texas budget proposal for fiscal years 2003–5. Instead of recommending dollar amounts, the proposed budget simply featured row after row of zeroes for each program and spending item. As the document was distributed, budgeteers quietly ignored it and returned to the actual process of allocating resources by looking at how they had done so in the past.

The findings from three state cases do not repudiate the view of previous empirical work or offer support for the strict model of performance budgeting. On the contrary, there was strong evidence of incrementalism and the low priority given to performance information. However, evidence from all three cases identifies one major use of performance information in resource allocation by agency representatives: as a means of advocating for policy issues and defending and expanding their budget. DOC staff in all three cases, even at the institution level, viewed defending and expanding resources as a primary use of performance information. They were encouraged in these beliefs by central agency officials and consultants promoting performance reporting requirements. One corrections manager in Vermont put it this way: "I think it provides a hell of a defense. When people come to rob you of resources of any kind, you can at least say this is what I need, this is where we are going, this is our plan. This is what you are going to do; this is the impact you will have on our plan."

A central budget official in Vermont echoed this view:

Performance measurement helps make the best argument for your programs. An example is human services. . . . That guy [agency head] had done a lot of good measurement, could tell you immediately how much it would cost, how many widgets, and he could also tell you his success or his outcomes for his various programs. And he did so well that normally he pretty much gets what he wants. He is pretty fiscally tight, but he really defends his purposes well. And another one who did it who does not usually do it is community colleges. They did the same thing. They basically strongly defended their policies and what they could do. And they were the two types of agencies that are normally least able to defend their programs. So I have seen people do it well. It's possible. I think it's the biggest help to anybody who is trying to defend their budget, to be honest.

Agency officials will use performance information in ways that call for increased funding. As one central budget official asked, "What agency in their right mind is going to include measures that are going to reduce the chance of success in getting their damn money?" For corrections, any help in winning resources is badly needed. Corrections is not a popular function. While many elected officials and members of the public want to see criminals given significant jail time, the resources required are given reluctantly. Without strong stakeholder support, performance information is an alternative way to persuade executive branch and legislative budgeteers to increase resources. Agencies use performance management to portray efficiency and effectiveness in management practices, and they emphasize needs by pointing to input measures or workload indicators, or output/outcome goals that require more funding. For example, the Virginia DOC strategic plan states: "Through the development of a strategic planning process in 1996 the Department of Corrections has achieved significant efficiencies in critical cost areas. The analysis of internal processes has enabled the Department to operate some programs with internal funding generated by more cost-effective operations."[20]

The claim is made in the context of a plea not to cut resources because the system is as efficient as it can be: "We have carefully reviewed all agency resources in preparing the strategies supporting our critical issues. We believe that further reallocation of existing resources will jeopardize the integrity of our public safety mission."[21]

How performance information was used varied to some degree in each state. Virginia used measures of efficiency and effectiveness to underline that performance management enabled cost cutting and high-quality service, and that any additional cuts were unwise. Vermont, meanwhile, used outcome measures that underlined the effectiveness of department-led experimental programs relative to traditional approaches in terms of lower cost and recidivism, and developed positive measures for corrections (e.g., postincarceration employment, hours, or dollar-value returned to the community). Alabama used measures intended to illustrate the state's desperate need for resources. Measures were largely inputs (e.g., number of officers, number of inmates, or workload indicators such as ratio of officers to inmates), and measures also advertised the need for additional inputs (e.g., percentage of state inmates in county jails and beds not occupied because of employee vacancies). Measures pointing to the lower costs of offenders diverted from the Alabama DOC system into alternatives to incarceration sought to reduce the flow of offenders into state facilities.

Basic Assumptions of the Interactive Dialogue Model

Proposals to integrate performance data and budgeting tend to assume that performance information is objective, standardized, indicative of actual performance, consistently understood, and prompts a consensus about how a program is performing and how it should be funded. The experience of the three states described above is contrary to these assumptions. Performance information is used, although not in a systematic manner. It is often presented by advocates seeking to support a predetermined position, trying to persuade others to look at the performance information they consider important and see it in the way that they do. The interactive dialogue model presented here seeks to fill this gap. It is based on a number of assumptions:

- Performance information is not comprehensive.
- Performance information is ambiguous.
- Performance information is subjective.
- Production of performance information does not guarantee use.
- Institutional affiliation and individual beliefs will affect selection, perception, and presentation of performance information.
- The context of dialogue will affect the ability to use performance information to develop solutions.

The interactive dialogue model assumes that simply because performance information exists, there is no guarantee that it is used. Whether it is used, and how it is used, depend on the motivations of potential users and utility of performance information to their goals. Because performance information will sometimes help to advance an argument, it is likely to be used—but not in the simplistic or deterministic way assumed by the strict theory of performance budgeting. The interactive dialogue model points to the ambiguity inherent in interpreting performance information. There is likely to be no single definitive approach to (a) interpreting what performance information means and (b) how performance information directs decisions. The meaning of performance information is constructed, and therefore the same performance information can support different arguments. The use of information will never meet some objective ideal according to Wildavsky because "the choice of problems to be solved, as well as the alternatives considered, is not specified but must be worked out by particular people with individual interests."[22]

The assumptions outlined above draw from previous theories. First, the study of organizations provides evidence of the ambiguity inherent in organizational life, the constructed and contested nature of discourse, and the potential for rival interpretations of performance information. Second, we know from the study of the policy process that the design of the budget process creates incentives for particular actors to advance arguments that reflect their institutional role and context, enhancing the potential for disagreement. Third, there is some limited evidence that the nature of dialogue routines affects the type of discussion and solutions generated. These theories are examined in turn.

Ambiguity in Organizational Life

The study of organizational life reveals its deep-seated ambiguity.[23] Feldman defines ambiguity as "that state of having many ways of thinking about the same circumstances or phenomena."[24] Ambiguity is likely to occur in issues where objectives or issue-definition is unclear, where there is a lack of clarity on causal mechanisms between organizational actions and outcomes, where it is difficult to interpret the past, and where the pattern of individual participation in different decisions is uncertain and changing.[25]

While more information might reduce uncertainty, it will not eliminate ambiguity, since ambiguity is created by different perspectives rather than a lack of information. Feldman suggests that ambiguous issues must be interpreted, a process by which actors give meaning to the issue: "Resolution is a matter of agreement rather than proof. To the extent that resolution occurs, it comes from shared understandings, not factual information."[26] While information helps actors interpret a policy issue, it does not necessarily foster consensus on decisions. According to March: "Organizational information processing seems to be driven less by uncertainty about the consequences of specific decision alternatives than by lack of clarity about how we talk about the world—what alternatives there are and how they are related to stories we think we understand, how we describe history and how we interpret it."[27]

Another approach to studying organizational life is to study its discourse, or how texts are created and exchanged between organizational actors. The literature on organizational discourse and narratives focuses on the ambiguity of these texts and assumes that the attitudes and behaviors of organizational actors are shaped by the discursive practices in the organization. Consistent with the literature on discourse is the growing attention to the concept of constructed narratives in political science and public policy.[28] These accounts present narratives as both a tool and reflection of political power, crafted to fit information in the context of a coherent story about a particular policy. This social constructionist approach represents what Fischer and

Forrester have termed the "argumentative turn" in policy debates.[29] Majone has made a similar point about policy analysis, which "has less to do with formal techniques of problem solving than with the process of argument."[30] Central to these perspectives is the idea that discourse is constructed by actors and is intended to influence others. Each text is rife with unspoken assumptions, although each text is also susceptible to rival interpretations.[31]

Performance information is as susceptible to social construction as other forms of discourse. Deciphering what constitutes performance can be difficult. Such variation in interpretation will increase when we face even trickier questions. What does performance mean? What are the next steps for the program? How should we budget on the basis of performance information? While performance information tells us something about a program, the data itself does not answer these questions.[32] Performance data, or simplified assessments of performance data, fails to tell us

- why performance did or did not occur.
- the context of performance.
- how implementation occurred.
- an understanding of outside influences on performance.
- how to choose which program measure is a priority.

The absence of this information makes it difficult to determine what performance actually means. Analysts are usually stuck with interpreting whether performance is satisfactory in light of previous performance or some target, implicit or explicit.

Even if you and I can agree on an appropriate performance measure and also agree on what the data means, we may still disagree on what to do next. Various plausible and logical options usually exist.[33] One person might decide that the type of action appropriate for the program is related to funding, where another sees a management problem. Even if two individuals agree that performance information should influence resource allocation, performance data does not tell us how. The classic example is a program with poor performance. According to Wildavsky:

> There are always competing explanations about why policies fail that may leave decision-makers uncertain over whether to abandon them. One hypothesis is that the theory behind the policy is bad and the more that is done the worse things will get. The other hypothesis is that the critical mass has not been reached. If more of the same thing were done then the policy would ultimately show good results. . . . If the ostensible purpose of a policy has not been achieved or does not seem worth the cost, one can usually discover other collateral objectives that have, in fact, been accomplished."[34]

Should funding be cut and the program abandoned as a failure, or should more resources be provided to help make the program a success? The ability to answer this question depends a great deal on our understanding of why performance failed to occur and whether it can be remedied, issues that are subject to disagreement. Values play a role. We are less likely to abandon programs that we feel have an important purpose.

Numbers fail to reflect trade-offs in public policies. Programs often have multiple goals that sometimes conflict with one another. As a result, the same program can be judged a success or failure depending on which measures are considered. Heinrich and Fournier's evaluation of which substance abuse programs were successful changed depending on the outcome measure used, leading them to observe: "The important question is not 'What structure or type of program treatment works best?' but 'What aspects of organization and treatment services work for whom, in what context, and toward what treatment goals?'"[35]

One response to the problem of trade-offs between goals is to pursue a type of comprehensive measure of performance that takes into account the multiple goals of a program. The PART described in later chapters is one such approach, and comprehensive measures are increasingly popular in the United Kingdom. The appeal of such a measure is the promise of converting the complexity of public programs into a fair and simple measure of success. But such comprehensive scores are still socially constructed. Questions of what to include and what weighting to assign to different parameters will significantly shape the overall score.[36] A study of comprehensive scores for local government and the health sector in the United Kingdom found that relatively minor changes in methods to construct the scores had significant impact on measured outcomes. Belying the reassuring idea of comprehensiveness, the authors of the study argued that the level of uncertainty and contingency associated with these measures should be better advertised.[37]

Given the ambiguity of performance information, we should put aside any assumption that performance information will make decisions simpler. Even if we accurately understood in advance the cost and outcomes of programs, that still does not provide a common basis for comparison since our willingness to fund services and specific levels of performance will depend on values. Indeed, the introduction of performance information simply adds related contextual questions: how do we know if more money will improve performance or be wasted? More broadly, how do we understand performance information, and how do we relate it to action?

The Role of Roles

Intelligent individuals with no particular axe to grind can disagree with one another about what performance information is appropriate, what it means, and what action it suggests. The potential for ambiguity to lead to disagreement becomes stronger in a political setting. In politics, actors play roles. They are representatives of ideologies, parties, programs, groups of citizens, organizations, and political institutions. This makes it more likely that the ambiguity of performance information will be exposed and used for subjective purposes. Consider the following example from a central agency official in Virginia, illustrating the importance of different perspectives in defining a policy issue.

> The challenge is to try to develop consensus on the objectives. Virginia has a system of mental health hospitals—over-capacity, under-utilized, expensive. We've had a terrible time trying to develop a restructuring plan for that system because . . . from the administration's perspective it's more of an efficiency issue, capacity issue. To the politicians, it's more of an economic development issue with the payroll in those places.

How an individual interprets and understands information will be shaped by their role. March and Olsen argue that individual behavior and preferences are endogenous to the organizational context of the individual.[38] Conditions of ambiguity and disagreement will therefore be exacerbated across political institutions that are designed to check one another and represent opposing viewpoints. The political arena is characterized by battles between rival actors to assert hegemony over issue definition.[39]

Brunnson has argued that organizations have strong incentives to use information to communicate the importance of their services and the values they represent.[40] As they seek to ensure that they present external values consistent with the demands of a changing environment, organizations will manipulate information to the point where external values may have only a weak relationship with internal ones. As long as the external values secure the legitimacy of the organization, and its funding, such an "organization of hypocrisy" is a natural and useful strategy. The use of performance information offers a means to communicate specific values, as exemplified by the different way that each DOC used performance information. Brunnson notes that few settings are better suited to the presentation of arguments to legitimate programs than the budget process.[41]

Information selection and use occurs in the context of different beliefs, preferences, and cognitive processes, and they will reflect organizational power and politics. Information providers will try to shape outcomes by choosing what information will be collected and highlighted. Each measure is representative of values and accompanied by the assumption that the organization should be making efforts that will have an impact on the measure.

Information can be used to advocate for a future state of affairs—and as a means to rationalize past behavior. Rationalizations are an important part of political discourse, justifying behaviors in the context of the public interest and seeking acceptance of these behaviors from others.[42] Multiple goals allow actors to retrospectively emphasize some objectives over others, a way of changing without appearing to change.[43]

March succinctly summarizes the potential to use information to represent values: "Information in organizations is not innocent."[44] Stone makes almost exactly the same point: "No number is innocent, for it is impossible to count without making judgments about categorization."[45] Stone notes that numbers are a frequently used symbol in establishing political narratives: "Numbers in politics are measures of human activities, made by human beings, and intended to influence human behavior. They are subject to conscious and unconscious manipulation by the people being measured, the people making the measurements, and the people who interpret and use measures made by others."[46] There can be political fights about numbers in terms of what is measured, how it is measured, what the measurement means. However, actors seeking to maximize the impact of numbers will usually present them in a way that downplays rival interpretation by not discussing how data was collected or what assumptions were made in creating information.[47]

Numbers can be used to tell stories, and sometimes to suggest that complex phenomena can be precisely defined and controlled. Numbers are powerful and offer the user a sense of authority because we associate data with objectivity and professionalism. According to Stone:

> In our profoundly numerical contemporary culture, numbers are symbolic of precision, accuracy and objectivity. They suggest mechanical selection, dictated by the nature of the objects, even though all counting involves judgment and discretion. By the time we are adults, the categorization part of counting is so much a second nature that we tend to forget about it. . . . Numerals hide all the difficult choices that go into a count.[48]

The same number can have multiple meanings, making it contestable.[49] To make performance information understandable, it needs advocates. Advocates direct attention to particular pieces of information, make sense of what it means in terms of resource needs, and offer decision suggestions to their audiences. They construct narratives and stories around what the performance information means and what it suggests should be done. The manager tasked with preparing performance information in the corrections field in Vermont commented:

> Understand that it is a basic principle of human nature that human beings are terrible statisticians, and especially orally. We do not understand numbers as spoken words; we understand them a little bit better visually, but still not very well. Understand that measuring policy is not a science. It is an art. It is words

and pictures and numbers. And you create impressions, beliefs, understandings, and persuasions.

Some authors have already begun to think about how performance or budget information is framed. Radin has argued that information is not neutral, pointing out that the many actors in a democratic setting are unlikely to agree on what is true or false: "One actor's 'fact' is another actor's 'value.' This has a direct effect on what is measured and how. When one scratches the surface, one is likely to find biases of various sorts within data systems."[50] Thurmaier and Willoughby note that budget information can also be framed in multiple different ways, that the budget process provides different actors with opportunities for mutual persuasion, and that the intensity of preferences held by program managers regarding their programs will usually be stronger than those of elected officials. We therefore expect to see different actors rely on different frames to present their agenda.[51] Doing so involves basic political skills. The limited relevance of performance information is illustrated by the fact that a single dramatic event can have a much stronger impact than a year's worth of performance data. The following comment came from a central budget officer in Vermont:

> Agencies come in and make cases of things. And some are successful and some aren't. And some are successful because they are right and they've made good case. Some are successful because they are just very good politicians themselves and they manage to rise to the top. . . . They can measure what is going to move people, and if they see there is a hot button here in the state [they will use it]. In Vermont right now we had a sixteen-year-old girl who was found dead in the Bronx or Brooklyn, New York. Turns out she had been taking heroin, prostituting herself, and ended up dead. This year and the next year, the commissioner of Social and Rehabilitation Services, it's a no-brainer for him to come in and say, "I need money for this kind of program. We are going to have to look at it." . . . Because it's a very popular issue right now in the legislature as well "What are we going to do about the sixteen- and seventeen-year[-old] kids that are in trouble?" They [the agency] go to legislature and they can say, "This is our budget and the administration also supports this new program for runaway youths." [If the administration does not support it,] they can go in and they say, This is our budget and somebody will clearly ask them—they do every year— "and what else did you see that was important for your agency to deal with that you just don't have the money to deal with?" And they'll go: "runaway youth programs." And all of the sudden the legislators will go: "Wait a minute, the administration didn't support this? We've been reading about it in the newspaper every day? How can they not see that is an important area?" . . . You can get

something that gets to the top of [the] list not so much because you know in a perfect world that [it] would have risen to the top but because a manager is looking at the process. He is looking at who is going to be involved in making the decision, where they come from, what moves them.

Research in psychology points to a confirmation bias in the selection and use of information in decision making—once decision makers have made up their minds on an issue, they will seek out information that supports their views and discount contrary information.[52] This insight helps us to understand why preferences formed by institutional norms become hard to displace, influencing the selection and perception of performance information. Confirmation bias can even affect the perception of the same information, with research finding, as Nickerson puts it, that "two people with initially conflicting views can examine the same evidence and both find reasons for increasing the strength of their existing opinions."[53]

The organizational discourse literature offers some insights into how roles shape how texts are created and whether they become embedded in discourse, that is, widely used by a target audience. Organizational actors are more likely to create texts that reflect actions that burnish their image, and so it is not surprising that organizations are likely to produce performance data in a way that makes them look effective or supports some other type of organizational argument. However, the existence of competing texts and rival perspectives lowers the potential for acceptance. Therefore, in an environment where actors represent different views and offer different interpretations, there is less chance of any single interpretation dominating. This is an important observation, given the pluralistic tendencies of public dialogue.[54]

Political roles shape how actors interpret, present, and use performance information. Conflict in interpretation will also be fostered by the norms and incentives associated with particular roles in the budget process, and observers of the budget process have noted how individuals tend to conform to role expectations.[55] Oversight committees will mix advocacy with a desire to exercise control over the agency. Central agency staff, the traditional guardians of the purse, are expected to manage and verify agency claims about performance and the implications for resources. In practice, central agency staff undertake this role of enforcer of measurement quality with varying degrees of intensity, although the role of the OMB during the George W. Bush administration represents a high watermark for such central control at the federal level (see chapters 7 and 8 for more detail).

Agency staff are likely to be advocates, using information to cast the agency in the best possible light and to argue for more resources. Sometimes the use of performance information goes beyond advocacy. Agencies have been found to select goals that will cast the agency in a favorable light, ignoring or dropping unflattering measures or goals over which they have limited control.[56] Agencies may "spin," or creatively interpret, measures.[57] Agencies may engage in the "churning" of measures, that is, changing such a high proportion of measures from year to year that it becomes difficult to identify cross-time comparisons.[58] In some instances, bureaucrats have been found to manipulate, distort, or simply lie about performance measures.[59]

One empirical example of how roles shape perspectives comes from a survey of state budgeteers and agency practitioners. Asked what were significant problems in performance measurement, 40 percent of agency practitioners point to "too many factors affect the results trying to be achieved," while only 14 percent of budget staff considered this to be a significant problem.[60] Clearly agency staff are more concerned with considering how outside factors shape performance results than budgeteers.

Dialogue Routines

The ability to persuade others depends a good deal on communication opportunities, or dialogue routines. DeHaven-Smith and Jenne argue that the treatment of discourse in public management has been limited, largely focusing on the ways in which participation opportunities are used to placate employees and the general public, and overlooking the ways in which discourse can actually affect decisions.[61] But the nature of such routines does matter. For example, Thurmaier and Willoughby found that states with regular and frank briefings between the governor and budget staff saw a stronger sense of budget staff affiliation with the governor and stronger policymaking capacity. Communication that allowed a closer relationship with the governor allowed state budget officers to have a higher percentage of their recommendations accepted, in part because they have a greater capacity to be persuasive and in part because they were more in tune with the preferences of the governor.[62]

Dialogue routines are important, in part, because managers tend not to spend their time reading performance data, but instead prefer verbally expressed information that is detailed and current.[63] Dialogue routines require a commitment of time by staff and a setting where performance data that might otherwise be ignored is considered. The interaction between knowledgeable staff can generate innovations and solutions that would not occur if such staff were acting by themselves. Such routines provide an opportunity to access information, make sense of this information, and persuade others.

Dialogue routines are important, not just because they prioritize performance information and identify solutions, but because they can change the attitude employees hold toward their tasks. DeHaven-Smith and Jenne point to Habermas's theory of communicative action to suggest that structured discourse can shape values and motivations, pointing to the "tendency for people to feel bound by their promises, to give reasons for their beliefs and actions, and to accede to the better arguments and more justifiable claims of others."[64] Dialogue forms a basis of social cooperation, and people feel committed to the agreements researched in such a context.[65] Interactive dialogue therefore acts as a social process that helps to create shared mental models, has a unifying effect, and helps to develop credible commitment for the execution phase.[66]

However, such routines appear to be rare in public discourse. The previous section on the role of roles suggests that the ability to foster problem-solving dialogue is reduced when multiple actors from different institutional settings are engaged because such a diversity of views reduces the ability to foster consensus. All else being equal, dialogue routines that are less institutionally diverse are more likely to feature the use of performance information to solve problems. For this reason, traditional budget routines have a limited ability to create dialogue that will generate solutions. Agency staff or stakeholders presenting information to the central budget office or testifying before the legislature have good reason to act defensively and will rarely address operational questions. In such situations, the trademark of interactive dialogue will be advocacy. Information will be used strategically by advocates who are fully aware that they argue in a decision environment that does not closely resemble a strict performance budgeting process.

Decision makers who receive budget information from agencies lack the time, interest, and capacity to make decisions on resource allocation based on performance information. The budget cycle is too short, and budgeteers have enough to do to make budget decisions incrementally. It is nearly impossible for them to make judgments on what mounds of performance information indicate for a particular functional area. This is true even if only a handful of performance measures is reported. There will never be enough information to substitute for the expertise and knowledge to enable substantive judgments to be made, and there will always be too much information for human cognitive processes to deal with. Of course, advocates are biased in their assessments, but all parties are aware of this, and it does not mean that they are wrong. In fact, the greater the degree to which they can use performance data to support their position, the less biased and more rational they appear.

The Interactive Dialogue Model and Decision Making

What does the interactive dialogue model tell us about decision processes and outcomes? In cross-institutional settings, there will be a variety of actors with different interpretations of performance data, each making different arguments about the actions implied. Incrementalism suggests that cognitive limitations eliminated the role of performance information in debate.[67] However, the interactive dialogue model suggests that no single actor attempts to develop a full account of all performance information; instead one actor uses only the information that is helpful to make arguments convincing. By selecting information consistent with prior preferences, advocates do not face an information overload. The actors using the performance information have different positions, motivations, priorities, and understanding of what the data means and what actions should result from the information. In short, the use of performance information is a subjective exercise and rarely removes much of the ambiguity from decisions. Once we incorporate the assumption of roles and advocacy, we expect actors to selectively present performance data in a context that supports their point of view and to discount conflicting information. The political nature of decision making will interact with, rather than be replaced by, performance information. Advocacy and ideology will continue to shape allocation decisions, using performance information as a tool. Rather than present information comprehensively, giving equal balance to all, actors will highlight specific pieces of data, offer plausible explanations for why performance occurs, and suggest how it can be improved.

Performance information, when used, will not necessarily engender consensus and agreement. This depends greatly on the homogeneity of the actors involved, their interpretation of the data, their ability to persuade others, and their power in the decision process. In some cases, what one group of decision makers concludes is a reasonable interpretation and an appropriate response may be completely at odds with another group looking at similar information. A simple example is how different regions have reacted to performance information about welfare-to-work programs. Fording, Schram, and Soss found that conservative regions in Florida were more likely than liberal regions to impose sanctions on job-seekers and push clients off the rolls if they received negative performance feedback.[68] Performance information mattered, but not in the same way for different groups.

The nature of the performance information is therefore not predictive of decisions. Different actors might take the same set of performance data and offer plausible and logical arguments for either option. In settings that limit a diversity of institutional views, many of the problems that arise from performance information ambiguity and subjectivity are reduced because there is a reduced incentive and potential for advocacy.

A model should be able to offer some falsifiable hypotheses. Based on the assumptions of the interactive dialogue model presented above, and the supporting literature, the following hypotheses about performance information and decision making emerge:

- Different actors can examine the same programs and come up with competing, though reasonable, arguments for the performance of a program based on different data.

- Different actors can examine the same performance information and come up with competing, though reasonable, arguments for what the information means.
- Different actors can agree on the meaning of performance information/program performance and come up with competing solutions for what actions to take in terms of management and resources.
- Actors will select and interpret performance information consistent with institutional values and purposes.
- Forums where performance information is considered across institutional affiliations will see greater contesting of performance data.
- Use of performance information can be increased through dialogue routines.

Conclusion: Assessing the Interactive Dialogue Model

Observations about the use of performance information at the state level prompted the search for an alternative model of performance information use. The next chapters seek to offer additional evidence to support this model. The range of evidence does not constitute a definitive proof of the model but supports the hypotheses above. Coming from multiple sources, the evidence therefore suggests that the model has a basic validity.

The next chapter narrates the development of new performance information by the George W. Bush administration and the resistance to the use of this information by Congress. Content analysis of congressional discussion of programs finds little discussion of performance. Congress has largely ignored new program evaluations and, in some cases, explicitly resisted the inclusion of more performance information in agency budget submissions at the expense of traditional forms of budget information. This is not just a federal issue. State legislators have pointed to distrust in executive branch data as a reason that they do not use the information.[69] Not surprisingly then, states where legislators have ownership of the performance management process and play a role in verifying performance information also see greater legislative use of that information.[70] These behaviors support the idea that the institutional setting makes a difference in the perception and use of performance information and that performance information produced by one institutional setting will may be ignored, resisted, and distrusted in another setting.

Chapter 8 examines the ambiguity and subjectivity of performance information. The Bush administration's PART evaluations provide an intriguing case to examine this issue, since the tool strives to be a transparent and objective way to assess program performance. The PART has prompted an evidence-based dialogue within the OMB itself and, in some instances, between the OMB and agencies. In other cases, agencies disagree with the OMB on the relevance of different types of performance information or evaluations, on the significance of such information for performance ratings, and on the significance of program ratings for performance. This illustrates the potential for ambiguity and subjectivity of a tool such as PART. Even within the OMB itself, the ambiguity of PART explains why OMB raters are not always consistent in evaluating programs. Chapter 8 also presents an experiment that illustrates how multiple actors can assess the same program and performance information and come to different but logical conclusions about how well the program is performing and what its budget should be. The chapter therefore provides both experimental evidence and evidence from assessing the use of PART of the ambiguous and subjective nature of information, the efforts of different actors to construct the meaning of that information, and the role that institutional setting plays in selecting and interpreting information.

Chapter 9 seeks to find positive contributions that the interactive dialogue model might have in fostering the use of performance information. To the extent that PART created an evidence-based dialogue, it did so by establishing new dialogue routines, where members of the OMB and agencies had to interact with one another. The experience of dialogue routines in Virginia and Vermont suggests that they can foster the use of performance information and identifies the characteristics of successful routines. Chapter 9 returns to the question of what makes dialogue routines successful. Dialogue routines are more likely to generate consensus and actionable solutions when they are agency/service centered, frequent, bring together authority (high-level actors) and operating knowledge (low-level actors), place pressure on actors to consider performance of their unit, and avoid defensive reactions.

Notes

1. For example, OMB's Circular A-11 budget guidance describes program assessment as "a determination, through objective measurement and systematic analysis, of the manner and extent to which Federal programs achieve intended objectives" (this information can be found at www.whitehouse.gov/omb/circulars/a11/current_year/s200.pdf). GPRA also calls for "more objective information on achieving statutory objectives, and on the relative effectiveness and efficiency of Federal programs and spending" and requires that agencies express goals "in an objective, quantifiable, and measurable form." (The language of GPRA can be found at http://govinfo.library.unt.edu/npr/library/misc/s20.html [accessed February 2, 2007]).

2. Wildavsky, *Speaking Truth to Power.*

3. In some ways, I use the idea of social interaction in ways that differ from Wildavsky. He portrayed social interaction as a democratic mechanism by which local governments and citi-

zens could provide feedback to the center on the plans they had imposed on them. My concep-tion of interaction is a little different. I am especially interested in interaction among members of the central agencies, agency staff, and political officials of the legislative and executive branch. I place less emphasis on the normative democratic elements of dialogue (though I believe that incorporating the views of implementers is almost always a good thing) than on its inevitability, and its inevitable subjectivity, given the range of people involved and their institutional loyal-ties. Wildavsky sometimes portrays rational analysts as battling political outcomes created by so-cial interaction (e.g., "practitioners of policy analysis seek to have it neither absorbed into social interaction not substituted for it," *Speaking Truth to Power*, 126), whereas the work presented here suggests multiple rationalities can coexist among analysts. Overall, however, I consider these differences to be distinctions of emphases and subjects studied. I see my work as building on Wil-davsky, rather than contradicting him.

4. Interestingly, the focus on roles that is so prevalent in his budgeting work is not repeated in his later discussion of social interaction models, and so I am drawing on different theories of Wildavsky to understand the use of performance information. Wildavsky and Caiden, *The New Politics of the Budgetary Process*, 5th ed.

5. Majone, *Evidence, Argument, and Persuasion in the Policy Process*, 1.

6. There are different perspectives on what constitutes an effective argument. Majone sug-gests that the key skills in crafting an argument are "the ability to probe assumptions critically, to produce and evaluate evidence, to keep many threads in hand, to draw for an argument from many disparate sources, to communicate effectively." See Majone, *Evidence, Argument, and Per-suasion in the Policy Process*, 22. Majone notes that there are many pitfalls or fallacies that can lead the analyst to make mistakes. Some of the most common pitfalls are focusing too much on mathematical models and technical language, using an overly formalized presentation style, and using data that is inadequate for the task. There is a broader literature on argumentation theory, e.g., Toulmin, *The Uses of Argument;* Walton, *Plausible Reasoning in Everyday Conversation*. Douglas Walton has argued that it is possible to assert standards for argumentation even when bias exists, *One-Sided Arguments*.

7. Key, "The Lack of a Budgetary Theory," 1138.

8. Grizzle, "Linking Performance to Decisions."

9. Joyce, *Linking Performance and Budgeting*.

10. Wildavsky, *Budgeting: A Comparative Theory of Budgeting Processes*.

11. Joyce, *Linking Performance and Budgeting*.

12. Lauth, "Budgeting and Productivity in State Government."

13. Melkers and Willoughby, *Staying the Course*, 2–4.

14. Wye, "Performance Management for Career Executives."

15. Aristigueta, *Managing for Results*.

16. Joyce and Tompkins, "Using Performance Information for Budgeting."

17. U.S. Government Accountability Office, *Performance Budgeting: States' Experiences Can Inform Federal Efforts*, 14.

18. Berry, Brower, and Flowers, "Implementing Performance Accountability in Florida"; VanLandingham, Wellman, and Andrews, "Useful, But Not a Panacea."

19. Lauth, "Zero-Based Budgeting in Georgia State Government."

20. Virginia Department of Corrections, *Strategy Performance Budgeting Plan 2000–2002,* F.1.

21. Ibid.

22. Wildavsky, *Speaking Truth to Power,* 14–15.

23. March and Olsen, *Ambiguity and Choice in Organizations.*

24. Feldman, *Order Without Design,* 5.

25. March and Olsen, *Ambiguity and Choice in Organizations.*

26. Feldman, *Order Without Design,* 144.

27. March, "Ambiguity and Accounting," 160.

28. Bridge and McManus, "Sticks and Stones"; Bridgman and Barry, "Regulation Is Evil"; Callahan, Dubnick, and Olshfski, "War Narratives"; Flood, *Political Myth;* Roe, *Narrative Policy Analysis;* Peelo and Soothill, "The Place of Public Narratives in Reproducing Social Order."

29. Fischer and Forrester, eds., *The Argumentative Turn in Policy Analysis and Planning.*

30. Majone, *Evidence, Argument, and Persuasion in the Policy Process,* 7.

31. Grant et al., eds., *The Sage Handbook of Organizational Discourse.*

32. Blalock and Barnow, "Is the New Obsession with Performance Management Masking the Truth about Social Programs?"

33. Toulmin, *The Uses of Argument.*

34. Wildavsky, *Speaking Truth to Power,* 218.

35. Heinrich and Fournier, "Dimensions of Publicness and Performance in Substance Abuse Treatment Programs," 63.

36. Majone, *Evidence, Argument, and Persuasion in the Policy Process,* 179–80. Majone's solution is not to seek any single objective measure but to "begin and sustain a wide-ranging dialogue about the meaning and implication of different sets of weights among producers and users of public services," 180.

37. Jacobs, Goddard, and Smith, "Public Services."

38. March and Olsen, *Ambiguity and Choice in Organizations.*

39. Kingdon, *Agenda, Alternatives, and Public Policies.*

40. Brunnson, *The Organization of Hypocrisy.*

41. Brunnson's work is relevant to understanding performance management in another way. First, as chapter 5 demonstrated, performance management itself is an institutional norm that public organizations must increasingly heed to satisfy their institutional environment. They do so through the creation of formal rituals of information collection and sometimes through what Brunnson calls double talk, i.e., supporting the ideology of performance management in public, even if they do not practice it internally.

42. Majone, *Evidence, Argument, and Persuasion in the Policy Process,* 2.

43. Wildavsky refers to this as retrospection. See *Speaking Truth to Power,* 139.

44. March, "Ambiguity and Accounting," 154.

45. Stone, *Policy Paradox,* 167.

46. Ibid., 177.

47. Majone, *Evidence, Argument, and Persuasion in the Policy Process,* 11.

48. Stone, *Policy Paradox,* 176–77.

49. Ibid., 169–70.

50. Radin, *Challenging the Performance Movement.*

51. Thurmaier and Willoughby, *Policy and Politics in State Budgeting.*

52. Nickerson, "Confirmation Bias."

53. Ibid., 187.

54. Phillips, Lawrence, and Hardy, "Discourse and Institutions."

55. Wildavsky and Caiden, *The New Politics of the Budgetary Process.*

56. Frederickson and Frederickson, *Measuring the Performance of the Hollow State;* Gregory and Lonti, "Never Mind the Quality, Feel the Width."

57. Hood, "Gaming in Targetworld."

58. Talbot, "Executive Agencies."

59. Van Thiel and Leeuw, "The Performance Paradox."

60. Melkers and Willoughby, *Staying the Course.*

61. DeHaven-Smith and Jenne, "Management by Inquiry."

62. Ibid., 165.

63. Mintzberg, *The Nature of Managerial Work.*

64. DeHaven-Smith and Jenne, "Management by Inquiry," 67.

65. Ibid., 69: "Administrative agreements reached in inquirement processes take on the character of vows. In part, this is because they are expressed publicly, but it is also a consequence of the content of the discourse leading up to decisions. As participants reveal their motives, expectations, and reasoning, and as they discursively adjust their intentions and beliefs, they are constructing their own identities as responsible professionals. To subsequently ignore agreements reached in this way is psychologically painful because it violates the individual's personhood."

66. Bossidy and Charan, with Burck, *Execution.*

67. Wildavsky and Caiden, *The New Politics of the Budgetary Process.*

68. Fording, Schram, and Soss, "The Bottom-Line, the Business Model, and the Bogey."

69. Joyce and Tompkins, "Using Performance Information for Budgeting."

70. Bourdeaux, "Do Legislatures Matter in Budgetary Reform?"

7

Performance Management under George W. Bush

This chapter looks to performance management reforms at the federal level to offer examples of the interactive dialogue model in action.[1] Why look to the federal level? The federal level of government offers an example of both the present and the possible future of performance management in the states and is of interest in its own right. The Government Performance and Results Act, passed in 1993, acted as a template for state governments seeking to foster their own version of performance management. GPRA required agencies to undertake strategic planning every three years and to provide annual performance reports and performance plans. States have looked to Bush administration efforts to integrate budgeting and performance information as an example for future reform. The OMB has asked agencies to reorganize their budget submissions around performance information, and the agency has started undertaking performance reviews of specific programs. This chapter presents agencies' perceptions on the future of performance management. While many of these initiatives, at least in their current incarnation, will conclude with the Bush administration, the basic thrust of the reforms is likely to continue in another form.

The President's Management Agenda

The President's Management Agenda (PMA) of 2001 heralded the most recent effort to introduce performance budgeting to the federal government, based on the seemingly indisputable premise that "everyone agrees that scarce federal resources should be allocated to programs that deliver results."[2] The PMA called for the integration of financial and performance information by increasing the quality and range of data available to decision makers, assuming that greater technical and allocative efficiency would result.

In the PMA, the Bush administration characterized GPRA as something of a failure:

> After eight years of experience, progress toward the use of performance information of program management has been discouraging. Agency performance measures tend to be ill defined and not properly integrated into agency budget submissions and the management and operation of agencies. Performance measures are insufficiently used to monitor and reward staff, or to hold program managers accountable. . . . The American people should be able to see how government programs are performing and compare performance and cost across programs. The lack of a consistent information and reporting framework for performance, budgeting, and accounting obscures this necessary transparency.[3]

Despite GPRA, the OMB report says, "agencies rarely offer convincing accounts of the results their allocations will purchase."[4] The cause of this failure, therefore, is laid at the door of agency staff. The remedy, according to the PMA, is for agency staff to integrate performance reviews with budget submissions and allocate costs to outcomes. The goal is to move budgeting to a point where politicians fund more effective programs and reduce or reorganize less effective programs.

It is difficult to argue GPRA has been problem free. Radin has pointed to the problems of GPRA, and the GAO has issued several reports finding that the quality of agency performance plans was sometimes low.[5] However, the OMB criticisms nettled the supporters of GPRA, primarily agency staff and congressional actors. These actors value GPRA because in addition to giving agencies the primary responsibility for developing performance information, it also directs a role for stakeholders and Congress in developing strategic goals. GPRA offers little direct role for the OMB. During the Clinton era, the OMB also had an uneasy relationship with the National Performance Review and was not directly involved in most of its activities.[6] The PMA was primarily authored by the OMB and returned the OMB to being the central actor in public management reform at the federal level.

The OMB pursued the goal of budget and performance integration in two ways. The first was to integrate more performance data into the congressional justifications (referred to as CJs by federal budgeteers). The second was to undertake performance reviews of all federal programs over a five-year period, using what the OMB characterized as a diagnostic tool called the Program Assessment Rating Tool. In some public statements, the OMB suggested that the integration of performance and financial information would move toward a strict model of performance budgeting, with relatively clear criteria for how to treat programs according to performance:

What has been missing is systematic use of these measures to make decisions. In particular, performance measures are not directly linked to the budget—and yet it is the budget that drives policy development, allocates resources, and has undeveloped potential to support better management. . . . In addition to funding high priority programs, the Budget devotes dollars to programs that are rated effective. The Budget proposes reforms for ineffective programs, reduces their funding or terminates them.[7]

This connection between performance and funding appears likely to become even stronger at a time when the government seeks to cut money from the budget and PART becomes the "primary tool" to judge how to focus resources on what works.[8]

Performance Integration in Budget Submissions

Every year the budget that the president proposes to Congress runs thousands of pages long. However, the documents that make up the president's budget are only the tip of the iceberg. Agencies submit even more detailed budget requests to Congress in the form of CJs. The CJs contain the type of detail that the clerks and other staff of appropriations subcommittees find essential in deciding what resources Congress will allocate to each agency. All agencies must follow common guidelines in presenting this information. The OMB sets these guidelines and distributes them in the form of Circular A-11. The OMB has changed Circular A-11 to foster greater integration between performance information and the budget process, requiring agencies to report on goals, objectives, and costs in an integrated fashion in their CJs.

In July 2003, the OMB asked agencies to integrate the annual performance plans required by GPRA into their fiscal year 2005 (FY05) budget submission:

To the extent possible, the full annual budgetary cost of resources to produce these outputs are to be requested in separately identified lines in the budget along with measures of what is produced—ready for monitoring and analysis of the effect of resources on performance. (This link between cost and production is routine in business, but rare in government.) Performance results, cost, and evaluations would provide feedback for a cycle of using linked performance and cost data year-round to improve budgeting and management.[9]

Agencies are following this guidance. OMB staff have examined these new CJs and view them as a major improvement in transparency. They accept that the process will take several iterations to work, but they see improvement in agency documentation in a short period and expect that agencies will continue to improve with experience, by learning from one another and negotiating with appro-

Table 7.1 Aligning strategic goals with resources—NASA's FY06 budget request. ($ million)

Appropriation summary: Science, aeronautics, and exploration			
	FY 2004 Sept. 28, 2004 Operating plan	FY 2005 Dec. 23, 2004 Operating plan	FY 2006 Budget request
Science	5,599.8	5,527.2	5,476.3
Solar system exploration	1,909.5	1,858.1	1,900.5
The universe	1,351.7	1,513.2	1,512.2
Earth–sun system	2,338.6	2,155.8	2,063.6
Exploration systems	2,573.7	2,684.6	3,165.4
Constellation systems	911.5	526.5	1,120.1
Exploration systems research and technology	676.6	695.6	919.2
Prometheus nuclear systems and technology	0.0	431.7	319.6
Human systems research and technology	985.6	1,030.8	806.5
Aeronautics research	1,056.8	906.2	852.3
Aeronautics technology	1,056.8	906.2	852.3
Education	230.4	216.7	166.9
Education programs	230.4	216.7	166.9
Total appropriation	9,460.7	9,334.7	9,661.0

Source: NASA's congressional justification, FY 2006

priations staff on how to satisfy their needs. One of the exemplar agencies in restructuring its resources according to goals has been NASA (see table 7.1).

The OMB has also argued that the alignment of budget accounts must support these efforts. The federal budget is organized into approximately 1,100 accounts that are based on an object, organization, process, or program. These accounts sometimes make it difficult to tie performance goals to accounts or capture "full costs" of programs. Both costs and goals can cut across multiple accounts. The OMB has complained that the accounts often fail to link clearly with goals and that many of the same accounts are focused on the same output or outcome. This makes it difficult for managers to focus on performance, and program activities often capture only inputs or a portion of the funding for an output.

The account structures are based on congressional interests and oversight, reflecting choices about how Congress wishes to exert control over agencies and frame resource allocation decisions. Congress has determined how it wants to receive information and has become used to and reliant on the nature of this data. The nature of the information shapes the nature of congressional relationships with agencies. Changes to the account structures, and to the type of information presented to Congress, are therefore somewhat risky, since they may meet with congressional resistance. In fact, the account structures are based in statute and cannot be changed without congressional permission.

Consistent with the claims of the interactive dialogue model, the changes to the CJs have prompted debate and disagreement about what information is appropriate for Congress, how this information is organized, and even the basis for calculating the information. Different perspectives in how to calculate performance information can be seen in the inconsistency between agencies in terms of how to allocate indirect or administrative costs. Some agencies dispersed all such costs across goals, some did for administrative but not inspector general costs, and others kept both as separate administrative costs. However, they all claimed to be doing "full cost" or "total budgetary resources."[10] There remains, therefore, some disagreement about what these terms mean among agencies. Agencies also varied the level of performance they allocated full costs to—strategic goal, strategic objective, performance goal, collections of programs, or programs. Most agencies used a mixture of two or more levels.[11] The ambiguity of budgeting categories extends to more basic classifications. Studies of state budgets have found that categories such as line-item or performance budgets are poorly defined, ambiguous, and overlapping.[12]

Appropriations committee staff in Congress offered little support for the changes. Most appropriations staff were broadly supportive of the idea of budget and performance integration, but they resisted the loss of traditional information they relied on for budgeting and oversight purposes (such as object class and workload information) and called for any new information to be supplementary. This behavior is consistent with the motivations of elected officials examined in chapter 4. Legislators will accept performance information as long as it provides an additional mode of control, but they are reluctant to adopt an executive-branch-designed mode of control that replaces tried and trusted methods of legislative oversight.

Appropriations staff made the following objections to the changes:

- The OMB failed to consult with congressional staff before delivering the new budget format.
- The information and new format did not meet appropriator's need.
- Some valued information was no longer visible or transparent.
- The addition of performance information made CJs overly cumbersome and difficult to use.

Some appropriations committee reports commended agencies for collecting performance goals for management purposes, but they stressed the importance of the traditional information for budget purposes. In some cases, appropriations subcommittees felt strongly enough to direct agencies in appropriations reports to stop or change the move toward budget and performance integration (see box 7.1 for examples).[13]

Box 7.1 Congressional reactions to OMB's budget and performance integration efforts

- The House Appropriations Committee directed the Veterans Administration (VA) "to refrain from incorporating 'performance-based' budget documents in the 2005 budget justification submitted to the Committee, but keep the Performance Plan as a separate volume." The following year, the VA still submitted a performance budget, leading to a sharper rebuke: "If the Department wishes to continue the wasteful practice of submitting a budget structure that will not serve the needs of the Congress, the Congress has little choice but to reject that structure and continue providing appropriations that serve its purposes."

- The Department of Housing and Urban Development (HUD) was told "not to submit or otherwise incorporate the strategic planning document or its structure into its fiscal year 2005 Budget Justification Submission to the Committee."

- Lack of consultation led to categorization at odds with congressional preferences. The House Appropriations Committee stated that the Federal Aviation Administration's (FAA) restructured budget "depends on overlapping budget categories and subjective judgments among agency officials concerning a program's predominant purpose."

- In addition, some types of information previously transparent were now no longer available, for example, individual expense items. For instance, a House Appropriations Committee report said that, "while the amount of performance data included in budget documents has increased, in many cases it has been at the expense of programmatic budget data and justifications that are critical to the work of the Committee." Elsewhere the same committee stated: "In the place of critical budget-justifying material, the Committee is provided reams of narrative text expounding on the performance goals and achievements of the various agencies."

- The House Appropriations Committee asked the FAA to abandon its performance budget format of FY03 and FY04 and to return to the FY02 format, saying, "After testing this structure for the past two years, the Committee finds that it is inferior to the previous structure."

- The House Appropriations Committee also asked the Department of Transportation (DOT) to return to the budget format of FY03, saying, "While the Committee remains interested in receiving performance information, in future budget submissions by the Departments of Transportation and Treasury, and independent agencies covered by this Act, these agencies are directed to refrain from including substantial amounts of performance data within the budget justifications themselves, and to instead revert to the traditional funding information previously provided. Performance-related information may be submitted under separate cover." Negative consequences were promised for agencies that ignored this directive: "If the Office of Management and Budget or individual agencies do not heed the Committee's direction, the Committee will assume that individual budget offices have excess resources that can be applied to other, more critical missions."

Sources: U.S. Government Accountability Office. *Performance Budgeting: Efforts to Restructure Budgets to Better Align Resources with Performance.* Washington, DC: GAO, 2005.

More frequently, congressional staff have expressed their displeasure directly to agency budgeteers or OMB staff informally. One OMB budget examiner made the following comment:

> The response on the Hill has been very much a mixed bag. The good govern-
> ment types and the government oversight committees are supportive, but they
> have very little clout. The appropriations subcommittees have been much less
> enthusiastic. My committee was outright hostile. They think that the perfor-
> mance information in the budget produced a lot of paper but nothing they
> found useful. We prepared two budget notebooks, a traditional one and a per-
> formance one. The committee clerk mistakenly took the performance one away
> on the weekend he was supposed to be looking at the traditional one. When he
> came back on Monday he called the agency and threw a tirade, telling them that
> this was useless and to never send it to him again.

Agencies found themselves caught in crossfire between the OMB and appropriations staff who disagree on the basis for resource decisions. The OMB wants a
budget that will prompt managers and appropriators to think in terms of performance. Appropriations staff want a budget that contains familiar information, will
help them get a sense of how money was spent in the past, and the workload demands for the future. An observer of the process from the GAO noted: "Agencies
do not want to antagonize committees. Some agencies complain they have to prepare two budgets: a performance budget for the OMB and a regular budget for appropriators." The OMB has advised agencies to consult with appropriations
committees, believing this is a key factor for acceptance of the information. Comments from the Clay Johnson, OMB's deputy director for management, reflect this:

> Well, agencies work with their individual appropriators. Maybe that is the most
> important issue, important factor. Like NASA [National Aeronautics and Space
> Administration] has been very successful. . . . And it is largely a function of the fact
> that Sean O'Keefe [former head of NASA] and his staff work very, very aggressively
> and closely with the appropriation subcommittees to get them to make that tran-
> sition, to understand what was not to be feared and how it was better to focus on
> these things rather than those things. It is our responsibility to help appropriations
> subcommittees make that change. They are used to seeing things lined up a cer-
> tain way, and when all of a sudden they get it a different way, I would be resistant,
> too. Well, they need help, and it is our responsibility, the agency's responsibility,
> to help them make that transition. But I am without any doubt that two years,
> three years from now all these appropriations subcommittees will be using per-
> formance budgets and be glad they are doing so, in my opinion.[14]

Appropriators want to be consulted on any revisions to budget format. However, appropriations committees and the OMB have very different views on what these consultations are intended to achieve. For appropriators, they want to make clear to agencies that old information is critical. For the OMB, agencies need to help appropriators understand and buy into the new approach to performance. In some cases, such as with NASA, these tensions have been resolved amicably. However, NASA was the only agency where the appropriations committee agreed to adjust the appropriations account structure suggested by the agency. The difference in preferences between appropriators and the OMB is real and will not go away easily.

This is not just a problem at the congressional level. State officials point to an inadequate link between the performance measurement database and the accounting/budgeting database as one of the most significant problems in limiting progress on performance budgeting.[15] Problems revealed in restructuring the CJs have made it clear that this is not only, or even primarily, a technical issue. The failure to make the link between categories of performance information and categories used for budgeting/accounting purposes is based on profound disagreements about what information should be presented to the legislature, as well as how it should be structured and calculated.

The Development of the Program Assessment Rating Tool

The development of PART was driven by Mitch Daniels, the first director of the OMB under Bush. Many OMB staff recall Daniels's personal belief in the importance of PART. One notes: "The director's view was that we had to be able to tell the public what worked and what didn't." Daniels also urged OMB staff to use PART as a nonpartisan tool to assess all programs with equal rigor. Another OMB staffer said: "Mitch Daniels said that to make PART credible is to show that we are challenging our own [Republican] ideology. And he encouraged OMB staff to do that."

The OMB did not have enough time to develop the PART tool for the FY02 budget proposal, and the pilot version of PART came with the president's FY03 proposal. OMB staff acknowledge that this first effort was less polished than they wished: "This was a subjective judgment about what worked and didn't from a performance standpoint a judgment about the budget. It was immediately challenged because it had not been done in a systematic way."

The OMB formed the Performance Evaluation Team early in 2002 to help create a more systematic tool. The team identified basic questions to ask of all programs and tried to identify what constituted acceptable evidence for answering these questions.[16] The team also set out the goal of evaluating all federal programs over a five-year period. A contentious issue that arose was the dividing line between program evaluation and policy decisions. There was a debate about whether PART should include a question asking, "Is the federal role critical?" The group decided against it and asked instead whether a program filled a specific need. Daniels would comment that the original question was "too subjective and could vary depending on philosophical of political viewpoints."[17]

The OMB has continued to apply PART and has sought to make minor improvements to the tool based on feedback. PART is essentially a set of thirty standard questions that OMB budget examiners, in consultation with agency representatives, use to assess federal programs. It is not an original evaluation of programs, but an analysis of relevant evaluations that have been previously completed. Programs can be rated as ineffective, adequate, moderately effective, or effective. If in OMB's judgment, programs fail to provide adequate information, they may fall into a separate category, of results not demonstrated. Over five years, the OMB has "PARTed" 1,016 programs, representing approximately 98 percent of the federal budget and resulting in the following program ratings:

- 18 percent are Effective.
- 31 percent are Moderately Effective.
- 29 percent are Adequate.
- 3 percent are Ineffective.
- 19 percent are Results Not Demonstrated.

The ratings are based on four weighted groupings of questions: program purpose and design (standard weight is 20 percent), strategic planning (10 percent), program management (20 percent), and program results (50 percent).[18] The OMB also developed variations of the tool to fit what it has identified as different types of federal programs: direct federal, block/formula grant, competitive grant, capital assets and service acquisition, research and development, regulatory programs, and credit programs. Appendix C provides a list of the standard PART questions and the particular PART questions for different program types. Single-page summary assessments of each program have accompanied President Bush's budget proposals to Congress. These summaries provided a numerical program score in the categories of purpose, planning, management, and results/accountability; the overall rating for the program; some key program performance indicators; qualitative observations of management problems and areas for improvement; and a budget recommendation for the program. President Bush's FY08 budget proposal no longer provided specific summaries of newly assessed programs. Instead, it directed legislators to www.expectmore.gov for both summary PART analyses and more detailed question-by-question breakdown of each analysis.

PART was developed with a degree of transparency and outside involvement that is unusual for the OMB. An external Performance Management Advisory Council brought together experts on performance management to comment on the development of the tool. The National Academy of Public Administration convened a workshop that gave feedback. The tool itself was publicly available, and the OMB has solicited comments from agencies, the GAO, and others.

As discussed in the next chapter, the application of the tool has also been transparent. Detailed assessments are available at www.expectmore.gov for every program rated, describing the reasoning and information used by budget examiners to respond to each of the PART questions. The basic framework of the relationship between budget examiners and agencies is now open to the public in a way that it has never been before. Those that disagree with the evaluations can critique the rationale for each assessment.

The OMB argues that PART is evidence based, systematic, and transparent. Mitch Daniels acknowledged that it was impossible to eliminate all subjectivity, but that PART at least added transparency to the existing process "and opens up any subjectivity in that process for discussion and debate."[19] The OMB has worked hard to ensure consistency, designing standardized questions, training raters, providing a ninety-two-page guide, and even forming a team to conduct a consistency check on 10 percent of the assessments.[20]

Does PART Affect Budget Decisions?

While most PART assessments do not focus on resource allocation, *every* PART summary is accompanied with a numerical funding recommendation to Congress. While in some public statements the OMB has leaned toward a strict model of performance budgeting, Daniels suggested that this was not the intention of PART:

> OMB does not view the PART as an automated approach to making budget decisions. A low PART score does not, in itself, signify whether a program needs more or less funding. The PART provides a tool for diagnosing how programs can be improved and it is from such diagnosis, as well as other information regarding the program, that budget and management decisions will be made. FY 2004 decisions will be fundamentally grounded in program performance, but will also continue to be based on a variety of other factors, including policy objectives and priorities of the Administration, and economic and programmatic trends.[21]

In private, OMB staff echo the belief that the connection between performance information and results is relatively loose and informed by other factors. In fact, most OMB staff see PART as being more about management than budgeting. One said: "PART's emphasis is to follow up actions on performance because there is so little room to change funding decisions. On funding we are working on the margins, but it is more useful to focus on management. We make budget decisions on every program, but for most programs it's a default decision."

A number of factors limit the impact of PART on funding decisions:

- Mandatory spending allows no discretion on setting the level of funding.
- Most budget items have strong political support, fostering incrementalism.
- Political promises and goals have higher priority over program assessments.
- Even if PART influences the president's proposal, legislators can still ignore PART.

The bulk of the federal budget is on automatic pilot because of entitlement programs, or strong stakeholder and legislative support, limiting cuts that can be made and continuing a trend toward incrementalism. An OMB official noted: "The reality is that there is a lot of pork every year, but it is tiny relative to the size of the budget. The big-ticket items have relatively strong popular support, and therefore it is hard to stop doing them. For example, the Rural Electrification Program was set up under Roosevelt to bring electrification to rural areas. It still exists even though it has accomplished its task.

In terms of politics, OMB staff accept that PART scores are unlikely to change White House commitments or legislative preferences. In some cases, they hope that PART assessments might affect the discussion of the performance of programs and lead to movement of resources to similar programs regarded as being more effective. In other cases, changes in context affect how PART assessments are treated. Before the 2004 presidential election, a number of education programs were rated as "results not demonstrated" or "ineffective," but the administration did not propose major cuts, and PART assessments talked about ways of improving management. In the aftermath of the election, the president placed a new priority on limiting spending, producing a budget proposal that allowed discretionary spending to grow 2.1 percent a year. Eighteen education programs were now proposed for elimination. The PART assessments for these programs had not changed. What changed was the political context.

Most OMB staff accept that PART does not offer a clear and predictable prescription for resource allocation. Effectively managed programs might face cuts or termination because they have completed their task and should be phased out, because elected officials believe they are not an appropriate task for the federal government, or because they are duplicative of another, more effective program. A budget examiner said: "If you are effective, or moderately effective, you are probably protected. If your program is rated at a lower level, you may have goals or problems that still need a federal solution. It might be struggling because of a lack of money or poor design. These are problems that can be fixed."

The weak relationship between PART assessments and funding proposals in the president's budget is reflected not only in comments among OMB staffers but also in quantitative analysis. This runs contrary to the strict model of performance budgeting that some have proposed. For instance, a for-profit training company and advocate of performance management, called the Performance Institute, issued a press release declaring that "Bush's '04 Budget Puts Premium on Transparency and Performance," pointing to a 6 percent increase for effective programs, while those rated ineffective gained less than 1 percent. However, this impression is somewhat misleading when one considers that the OMB's own analysis for FY04 found that programs graded as effective did gain 6.4 percent, but that moderately effective programs gained 6.6 percent, and those rated adequate did even better, enjoying an 8.1 percent increase on average. Ineffective programs gained just 0.07 percent, but programs that were categorized as "results not demonstrated" gained 4.4 percent.

Another way of looking at how PART influences the president's proposal is to look at the PART characteristics of programs listed in the *Major Savings and Reforms in the President's 2006 Budget,* which identifies major proposed cuts for the FY06 budget.[22] Overall, most justifications of funding reductions fail to mention PART because PART was not assessed for the programs cut. Of the ninety-nine programs listed under program terminations, just thirty-two had undergone PART assessments, and only twenty-three of the fifty-five programs slated for major reductions were PARTed. Clearly, PART assessments were not a precondition for funding cuts.

If a program slated for termination or reduction has been PARTed, the assessment was likely to have been "results not demonstrated" or "ineffective." Of the thirty-two programs proposed for termination that had undergone PART assessments, sixteen of the assessments were deemed "results not demonstrated," ten were considered "ineffective," and six were "adequate." Of the twenty-three programs proposed for major cuts that had been PARTed, nine had "results not demonstrated," four were "moderately effective," eight were "adequate," and two were deemed "ineffective."

Other quantitative evidence provides stronger support for the idea that PART assessments have a significant but not powerful relationship in explaining proposed budget increases. The GAO finds a significant relationship between PART scores and proposed budgetary increases for FY04, although PART scores explained only a small portion of the variation.[23] Gilmour and Lewis also demonstrate a positive relationship between PART scores and proposed budget increases for both FY04 and FY05, even when controlling for other possible explanatory factors such as program type, program age, and political factors.[24] They find that PART assessments matter to the president's proposed budget, but they also find that it explains only a small portion of the variance of budget changes. PART assessments had a stronger impact on smaller programs in FY04 because, Gilmour and Lewis suggest, such programs have less entrenched support. Perhaps the results also reflect reluctance on the part of the OMB to make major changes in actual dollar totals—cutting 20 percent of a program may be less daunting if the total program is $1 million as opposed to $100 million. However, this result is not replicated with the FY05 data. Of the various PART categories, some matter more than others in influencing budgeting changes. Most important is program purpose and design, positively and significantly related to budget changes in both years. We would expect that program results category, worth 50 percent of the PART grade and the rationale for performance reforms, should be positively and significantly related to budget changes. They were in FY04, but were less important than program purpose and design. Program results were not a significant predictor of budget changes in FY05.

On balance, the quantitative evidence suggests that programs deemed as ineffective or not demonstrating results are more vulnerable to program cuts or termination, but again, this relationship is not terribly strong. The data is consistent with the views of OMB staff whom I interviewed, who suggested that when looking for cuts, it was natural to turn to PART to indicate candidates for reduction but that programs with weak performance may have strong supporters capable of preventing major cuts. There are plenty of examples of programs with poor PART ratings receiving increases, while programs deemed effective have been cut. The strict model of performance budgeting—that performance will be rewarded and failure punished—does not explain the results cited above. If PART does influence even the president's proposal, its impact is not very great and is largely driven by the program purpose and design section of PART, not program results.

Dialogue in Congress about Performance

Once PART recommendations move to Congress, there is an even looser connection with actual budget decisions. An OMB budget examiner said, "There is still a disconnect between the bureaucratic desire to analyze programs and congressional imperatives on how to fund. Recommendations, if they are not met with political favor, will probably not be implemented."

Changes to the budget format and the creation of PART represent a bet by the OMB. The OMB is wagering that changing the format of budget information will change decision making. Intuitively, this makes sense. Decision makers with different types of information should behave differently, or at least discuss their decisions in different ways. Grizzle's content analysis of two state budgets argued that budget format had an impact on the nature of the discussion that legislators had about agencies.[25] With line-item budgets, legislators appeared to talk about control. More expansive program budgets saw greater discussion of management issues. In short, the type of information presented made appropriators more likely to talk about one aspect of budgeting rather than another, although it is also possible that the causal effect worked in the other direction, that is, legislators selected a budget format consistent with their view of the agency or the budgeting process, for example, choosing a line-item budget format when they cared most about control. The federal experience described in this chapter suggests that new formats are less likely to have an impact if they are imposed on decision makers who are used to and prefer older categories of information.

This section examines the degree to which Congress considers performance information at a time when the Bush administration seeks to make performance data more important. Joyce has argued that we should not look to the legislature as the only venue in which performance might be discussed.[26] But if PART and agencies' performance budgets are to have an impact, it is reasonable to hope that *some* discussion of performance leaks into the legislative branch. To test whether and how performance information was examined, one can look to two key records of legislative discourse: (1) appropriations bills with corresponding conference reports, and (2) committee hearings held by the oversight committee and the relevant appropriations subcommittee.[27] Appropriations bills and conference reports are written by the actors in the legislature that agencies have most reason to listen to—those that provide them with resources. Hearings provide a more diverse setting by including testimony from executive branch officials and stakeholders while allowing legislators to solicit views and ask tough questions about performance.

I undertook a content analysis of these texts for the FY04 budget in the areas of defense, education, social security, homeland security, health and human services, and transportation. The analysis was relatively simple—I looked for any mention of the term *performance*.[28] The term *performance* was mentioned 391 times in the documents examined. This sounds impressive until we consider that the texts examined total 3,257 single-spaced pages, meaning that *performance* was mentioned slightly more than once in every 8 pages of appropriations or hearings.

When references that indicate the use of the term to indicate action (the performance of duty) or those that bore no reference to a public program are removed, the number of mentions drops to 353. Two other ways of discussing performance are to use the term to characterize some standard associated with materials (e.g., instrument landing systems are up to FAA performance specifications) or to characterize a program as using some sort of performance tool (e.g., use of pay-for-performance, performance-based contracting). Neither use tells us much about actual program performance, and they largely indicate the attraction of attaching the term to cast an object in a positive light. Once we discount those mentions, 234 mentions of performance remain, or 1 for almost every 14 pages of legislative talk.

What's left? The remaining mentions of performance can be divided into four categories that have consequence for our understanding of how the concept of performance is discussed. The first category is a statement about future performance, indicating the expectation about a program's potential achievement, or speculating on the effect of management innovation or additional funding on achievement. This category of performance was mentioned 57 times. The second category is the discussion of the use of performance information. The use of performance information was mentioned 21 times. The majority of references about use came in appropriations bills, urging agencies to use performance information, particularly in making decisions about contracts or grants. For example, a House appropriations bill urged that a program "use a portion of the increased funding provided to increase support for existing health centers based on performance-related criteria in addition to site and service expansion applications."[29] The documents examined show no discussions of legislators using the information themselves.

Perhaps the most interesting finding from the content analysis is that the lack of use by legislators (or at least lack of discussion of use) of performance information stands in stark contrast to a consistent demand for more data. Mentions related to the creation, development, funding, or presentation of data on program implementation occurred 109 times. These mentions came primarily in the form of legislative requirements in an appropriations bill (73 times). Forty-nine of these references came from the area of education, where policymakers called for program after program to develop performance measures. An example is the following:

> The Committee fully expects that the Uniform Management Information and Reporting System, required by the No Child Left Behind Act, will be developed and implemented so that data and other pertinent information is collected in a uniform manner both within a particular State and across all States, and that it be reported by every State to the Secretary of Education. The Committee looks forward to reviewing such information in future program performance reports and congressional justifications.[30]

The robust demand for the creation of performance information shows that Congress is perfectly capable and willing to require what it considers to be relevant performance information from agencies, which helps explain some of the resistance that congressional actors have shown toward OMB efforts to revise the CJs. It is not so much that Congress is opposed to performance information, but it wants to decide when and how such data will be created.

The final category is discussion of performance as actual achievement, where an actor portrayed a program as effective or ineffective. This category of performance was mentioned 47 times. It was mentioned mostly by either executive branch officials (24 times) or program stakeholders (16 times), both of whom where generally supportive of the program. An example comes from James Roche, secretary of the Air Force, at a hearing of the Defense Subcommittee of the House Appropriations Committee, on March 19, 2003:

> I'm proud to report our proposed budget increases investment in new technologies by five percent over the last year. Next year we'll fund 22 FA-22s if the budget is approved, continuing our move to a sustained production rate. We are attempting to get stability in this program so as to replicate what occurred with the C-17 where we can bring cost down and increase reliability. Mr. Chairman, you remember very well the C-17 and some of the terrible days it went through, and it barely survived. And yet today we will receive a C-17 and within 48 hours it's in the area of operations doing its mission, without any additional work. The FA-22 program is improving. It's currently meeting or exceeding all key performance requirements.

There are only 7 instances when discussions of actual achievement of programs suggest that performance was less than satisfactory. Such discussions tended to be abstract, without reference to any benchmark or performance target. Instead, the general need for improvement is mentioned and honored by those involved. Actual quantitative performance indicators were mentioned to reflect program achievement only 9 times, or once for every 362 pages of text.

The discussion of number of references to performance gives us some sense of the type or frequency of mention of performance, but it gives us little sense of whether there were coherent discussions of performance, characterized by an iterative dialogue that examined evidence, or at least advanced some logical claims. Such discussions were largely absent in the texts examined. Performance was mentioned quickly, not at great length, and not intended to prompt a discussion. The one exception was the area of education, where stakeholders in hearings offered serious discussions of the effects of performance standards and made clear and testable arguments about what factors led to educational performance. Overall, although mention of performance occurs, the quality of the discussion in these formal settings is low.

What generalizations can be made from the findings?

- Mention of performance is relatively rare; discussions of actual program performance are even rarer.
- The quality of discussion about performance is poor, usually mentioned in passing, and discussed in an abstract fashion.
- The use of the term *performance* is consistent with institutional interests. Legislators are likely to ask for more information about program performance to help satisfy their oversight function. Executive branch officers and program supporters are more likely to talk about program achievement, defending their record and pointing to the benefits of their programs.

Is PART Partisan?

A barrier for PART is its perceived partisan origins. PART shares many of the same performance management assumptions as GPRA, which enjoyed bipartisan support. But unlike GPRA, PART was established through an administrative procedure and has become associated with President Bush and the Republican Party. This affects both how PART is perceived and its potential for continuity.

The OMB argues that PART assessments are not influenced by partisan preferences, but the agency acknowledges that resource allocation decisions are. Many Democrats in Congress do not accept this distinction and regard PART with suspicion. They view it as a White House tool to cloak ideologically based attacks on traditionally liberal programs under the neutrality of management. The legitimizing use of the language and norms of good management makes the attack of such policies less contentious, avoiding the conflict-laden policymaking process by targeting the policy-delivery process.[31] For example, social services may have a more difficult time than other programs in generating the kind of results that will satisfy OMB examiners. Critics also point out that PART does not assess tax expenditures, which are less likely to be traditional Democratic programs.

The White House has not been able to convince many in Congress that PART is not partisan. In part, this is because it explicitly feeds into the highly political budget process. In addition, the deep rancor between the parties, especially in the House, reinforces partisan tendencies, as does Democrats' particular distrust of anything associated with President Bush. There has also been an uneasy relationship between legislators of both parties, especially in the Senate, and the political appointees of the Bush OMB. Mitch Daniels was seen by some as disrespectful of the traditional prerogatives of Congress. One point of contention was a statement in the PMA that "all too often Congress is a part of the government's problems. Many members find it more rewarding to announce a new program rather than to fix (or terminate) an old one."[32] The president's 2003 budget proposal illustrated this point by including a cartoon of Gulliver tied down by Lilliputians, with the caption, "Many departments are tied up in a morass of Lilliputian do's and don'ts."

Perhaps the best barometer of congressional attitudes is seen in efforts to institutionalize PART into statute. H.R. 185, the Program Assessment and Results Act (known as the PAR Act, or PARA) was introduced in 2004 and 2005 by Representative Todd Russell Platts, a Republican from Pennsylvania. Platts was the chair of the House Subcommittee on Government Efficiency and Financial Management, which is a subcommittee to the House Committee on Government Reform. The PAR bill claimed to build on GPRA and sought to "provide congressional policy makers the information needed to conduct more effective oversight, to make better-informed authorization decisions, and to make more evidence-based spending decisions that achieve positive results for the American people."[33] The bill did not call explicitly for PART but for something that sounds very similar: an evaluation program that assesses all federal programs within five years, to be conducted by the OMB using criteria of its choosing.

The bill was, in effect, a proxy vote for or against PART. The outcome was not encouraging for PART advocates. The act failed to receive a floor vote. At a subcommittee meeting, Democratic proposals to amend the PAR Act were defeated, and the bill was reported by a party-line vote. In political terms, PAR was a partisan piece of legislation, mirroring the partisan disagreements on PART. Edolphus Towns, a Democratic member of the subcommittee, said: "The subjective nature of PART seems to negatively impact the amount of reliable data it provides due to chronic disagreement between OMB agency officials on long-term performance measures of unreasonable thresholds in satisfying PART standards."[34]

Conclusion

OMB officials did not perceive PART to be a partisan tool. But the broader political perception that PART was a mechanism of one party became a self-fulfilling prophecy—the only legislators paying attention were Republicans, over the objections of Democrats. The political ascendancy of Democrats in 2006 weakened the potential for PART to survive, and new presidents tend to establish their own approach to management. PART therefore offers a high-profile example of the way in which seemingly neutral performance management reforms become, for better or worse, the property of one party over the other, thereby weakening both its present-day use and long-term survival. It also illustrates that the legislature may be unwilling to go along with management reforms that weaken its institutional powers, even when the same party has control over both the executive and legislative branches.

The results of the content analysis reported in this chapter further suggest that few legislators are paying much attention to performance information generally. It is important to note that the content analyses came from a single year, and it is reasonable to argue that such discussions will take place in a variety of venues. The Bush administration has aimed at changing the nature of legislative discussion of performance by changing budget formats and creating program evaluations, and the administration hopes that performance information will come to shape budget decisions to a greater degree. This limited test of legislative talk about performance suggests there is much scope for improvement. There is, therefore, a challenge for Congress and state legislatures to improve their facility with the language of performance.[35] On the other hand, one might argue that there is little incentive for legislatures to change their use of performance information or any reason to expect that they will. The challenge, therefore, is to change our expectations of what legislatures do with performance information.

Notes

1. Portions of this chapter and chapter 8 appeared previously in Moynihan, "What Do We Talk about When We Talk about Performance?"

2. U.S. Office of Management and Budget, *The President's Management Agenda,* 27.

3. Ibid., 27–28.

4. Ibid., 27.

5. Radin, "The Government Performance and Results Act (GPRA): Hydra-Headed Monster or Flexible Management Tool?"; Radin, "The Government Performance and Results Act and the Tradition of Federal Management Reform."

6. Moynihan, "Public Management Policy Change."

7. U.S. Office of Management and Budget, *Analytical Perspectives,* 3.

8. Comments of Robert Shea, the most senior OMB political with responsibility for PART; Gruber, "The Big Squeeze."

9. U.S. Office of Management and Budget, *Analytical Perspectives,* 3.

10. Disagreements about how to allocate costs can also cut across political institutions. In FY03 the OMB decided it would allocate retirement costs to agency programs. Congress disagreed with this approach and excluded this cost allocation from its appropriations report, forcing the OMB to stop the practice.

11. U.S. Government Accountability Office, *Performance Budgeting: Efforts to Restructure Budgets to Better Align Resources with Performance.*

12. Howard, "State Budgeting," 199.

13. U.S. Government Accountability Office, *Performance Budgeting: Efforts to Restructure Budgets to Better Align Resources with Performance.*

14. Johnson, *Testimony before the Subcommittee on Government Efficiency and Financial Management,* 38.

15. Melkers and Willoughby, "Staying the Course."

16. The team also performed the role of determining what the official OMB position would be on a number of questions the exercise would raise, e.g., How do PART scores relate to budgeting? What is the relationship between PART and GPRA? The recommendations of the team can be found at www.whitehouse.gov/omb/mgmt-gpra/pmac_part_revisions.pdf.

17. Daniels, *Program Performance Assessments,* 1.

18. OMB examiners may adopt an alternative weighting of questions they consider appropriate; see U.S. Office of Management and Budget, "Budget Procedures Memorandum No. 861" (available at www.whitehouse.gov/omb/budget/fy2005/pdf/bpm861.pdf), 2003, 15.

19. Daniels, *Program Performance Assessments,* 3.

20. The *Guide to Assessing the Program Assessment Rating Tool* is available at www.whitehouse.gov/omb/part/fy2006/2006_guidance_final.pdf.

21. Daniels, *Program Performance Assessments,* 4–5.

22. U.S. Office of Management and Budget, *Major Savings and Reforms in the President's 2006 Budget.*

23. U.S. General Accounting Office, *Observations on the Use of OMB's Program Assessment Rating Tool for the Fiscal Year 2004 Budget.*

24. Gilmour and Lewis, "Assessing Performance Budgeting at the OMB."

25. Grizzle, "Does Budget Format Really Govern the Actions of Budgetmakers?"

26. Joyce, *Linking Performance and Budgeting.*

27. The approach undertaken is informed by Schick's critique of a previous content analysis of committee reports, undertaken by the Congressional Research Service, which suggested the growing use of performance terminology. Schick dismissed the analysis as proving only that "buzzwords buzz around"—that elected officials knew enough to speak in the language of performance management—"but such verbiage should never be mistaken for usage." My content analysis focused not just on committee reports but also on appropriations legislation (the "best place to look" for true evidence of the impact of performance management, according to Schick). My analysis of the mentions of performance also seeks to characterize the context and nature of use, rather than simply report the number of mentions. In doing so, the results appear to support Schick's contention that performance concepts may be mentioned, but performance data is rarely used. Schick, "Getting Performance Measures to Measure Up."

28. *Performance* is one of a number of synonyms that could have been used. The content analysis is not intended to be comprehensive, covering all possible discussion of results, but to provide a basic indicator of whether results were discussed at all. Since the term *performance* is familiar to legislators and is commonly used (e.g., the Government Performance and Results Acts requires agencies to produce performance reports), it is expected to provide a good indicator of the level of discussion about results.

29. U.S Congress. *Departments of Labor, Health and Human Services, and Education, and Related Agencies Appropriation Bill,* 2004, 23.

30. Ibid., 145.

31. Evelyn Brodkin has observed such a pattern in Richard Nixon's treatment of welfare programs. The Nixon administration was unable to find legislative support for policies to cut welfare

spending, but it achieved these goals through administrative means under the justification of reducing waste, fraud, and abuse. See Brodkin, "Policy Politics."

32. U.S. Office of Management and Budget, *The President's Management Agenda*, 6.

33. U.S. Congress, *The Program Assessment and Results Act*, Section 4.

34. U.S. Congress. House Subcommittee on Government Efficiency and Financial Management, *Should We PART Ways with GPRA*, 5.

35. To this end, the GAO has prepared guides for Congress on how to make intelligent queries about performance information arising from GPRA. See, for example, U.S. Government Accountability Office, www.gao.gov/new.items/gpra/gpra.htm (accessed November 5, 2007).

8

PART and the Interactive Dialogue Model

This chapter attempts to use the early experience with PART to further illustrate the interactive dialogue model. I examine the potential of PART to create an evidence-based dialogue. Many stakeholders consider PART to be subjective, which makes them less likely to accept its claims. Even without these disagreements there is much ambiguity associated with the link between PART assessments and budgeting, as demonstrated by an experiment where subjects examined the logic behind OMB recommendations.

Evidence-Based Dialogue

OMB staff argue that PART is designed to elicit an evidence-based dialogue with agency staff and to generate a variety of recommendations related to management, funding, program design, and program assessment methods. The basic rationale underlying the concept of evidence-based dialogue is that by (a) having a third party develop a simple assessment score for each program and (b) attaching it to a critical process of the budget, all stakeholders are prompted to respond. If they agree with the evidence presented by the OMB, they will take it into account in their decisions. If they disagree, they have to explain why, relying on evidence rather than rhetoric.

The OMB sees PART as prompting evidence-based dialogue in a number of ways:

1. *Third-party program review with a clear opinion:* PART seeks to deal with the perceived unreliability of agency self-reporting and the problem of information overload. For decision makers who cannot make sense of or even who distrust mounds of performance information, the OMB offers to wade through program data and give, along with a moderately detailed assessment, a simple answer to the question of whether the program is working or not.

2. *Greater emphasis on performance:* The basic focus of PART is performance, and the existence of the tool has increased discussion of program performance, at least in the budget preparation process within the executive branch. Agency staff have paid more attention to performance measures in day-to-day management as a result of PART, which they view as more relevant than the actual PART ratings and recommendations.[1]

3. *The standard of proof is positive evidence of results, rather than an absence of obvious failure:* Programs are not given the benefit of the doubt if they cannot produce performance information. If there is a lack of information about the success of a program, or if the OMB disagrees that the measures in place are valid, then a program will be rated as "results not demonstrated." This raises the burden of proof to require actual evidence of program effectiveness.

4. *The burden of proof rests on agencies:* The OMB sees its role as assessing existing evidence on performance, but it expects that agencies will collect and present this evidence. This has prompted a renewed interest in program evaluation at the agency level, as agencies have an incentive to disprove ineffective ratings or to replace "results not demonstrated" ratings.[2] Agencies can convince the OMB to do reassessments only if agencies have collected new evidence of program performance.

5. *Entire programs are evaluated on a regular basis:* PART requires that the overall performance of all programs be examined over a five-year period. This is a major change to the traditional approach of budgeting, where programs are usually only given a thorough evaluation when first proposed or when Congress requests the GAO to do an assessment. For most programs, the annual budget review does not extend beyond examining whether the additional increment requested is justified by service demands and costs. PART offers regular assessments of entire programs along with its funding recommendations, suggesting a willingness to make dramatic cuts where the evidence merits it. One budget examiner at the OMB compared her experience under the Clinton and Bush administrations: "During the Clinton era our efforts were almost exclusively focused on new programs, new Clinton initiatives, or congressional initiatives. Eighty to 90 percent of programs were not being analyzed by the OMB. And if the OMB are not doing it, the policy officials at the agency are not asking questions about programs. By forcing the OMB to review everything on a five-year schedule, this forces agencies and the OMB to have a dialogue about programs that had been neglected for years."

6. *The routine nature of PART creates an incentive to engage:* In addition to assessing all programs over a five-year period, reassessments of some programs take place when new evidence warrants it. However, even programs that are not fully reassessed are examined to see if they have followed up with management recommendations. The FY06 PART analyses were accompanied with a record of all programs that have been evaluated in FY04 and FY05 and a survey of whether

management recommendations made as part of these previous assessments were implemented. The results? Two hundred four recommendations had been completed, 46 had seen no action taken, and 516 recommendations led to action being taken, but not yet completed. Although agencies and the OMB can disagree about what constitutes completion of recommendation, or action taken but not yet completed, this routine attention to programs makes it difficult for agencies to forget about PART once the assessment has taken place. However, since PART is an administrative requirement, it could be overturned by a new administration.

The systematic and evidence-based nature of PART has, say OMB staff, allowed them to make evaluations that run against the ideology of the Bush White House or strong stakeholders. One OMB budget examiner noted the following:

> There is lots of self-censorship among OMB officials because there is not appetite for bad news at a political level. PART is a license to take forward discomforting information. An example is Even Start. A lot people on the Hill like it, and it is consistent with the priorities of Laura Bush. But we have three national evaluations that have not shown positive outcomes. The administration was willing to cut it at first and, now, to eliminate it. This has gotten a lot of people on the Hill angry. But our [OMB] leadership has recognized that it is important to stick to our principles.

In contrast to GPRA and state performance information systems, PART requires a central agency to develop its own data and is work intensive. As a result, PART has more influence on OMB decisions. The most prominent impact of PART is its inclusion as part of the president's budget proposal. Within the OMB, the decisive debate that underpins this budget proposal is the Director's Review. The review begins at the end of October each year, and each session covers a major function, for example, education. The review is chaired by the OMB director and includes the OMB deputy directors and senior staff with responsibility for the area being examined. White House policy staff are frequently invited to the reviews. Individual OMB budget examiners discuss specific issues and offer recommendations, and in this context they will sometimes refer to PART assessments:

> It is brought up in the context of budget recommendations, and usually when we are taking a critical stance on a program, i.e., trying to cut the program's budget. In the review we will usually just refer to the summary assessment. We do not bring it up for every program PARTed, but in the oral discussion we do not discuss every program either. . . . PART is not just about budgets, and sometimes it is discussed in the context of how to fix a program.

The written PART assessments and summary assessments are available at the Director's Review, but budget examiners also provide one- or two-page tables that summarize the PART scores for all programs examined in that function alongside funding recommendations. PART assessments are not examined one by one (this is true also of individual program budget recommendations), and the influence of PART, if real, has been at the margins. Consistent with evidence presented in the previous chapter, it seems that PART is frequently invoked in the context of budget cuts. One OMB staffer considered how the discussion at the Director's Review has changed as a result of PART: "It is not clear that it has changed it that much. There are better discussions of performance. If there is a discussion to terminate the program and PART findings show it is not effective, this helps the recommendation."

The Ambiguity of PART

One of the assumptions of the interactive dialogue model is that performance information is ambiguous, holding different meanings for different individuals at the same time. PART assessments rely on such information, and therefore it is be based on data that may be subject to ambiguity. PART itself is a form of performance information since it grades all programs on a common scale. This section examines the aspects of PART that have fostered ambiguity.

OMB staff consider PART to be a systematic tool that, as much as possible, minimizes the subjectivity of the budget examination process. Some OMB staff acknowledge what they see as minor problems with the tool. For instance:

> We are not necessarily able to compare PART scores across agencies. Examiners with different agencies will have different approaches. Some agencies will be less willing to fight with the budget examiner. Other agencies will be more willing to fight to make sure their score is high. The OMB has done consistency checks, but each branch will have their own relationships and culture, which will color the assessments.

OMB budget examiners also understand terms, apply standards, and interpret data in different ways. In reviewing PART, performance measurement expert Harry Hatry noted, "Any ratings of program purpose and design, strategic planning, and program management are bound to be heavily subjective."[3] For instance, how does a rater evaluate the performance of a program that is categorized as "results not demonstrated"? The use of the "results not demonstrated" categorization is itself ambiguous. It is sometimes applied if there were inadequate performance information, but in other cases it is used if the OMB and agency simply disagree on what are appropriate long-term and annual performance measures for the program, or according to one budget examiner, if the program looked like it would receive a poor grade but the agency pleaded for more time to turn the program around.[4] The understanding of what constitutes "independent and quality evaluation" is also a source of disagreement between agencies and the OMB.[5]

The wording of some important questions also gives rise to ambiguity, for example, whether a program is "excessively" or "unnecessarily . . . redundant or duplicative of any other Federal, State, local, or private effort"; whether a program design is free of "major flaws"; whether a program's performance measures "meaningfully" reflect program purpose; and whether a program has demonstrated "adequate" progress in achieving long-term performance goals. The use of such imprecise terms invites a variety of interpretations.[6] There has been inconsistency among OMB budget examiners on the meaning of terms such as *ambitious, outputs, outcomes,* and *having made progress.*[7] Agency officials have complained that OMB officials use different standards for defining what measures are outcome oriented.[8] Even efforts to standardize responses through the use of "yes/no" responses created problems, since different OMB staffers had different standards for what constituted a "yes."[9] Disagreement on the meaning of terms between OMB examiners illustrates not only the ambiguity of the meaning, but also the fact that examiners have a great deal of discretion placed in their judgment, even in the context of tools such as PART.

The ambiguity of the exercise means that the final scores depend upon the individuals involved. Agency staff believe that OMB program examiners who are skeptical of a program are likely to lower a PART score, while OMB staff see agency counterparts who are willing and capable of arguing with the OMB as effective advocates in increasing PART scores. More broadly, Frederickson and Frederickson have argued, the success of agencies at convincing the OMB to accept their approach to performance management is partly because of the prestige, political influence, and professional expertise of the agency.[10] This point also underlines the importance of communication and persuasion in the PART process. Gilmour's interviews of agency officials found that they responded to PART not by undertaking strategic change to foster actual performance improvement, but by finding ways to better communicate the value of existing activities. In short, agency officials viewed PART more as an exercise in argument rather than management.[11]

The Subjectivity of PART

The interactive dialogue model assumes that performance information is not objective, but selected, measured, and presented in ways that reflect the biases and interests of the actors presenting it. PART has become criticized as a means for the

OMB to exert its influence on performance management. These criticisms, whether accurate or not, affect the way in which PART is perceived. As a result, PART will struggle to generate a real dialogue with other actors and will simply be dismissed because it lacks credibility.

According to the organizational discourse literature, a mutually constitutive relationship exists between power and discourse. Those with power, legitimacy, and resources have a strong opportunity to shape how discourse is constructed in ways that sustain their authority and promote their perspective.[12] The way in which information is presented will also affect acceptance, as genres of texts that are recognizable, interpretable, and usable to others, or texts that draw on previously established texts, are more likely to become embedded in discourse.[13] Applying this insight to the public sector, central agency officials using the traditional budget format are in a relatively strong position to push performance information into the budget discourse. This OMB has done so with PART, although it has struggled to engage agency staff, and particularly Congress, in its version of evidence-based dialogue.

The OMB considers PART as a politically neutral tool, as have other proponents of performance management reforms in the past. "How can men account for so foolish a statement?" asks Wildavsky.[14] Such faith in the apolitical nature of performance management tools overlooks their centralizing tendencies. PART represents the interests, biases, and views of the OMB. The assessments are done in the spring and summer, prior to agency budget submissions, and then incorporated in agencies' budget requests prior to the OMB review process in the fall. In tying PART to the budget process, OMB has used its most powerful tool to give PART prominence in key decisions. The OMB can define issues and shape interpretation by choosing what information is considered relevant and important, how to define a program's purpose, which programs are classified as succeeding or failing, and which programs are recommended for greater resources.

Radin points out that many federal programs have multiple and conflicting goals, while the PART tool is designed on the assumption that there is only one dominant performance goal.[15] Clearly, having the power to decide what that goal will be, while excluding other goals or measures, will affect how success is understood. One OMB official noted that "there have been lots of disagreements between agency staff and OMB staff about what constituted an outcome." For example, Radin has shown that PART has systematically excluded equity goals. Unless equity is a primary goal of the program, PART does not try to measure equity. Even for programs where equity was a stated goal, results were rarely disaggregated by ethnic group or income level.[16]

To the extent that PART can help set the policy agenda by changing the nature of discussion about a program, then controlling PART represents a form of power and influence for the OMB and the White House. One OMB official suggested as much, saying: "I would like to believe that this is objective, but performance management is such a slippery slope, so it's easy to take this stuff and make it political. . . . PART is a gate-keeping process. It's a framing device. It affects how policies are defined and framed, which affects how issues are viewed. There is a lot of subjective bias even though it is an 'objective' tool."

Not surprisingly, agencies and stakeholders have been suspicious of PART. While GPRA encouraged stakeholder involvement, the design of PART tends to exclude third parties from providing input. Radin has argued that this limits the analysis that goes into programs and eliminates a check on OMB biases.[17] OMB Watch, a government watchdog group, describes PART as a subjective tool used by the OMB to enhance its influence, warning that "relying too heavily on the PART ratings not only will gradually remove Congress from its funding and oversight responsibilities granted under the Constitution, but also will continue to close the door on opportunities for outside stakeholder interests to be infused into the congressional budgeting and evaluation process."[18]

OMB Watch has offered other criticisms of PART: It is overly simplistic, with a rating scale that does not explain why a program might fail and that is unable to recognize that some programs are more complex than others. PART favors programs with simple clear goals that are easily measurable and provide short-term impacts, but many federal programs do not look like that. Programs that provide competitive grants or block grants have a harder time coming up with unitary outcome measures of success and are about half as likely to be graded "effective" or "moderately effective." Adam Hughes of OMB Watch testified before a Senate subcommittee that

> PART is so limited and distorted a tool that it should be used neither for management nor for budget and appropriations decisions. Both by the design of the tool and as the mechanism is implemented, PART systematically ignores the reality of federal programs and judges them based on standards that are deeply incompatible with the purposes that federal programs are expected to serve. As one agency contact memorably explained to us, PART assessments are tantamount to a baseball coach walking to the mound to remove his pitcher and then chastising him for not kicking enough field goals as he brings in a reliever.[19]

The OMB and agencies have clashed on what sorts of evaluations are useful and credible, and they frequently have different expectations about what sort of information evaluations should produce.[20] Agencies offer traditional complaints: that measurement is inexact, that some programs are more difficult to measure than others, and that there is often a significant lag between program treatment and outcome. PART has created transaction costs for agency staff in terms of data collection and evaluations, even as agencies are constrained by limited resources and the mandates of the Paperwork Reduction Act.[21] OMB Watch reports that many agency managers saw PART as a compliance exercise that encouraged gaming to avoid negative scores.[22]

Agencies are also concerned about the OMB emphasis on outcome measures. The OMB, consistent with the language of GPRA, sees agencies as responsible for achieving national goals, even if agencies do not fully control these outcomes. Agencies prefer output measures that reflect effort and inform process improvement. They argue that many programs are better suited for outputs because of external factors that affect outcomes. They try to convince the OMB that such output measures are valid, and in some cases, they argue that what the OMB considers an output is actually an outcome.[23] The difference in perspective points again to the importance of role—central agencies demand solutions to policy problems while agencies want to be accountable for what is under their control. Frederickson and Frederickson document how agency control over outcomes has weakened with the growth of the hollow state.[24] One irony of recent public management reform is the growing push to hold public managers accountable for performance even as third parties increasingly provide services. The relationships between public managers and these third parties (who themselves are often politically active stakeholders) often fail to resemble a contract specified by an informed principal. Instead, these relationships rely on collaboration about management and the nature of the measurement system in place.[25]

Agency staff are also likely to disagree with the PART assessments of a program's purpose. Staff are more likely to view the purpose of their activities as self-evidently valuable. If agencies disagree with the budget examiner's decision, they can appeal to political appointees in the OMB, but they are generally not successful. While PART is a relatively transparent process, it is still dominated by the OMB and largely excludes stakeholders and Congress. However, this does not prevent the agencies from using PART for advocacy purposes. Agencies have sometimes succeeded in using PART to argue for greater resources, either for the program as a whole or for new evaluation efforts.[26]

A basic area of disagreement is how the PART assessments categorize programs. The OMB has defined programs in terms of the decision blocks that they make every year as part of the budget. For instance, they may distinguish between discretionary and mandatory aspects of spending in a particular area, while Congress does not. In other instances, the OMB might define programs more broadly than Congress or agencies do, aggregating areas of spending that congressional subcommittees treat separately. As Wildavsky noted many years ago, defining a program is a contested and important activity: "Programs are not made in heaven. There is nothing out there just waiting to be found. Programs are not natural to the world. . . . There are as many ways of conceiving of programs as there are of organizing activities."[27]

In undertaking PART, OMB budget examiners consider themselves to be evaluators, not just bean counters. The scope of their influence enforces a norm that they need to consider management issues as well as budget issues.[28] PART offers another way to summarize and analyze evaluation information about programs, formalizing existing analytical practices that budget examiners already perform. PART therefore reflects the professional norms of budget examiners and the OMB. To supporters of the OMB, those values include political neutrality and ensuring the probity and efficacy of public spending. To critics, the OMB and PART represent an effort to exert top-down control through one-size-fits-all tools, as well as a strong and increasing deference to presidential preferences.

PART can also be seen as an OMB response to being sidelined from performance management during the Clinton administration. One OMB budget examiner noted: "A problem with the National Performance Review—which the OMB was not really involved in—was that it was not tied to the budget process. Therefore, it had less impact on budget and management decisions. PART is much more empowering for the OMB."

OMB staff also critiqued GPRA as failing to measure outcomes and producing information that had weak connections to program activities. PART is characterized as the vehicle that will finally make GPRA useful: "PART is systematic. GPRA did not provide a systematic framework for how you do it. GPRA is nebulous. How you use the information is not clear. PART put a structure in place to use GPRA. PART is not inconsistent with GPRA, but builds on it."

In fact, there has been no easy marriage between PART and GPRA. The GAO has pointed to the tension between PART and GPRA, suggesting that PART was an effort by the White House and OMB to substitute their judgment for the stakeholder interests fostered by the GPRA framework.[29] GPRA was intended to invite stakeholders and Congress into the goal-setting process while PART is tied to the executive preparation phase of the budget process, which excludes outside actors. Because of the PART process, agencies are frequently forced to develop annual goals without consultation with key stakeholders, who are presented with new or revised goals without a chance to offer meaningful input.[30]

OMB raters often deem existing GPRA measures as unsatisfactory and have used PART recommendations to prioritize the type of performance information that the OMB values. In its analysis of the FY02–04 PART summaries, the GAO found that the majority of recommendations have been in the area of improving assessment methods—52 percent of the 2002 recommendations, 59 percent in 2003, and 58 percent in 2004.[31] These recommendations will not directly improve the performance of these programs but are designed to generate more or better performance data, making it easier for OMB examiners to assess whether a program satisfies the PART standard of success. The high percentage of assessment recommendations indicates OMB dissatisfaction with existing performance information used by agencies, as does the high number of programs that are classified as "results not demonstrated." But the GAO study found that these recommendations were the most frequent PART recommendation regardless of the deficiencies of the program or the program's PART rating.[32] In this, at least, the OMB resembles Congress. Both bodies have used performance management to demand ever-more performance information from the agencies under their purview.

The attitude of Congress toward PART has ranged from indifference to occasional hostility.[33] One OMB official said, "I don't want to say they don't care, but they don't care. They hold the purse strings and are proud of that role. They do not like to be told how to allocate money because of what a performance measure says." Congress already has performance information from GPRA and can force agencies to produce any sort of program performance data it feels necessary. There are also many other sources of performance information relevant to budget decisions: GAO reports, inspector general performance reports, requests to agencies, testimony, think tanks like the Brookings Institution and Urban Institute, the National Academy of Public Administration, constituent complaints, and anecdotal information. One might expect that so much potential information would create a demand for a tool that promises to reduce the complexity of performance data, such as PART. But Congress has resisted, as much because of the messenger as the message. Legislators at both the state and federal levels have shown a tendency to distrust the objectivity of any performance information emanating from the executive branch. An OMB budget examiner conceded that "they may just disagree with the results. Based on the same information, they come to different conclusions." Congressional staff indicated that they are suspicious of the PART tool, of how the OMB defines a program, what information they use to define performance, and the actual PART ratings.[34]

Even if legislative committees were to accept PART analyses, they may believe that PART is simply inconsistent with their priorities or the priorities of major stakeholders. After presenting PART information, one budget examiner recalled being told by an appropriations subcommittee clerk that "your proposals are for your priorities. We need to fund our priorities." One instance where committees may use PART recommendations is if interest groups are weak and cuts are needed to provide money for other programs.

The OMB hopes that, even if Congress disagrees with the evaluations, PART will force a discussion between the executive and legislative branches in terms of performance. However, Congress is under no requirement to enter into such a discussion and thus far has largely refused to engage with the OMB. While the OMB has improved the supply of performance information, there is not yet, and perhaps will never be, a strong legislative demand for its product. At best, interest groups or agencies that find PART useful may bring it to the attention of legislative supporters.[35] It is worth noting that Republican control over both the Senate and the House during the Bush administration provided the most favorable possible political context for PART to affect legislative decision making. That it has had only marginal influence suggests the importance of institutional roles relative to partisan loyalties when it comes to public management reforms that affect decision making.

An Experimental Test of the Interactive Dialogue Model

The interactive dialogue model hypothesizes that because of the ambiguity of performance information, different actors can examine the same programs and disagree on what performance data is relevant and what the same performance data means. Even if they agree about performance, they can disagree about what actions to take in terms of management and resources.

This section seeks to further illustrate the interactive dialogue model by testing these claims through an experiment using graduate students in public affairs programs at the Bush School of Government and Public Service at Texas A&M University and at the La Follette School of Public Affairs at the University of Wisconsin–Madison. The experiment describes variation between PART program ratings and budget recommendations made by the OMB examiners and subjects familiar with but not directly involved in the political process. The existence and reasons for such variation support the idea that different actors can employ logical warrants to interpret the same information differently.

In the experiment the subjects were asked to take the position of a staff analyst for a congressional committee and analyze three to five programs overseen by that committee and evaluated by PART. The subjects were instructed to examine the OMB's PART assessments but also to become an expert on the programs in their own right, undertaking research by examining the agency's strategic plan, performance report, website, agency, appropriate think tank reports, GAO reports, newspapers and professional magazines, and any other relevant sources, such as stakeholder views. The subjects were asked whether they considered the OMB evaluation to be "fair and accurate, and for each program explain why you agree or disagree with the OMB solution" and to develop funding recommendations to provide to their committee.[36] Performing such an experiment is possible only because the PART process is so transparent, allowing subjects access to a high level of detail for each of the analytic categories that make up the PART score and rating, the process of reasoning behind the OMB responses, and the relative importance of these factors.

It should be noted that the purpose of the experiment was not to replicate the decision of an OMB or congressional analyst specifically, but to examine whether individuals with general policy analytical skills can look at the performance information for a specific program and come to different—though logical and defensible—assessments. Other research has relied on graduate students in public affairs as the basis for generalizing to the behavior of public officials, particularly in the area of information processing and decision making.[37] Such subjects have training in policy analysis and public management, largely intend to make their career in public policy, have worked on practical projects with real public organizations, and are required to intern with public organizations. Frequently they have previous experience working in government, and many will occupy positions as policy analysts or public managers at different levels of government.

Thirty-five subjects evaluated 128 programs, distributed across three years of PART summaries. The resulting data provides two decision points to compare subject and OMB judgments, the PART program rating (where "ineffective" was given a score of one, "results not demonstrated" is two, "adequate" is three, "moderately effective" is four, "effective" is five) and a budget recommendation.[38] Since 128 programs were evaluated, there are a total of 256 potential decision points. For three evaluation decisions and two program budget decisions, the subject did not express a decision.[39]

Of the 125 valid program-rating decision points, the subjects agreed with the OMB assessment eighty-five times and disagreed forty times. Those forty disagreements included five instances where the rater had assessed the program two or more points above the five-point scale set by the OMB, thirty instances of judging the program one point above the OMB scale, two instances of being less generous than the OMB by one point, and three instances of rating the program two points or more lower than the OMB. There was less agreement in terms of actual funding decisions.[40] The raters agreed with the OMB assessment on only 65 of 127 occasions. The raters were somewhat more likely to recommend increased funding (on 40 occasions) than to cut it (on 22 occasions). Comparisons of correlations between PART evaluations and budget recommendations for the sample suggest that the decision behavior of the subjects was similar to OMB officials. For both groups, PART ratings were positively correlated to proposed budget increases, indicating that programs that were rated as better performers tended to receive higher scores. Subjects willing to disagree with the OMB on the PART score were also more likely to disagree with funding allocations. Disagreement on the evaluation and disagreement on the budget recommendation is positively correlated at 0.433, significant at 0.001 (two tailed).[41]

What conclusions, albeit tentative, can be reached? First, raters were generally reluctant to disagree with the OMB's ratings. While the next section discusses the reasons for disagreement, it is first worth considering the reasons for agreement. The subjects pointed to the information advantage enjoyed by the OMB and the persuasiveness of the PART format, which allows the OMB to lay out detailed information to support its recommendations. One subject pointed to what she saw as the tight logical connections between the information presented and recommendations: "Everything in the PART analysis was clearly laid out; they presented information and came to conclusions as a result of that." To be sure, the PART summaries are persuasive and, unless someone is deeply interested in the program and has the basis upon which to form a contrary opinion, a person is likely to accept the OMB version.

Any experimental approach largely excludes consideration of institutional pressures that actual analysts face. As noted in chapter 5, institutional roles are likely to influence the assessment of PART. Agencies, stakeholders, Congress, and the budget office are likely to have their own views of a program that shapes how they interpret performance information. There was limited qualitative evidence of the role of roles in the fact that the subjects were more likely to challenge the PART assessments if they had some prior knowledge of the program or if they could find another respected resource, such as the GAO or a think tank, to support alternative interpretations of program dynamics and performance information. A number of the subjects felt that if they had had access to agency officials, they would have had a better basis for challenging the PART outcomes. One subject, who had experience working in the federal government, commented, "There was insufficient evidence for me to disprove their rating. We were looking at public documents, not talking to officials. If you talk to program staff you can find direction to get supplemental information that can help you advocate a position."

The experiment therefore underestimates the likelihood of disagreement between parties because agency officials and legislative committee staff will not suffer from the same measure of information asymmetry as the experiment's participants. We can expect that agency actors, stakeholders, and committee staff will have more strongly held preferences, be in a better position to launch plausible alternative interpretations to the PART summaries, and be more motivated to do so. Because the experiment takes place among public affairs programs from two quite different schools, there are some limited quantitative insights to be gained on whether different institutional settings (being a student in one public affairs school or another) results in different decision outcomes. The likelihood that this is the case increases because of marked differences between the schools, even though the content of both public affairs programs is similar and the context of the experiment was the same.

The students at the Bush School tended to be more conservative, more critical of government programs, and more likely to resist increases in federal government spending. Students at the La Follette School tended to be more politically liberal and more supportive of government programs. In part, this is because of geography—students at the Bush School tend to be from Texas and other southern states while the La Follette School attracts more students from the more liberal Midwest and Northeast. In part, it is because of self-selection. Conservative students are more likely to be attracted to a school that commemorates a former Republican president and is part of a university with a conservative student body and city. Liberal students will lean toward a school that celebrates the achievements of an icon of the progressive movement and is situated in a very liberal city. Differences in perspectives will also be shaped by the institutional setting, and the norms and values established by fellow students and professors will shape an understanding of what is appropriate behavior.[42]

The results of the experiment support the hypothesis that institution matters to decision outcomes. Students from Wisconsin were significantly more likely than Texas A&M students to disagree with OMB officials about what PART assessments or budget a program deserved. Not only were Wisconsin students more likely to disagree, but the nature of their disagreement also differed from their Texas A&M counterparts in a way consistent with a more liberal perspective. Students at Wisconsin were significantly more likely than A&M students to propose that programs receive a PART score above what OMB officials had recommended, and they were more supportive of increasing program budgets above what OMB officials had proposed.[43]

The Logic of Disagreement

The primary goal of the experiment was not to focus on the role of institutional differences but to uncover the logic that underpins disagreement about the same information. The results help us understand how performance information is interpreted and, in turn, used. In doing so, the experiment helps to shed light on the actual experience of PART. A GAO report has noted that "OMB and agencies often have conflicting ideas about what to measure, how to measure it, and how to report program results."[44] Box 8.1 summarizes the rationales subjects used when disagreeing with the grades and the funding decisions.[45]

Program complexity
Many subjects questioned how performance was assessed. One complaint was that functions that were inherently difficult to measure were forced to fit into the PART framework and as a result were more likely to be considered ineffective or categorized as "results not demonstrated." One reviewer noted, "A lot of the programs that I evaluated, it was so difficult to quantify the results, so the program took a

---

Box 8.1   Arguing about performance information: Rationales used in disagreeing with PART

- Program complexity: Program function is too complex to adequately measure; program outcomes are driven by external factors.
- Data problems: Underlying data is unreliable or misses key goals.
- Alternate interpretation: Existing measures are valid but have been incorrectly interpreted.
- Expert opinion supports our view.
- Punish poor performers: Programs categorized as "results not demonstrated," as having poor financial controls, or that have achieved their original goals should not receive increases in funding.
- Support winners: Programs with strong positive assessments should receive higher funding.
- Fair play: There should be consistency across PART assessments and rewards—other programs with similar PART scores received more or less funding increases.
- Improvements are being made: Program problems, while real, are being eliminated through improved planning and management; program cuts are not appropriate at this time.
- Need for services: A clear relationship between resources, need, and program delivery trumps performance information.
- Political needs: Stakeholder and congressional views trump performance information.

---

hit because it was something that was almost immeasurable." In addition the outcomes of many programs were frequently beyond the control of the program, making assessments of program effectiveness appear somewhat arbitrary. For example, a reviewer of the Job Corps program noted that success depended a good deal on economic conditions. Another example is the Public Diplomacy program in the State Department, which has the goal of improving the image of the United States in foreign countries. This program was criticized by the OMB for lacking useful performance measures and judged to have not demonstrated results. The subject assessing the program pointed out that multiple factors shape international public opinion and that actions of State Department embassies will have only a marginal impact, making it difficult to develop reliable outcome measures. He argued that "a program should not be penalized because it is operating in a complex situation where measurable success is uncertain."

Data problems: Underlying data is unreliable or misses key goals
Some experiment subjects argued that the OMB was using unreliable data or inappropriate measures. One person criticized a proposed cut to the Even Start literacy program, arguing that poor performance reporting mechanisms between

grantees and the Department of Education, rather than actual program failure, were responsible for the "ineffective" rating and that more data was needed.

Another subject argued that OMB assessments of social programs seemed more concerned with preventing waste, fraud, and abuse than with ensuring that eligible participants received a service. Similarly, a subject reviewing the School Breakfast program argued that the OMB was overemphasizing the number of ineligible students receiving aid and not placing enough emphasis on the number of eligible students not receiving aid.

Some subjects argued that the OMB unfairly rated programs as performing poorly or unable to demonstrate results even when relevant and insightful outputs existed. For an education program, TRIO Support Services, the subject pointed to a study showing that program participants had a 9 percent higher rate of completing a bachelor's degree than people in the control group, suggesting that the OMB's "results not demonstrated" rating underestimated program performance.

Sometimes subjects argued that the OMB sought overly complex outcome measures or focused too greatly on narrow efficiency measures when straightforward measures of benefits received were the most appropriate. In examining the Veterans Home Loan program, the reviewer argued: "I disagree that additional long-term outcome measures are required. This program gives loans to veterans who want to get houses. The percent of veterans who could not have gotten houses without the program is an adequate measure for a straightforward program." Similarly, for the Montgomery GI Bill, the program was classified by the OMB as "results not demonstrated" for failing to have adequate outcome measures, and the program was regarded as failing to demonstrate progress to meet its outcome goal because of concerns over claims-processing times and payment accuracy. The subject argued that the goal of the program was clear and that measures of use of educational benefits provided a straightforward way to demonstrate that the program was delivering its main goal.

Alternate interpretation of performance information
The subjects also interpreted performance data in ways at odds with OMB examiners. One subject argued that a program dedicated to the development of hydrogen technology should receive a higher evaluation, based on alternative interpretation of the context of the program. The subject argued that the program had contributed real progress in moving from a petroleum-based economy and was meeting difficult-to-measure benchmarks on the way to a very ambitious and important long-term goal that required patience.

Alternate interpretations tended to highlight the ambiguity of PART language. For example, one subject disagreed that the program problems that the OMB had pointed out rose to the level of being a "major flaw." Another subject argued that given the goal of the Small Business Surety Bond program to increase bonding rates by 10 percent, the OMB assessment that the program failed to have "ambitious targets" was misplaced. A mixture of sarcasm and frustration was evident in the subject's comment that "perhaps if they instead attempted to increase bonding by fifteen percent it would have been considered ambitious." Another subject questioned the OMB assessment that the Job Corps program was achieving its goals only to "a small extent." The subject pointed out that Job Corps came relatively close to meeting its key goals for graduates moving to employment, further education, or the military during a relatively weak period of economic performance.

Expert opinion supports our view

Subjects frequently used third-party evidence that contradicted the OMB and supported their own interpretation. This helped subjects in two ways: overcome information asymmetry and boost their credibility in making claims. For instance, a student examining Commodity Supplemental Food Program pointed to an analysis by the Center on Budget and Policy Priorities that argued that the OMB omitted key evidence from its analysis. Another subject who disputed the OMB finding that the Urban Indian Health program was redundant pointed to a GAO report that showed that this population was underserved. A subject reviewing the Trio Upward Bound program incorporated the views of professional education groups to argue that the OMB was using the PART process to try to change the mission of the program from serving disadvantaged students entering college to focusing on high school dropouts. This illustrated how PART recommendations, by seeking to shift programmatic resources to different client groups, clearly go beyond management recommendations and enter the realm of policy changes. What is interesting is that the OMB had originally pushed for focusing on high-risk students by pointing to evidence from another third party—an independent contractor study that had found the program was most effective at targeting dropouts.

Punish poor performers and support winners

In some cases the subjects agreed with the PART assessments but felt that the OMB had not followed through on the logic of its analysis because of a failure to cut, or at least limit, the growth of poor performers or programs that had completed their missions. An example comes from the Project-Based Rental Assistance program. The OMB rated it as "ineffective" but recommended only incremental funding changes. The subject agreed with the PART summary but recommended zeroing out the program and moving the money to another housing voucher program that was deemed moderately effective. The alternative program was described in the PART assessment as having advantages in terms of greater individual choice, cost-effectiveness, less federal liability, and more local regulation. The subject, therefore, was not contradicting the PART analysis but pushing the implications of the analysis to its logical conclusion, that is, take funds from a program that is not effective and put it toward a similar, more effective alternative. OMB examiners had used the same logic elsewhere.

Other subjects argued that programs should be able to demonstrate results before gaining large increases. One subject who looked at different education programs argued for the principle that programs categorized as "results not demonstrated" should receive very limited increases, if any, and consistently cut proposed increases to these programs. One subject spelled out the logic of this approach: "Is there really an incentive to create effective performance measures if the program will receive increased funding regardless? If the priority is to institutionalize the PART as an effective evaluation tool, the Appropriations Committee should react to poor PART evaluations with budgetary restraint." A related argument was that adequate financial controls needed to be in place before increases were made. A subject objected to a proposed funding increase for the Student Aid Administration, citing a GAO report that found ongoing problems with fraud and error.

Fair play

Of course, it is unlikely that program advocates will make the type of arguments outlined above to cut funding. However, agency advocates are capable of using the logic of this approach—a consistency between performance, evaluation, and funding—in situations where programs gained positive evaluations but received lower increases than programs with similar or lower ratings. The argument for treating a particular program consistently with other programs appeals to a logic of comparative "fair play" that agency advocates have long used to push for maintaining parity in increases.[46] For example, one subject explicitly cited the PART budgeting patterns themselves in arguing for a greater increase, pointing out that her Soil Survey Program, which was rated "moderately effective," was receiving only a 1 percent proposed increase while other programs with the same rating were receiving an average 8 percent increase during that fiscal cycle.

The fair play logic also applies to how PART ratings are arrived at. Agencies can argue that the OMB should treat programs similarly and assess them using the same standards in the name of consistency and fair play. This argument is most effective when the agency can find examples of what appears to be inconsistency in how the OMB evaluates programs. For example, a subject who assessed the similar Youth Activities and Jobs Corp program, which both target disadvantaged youth, noted that the Youth Activities program had a lower rating because it only affected a fraction of possible participants. The OMB failed to make the same criticism of the Jobs Corp program, even though it served a much smaller portion of a larger target population.

Improvements are being made
Advocates can call for more favorable ratings or funding if they can make a plausible case that they are making changes to improve effectiveness. The logic here is, "be patient, we are fixing the problem." For example, in the Farmland Protection Program of the Natural Resource Conservation Service, the OMB proposed, and the subject agreed, that increases were justified despite a "results not demonstrated" rating because the agency was in the process of creating a plan to remedy the program shortcomings. Another subject student disagreed with the OMB penalizing a program for lacking long-term measures because the program was in the process of creating these measures. In the context of budget decisions, a corollary to this argument is that more resources are needed to facilitate improvements and that cuts will hamper change. Accepting that program problems exist, and having a management plan to remedy those plans, therefore becomes a credible tactic to delay or prevent budget cuts.

Clear need for services
Subjects often disagreed with negative PART evaluations and called for higher funding where they saw a clear relationship among resources, need, and delivery of appropriate services. Such an interpretation views performance measures as secondary to factors that drive program demand. The program needs the resources to do its job. Both the subjects and the OMB applied this logic to nonentitlement spending where program resources were perceived as central to achieving a vital function. This reflects the finding of Gilmour and Lewis that the program purpose and design scores, which represent the perceived importance of the function, were the only elements of the PART analysis that had a significant influence on OMB funding recommendations for both FY04 and FY05.[47]

Examples that the subjects identified include a program that provided tangible benefits to sympathetic groups (such as the GI Bill, Veterans Home Loans, and Veterans Burial Benefits), a program designed to deal with the growing problem of cybercrime, and a safety and security program for nuclear materials. A subject rating Wildland Fire Management pointed to the saliency of the program in light of recent wildfire disasters. Another subject called for raising funding for the space shuttle mission above the president's proposed increase, citing the Columbia disaster and the need for a greater investment in safety. The National Forest Improvement and Maintenance program was criticized and recommended for cuts by the OMB because of a maintenance backlog. The subject reviewing that program argued that the backlog stemmed from lack of adequate resources and recommended a funding increase. The argument was based on a logical interpretation of the information contained in the program's PART analysis, to the effect that reducing the backlog was central to agency goals, was directly related to resources, and was underfunded.

Stakeholder and congressional views

In rare cases, the subjects discounted the role of PART because of political concerns. One subject argued for higher increases in funding for the Veterans Administration Medical Program for largely political reasons, noting that the secretary had lobbied for a higher level of funding and that pursuing such an increase would raise stakeholder trust. A broader political observation is that the PART will face political conflict because it is designed to counteract the legislative tendency to create duplicative programs and the OMB has shown a willingness to aggregate or cut overlapping programs. A number of the subjects pointed out that Congress deliberately seeks to divert resources to specific groups regardless of duplication with other programs. For example, a program exists to provide housing loans to veterans. The OMB has pointed out that the program overlaps with similar housing programs elsewhere and reduced its PART score as a result. The subject evaluating the program noted that "Congress wants to target programs directly to certain groups; the OMB should allow Congress to express its will. Program redundancy is not a design flaw, but rather a reflection of political priorities." This simple observation underlines the point that the basic purpose of many programs is to reward or support certain political groups, and simply providing those resources is a primary performance measure in the eyes of Congress. Some have argued that the OMB is using PART to disagree with the way Congress designs programs "using the rhetoric of results rather than a direct statement of its disagreement with Congress."[48]

Conclusion

The OMB perceives PART as a way of creating an evidence-based dialogue within the OMB, agencies, and Congress, and across those institutions. PART's transparent and persuasive nature enables it to win over disinterested parties in most cases. In constructing PART, the OMB used its legitimacy and central position in the budget process to great effect. Preliminary evidence suggests that PART is having an impact on decision making within the OMB and in interactions between the OMB and agencies, albeit as a minor influence. Two barriers limiting the use of PART by agencies and Congress is its perceived subjectivity, reflecting the views and biases of the OMB, and the perception that it is a partisan tool. Both factors reduce the likelihood that PART analyses will be welcomed and weaken efforts to institutionalize program assessments.

Perceived subjectivity and partisanship also affect *how* PART is used, along with the basic ambiguity of both the PART scores and the performance data used in constructing the scores. Other parties are likely to resist PART assessments unless they align with their views. The basic ambiguity of PART assessments was demonstrated in the experiment described in this chapter. The subjects examining PART assessments were able to use logical warrants to come to different conclusions on what the underlying data meant for creating PART scores and what the PART scores meant for budget decisions. The plausible nature of the subjects' arguments is demonstrated by the fact that OMB examiners employed many of these same rationales—on what constituted a reasonable basis for assessing performance, on how tightly evaluations should connect to funding, on the importance of demonstrating results, and on the relative importance of program need and the connection of resources to service delivery. However, neither the OMB nor the subjects used these rationales in the same way for every decision, suggesting that how performance information is used depends partly on the performance information, partly on the decision makers involved, and partly on the nature of the decision to be made.

Such disagreement will increase when the actors involved in making decisions represent particular roles and institutional interests. This insight should guide our expectations about the conditions for useful dialogue routines. In instances where programs are relatively simple with clear goals, costs, and benefits, there is greater chance of avoiding ambiguity and generating agreement. Thurmaier and Willoughby draw on research in psychology to make the point that on some issues—particularly those perceived as simple or where actors have familiarity or direct experience—actors are more likely to have strong exogenous preferences and are less prone to persuasion.[49] There is also greater potential for agreement in decision situations that feature a relatively homogenous set of decision makers and interests, a theme explored in the next chapter. However, in most instances, the goal of reforms like PART should be to change how decision makers talk about programs, rather than foster consensus or make decisions easier. As Richard Nathan argues, PART should not be seen as a tool to simplify the policy world. Instead, its real value is in complexifying decisions—prompting a serious dialogue about performance, including discussion about the reliability and limitations of the data and the context of performance.[50] The interactive dialogue model suggests that such a discussion is more likely to occur when a wide range of actors is involved and competing to define performance.

Notes

1. U.S. Government Accountability Office, *Performance Budgeting: PART Focuses Attention on Program Performance, but More Can Be Done to Engage Congress,* 17.

2. U.S. Government Accountability Office, *Program Evaluation.*

3. Hatry, *Comments of the Members of the Performance Advisory Council* (available at www.whitehouse.gov/omb/budintegration/pmac_030303comments.pdf), 2003, 8.

4. U.S. General Accounting Office, *Observations on the Use of OMB's Program Assessment Rating Tool*, 25.

5. Ibid., 24.

6. Brass, "The Bush Administration's Program Assessment Rating Tool," 21.

7. U.S. General Accounting Office, *Observations on the Use of OMB's Program Assessment Rating Tool*.

8. Ibid., 21.

9. Ibid., 7.

10. Frederickson and Frederickson cite the National Institutes of Health and the Centers for Medicare and Medicaid Services as two agencies whose professional status, prestige (especially the National Institutes of Health), and political influence (especially for the Medicare program) allowed them to shape their implementation of performance management. Frederickson and Frederickson, *Measuring the Performance of the Hollow State*.

11. Gilmour, *Implementing OMB's Program Assessment Rating Tool*.

12. Hardy and Philips, "Discourse and Power."

13. Phillips, Lawrence, and Hardy, "Discourse and Institutions."

14. Wildavsky, "The Political Economy of Efficiency," 308.

15. Radin, *Challenging the Performance Movement*.

16. Ibid., chapter 5.

17. Radin, *Testimony to the Senate*.

18. Hughes, *Testimony to the Senate*.

19. Ibid.

20. U.S. Government Accountability Office, *Program Evaluation*.

21. Radin, *Testimony to the Senate*, 4. Radin also points out that some agencies are under specific legislative direction not to collect data that the OMB seeks. She points to the example of the Consumer Product Safety Commission, which is prevented by Congress from using cost–benefit analysis for some programs and was penalized in its PART evaluation as a result.

22. Hughes, *Testimony to the Senate*.

23. U.S. Government Accountability Office, *Performance Budgeting: PART Focuses Attention on Program Performance*, 7–8, 37–38.

24. Frederickson and Frederickson, *Measuring the Performance of the Hollow State*.

25. Ibid., chapter 8; see also Radin, *Challenging the Performance Movement*, chapter 7.

26. U.S. General Accounting Office, *Observations on the Use of OMB's Program Assessment Rating Tool*, 16–17.

27. Wildavsky, "The Political Economy of Efficiency," 302.

28. White, "Examining Budgets for Chief Executives"; Martin, Wholey, and Meyers, "The New Equation at the OMB."

29. U.S. General Accounting Office, *Observations on the Use of OMB's Program Assessment Rating Tool*, 31–32. A more detailed comparison of GPRA and PART can be found in Radin, *Challenging the Accountability Movement*, chapter 6.

30. U.S. Government Accountability Office, *Performance Budgeting: PART Focuses Attention on Program Performance*, 8.

31. Ibid.

32. Ibid., 22.

33. This observation has been made anecdotally, based on interviews with OMB and congressional staff. It received further support when the GAO noted that "it is not clear that the PART has had any significant impact on congressional authorization, appropriations, and oversight activities to date. Moreover, it is unlikely that performance information will be used unless it is believed to be credible and reliable and reflects a consensus about performance goals among a community of interested parties." U.S. Government Accountability Office, *Performance Budgeting: PART Focuses Attention on Program Performance,* 44.

34. U.S. Government Accountability Office, *Performance Budgeting: PART Focuses Attention on Program Performance,* 8, 42–46.

35. This would be consistent with a fire-alarm approach to policymaking. McCubbins and Schwartz, "Congressional Oversight Overlooked." The OMB has made access to information easier though a more user-friendly website that provides PART analyses: www.expectmore.gov.

36. Students were required to provide a written memo of about seven single-spaced pages explaining their decisions. They also had to present their findings before the class, which operated as a mock legislative committee, asking pointed questions about the recommendations. After one session, a group of eight students served as a focus group to discuss in greater detail the reasons for the decisions they made. In the analysis that follows I quote student comments made during the focus group or from their memo. The experiments took place between 2003 and 2005, inclusive.

37. Bretschneider, Straussman, and Mullins, "Do Revenue Forecasts Influence Budget Setting?"; Coursey, "Information Credibility and Choosing Policy Alternatives"; Wittmer, "Ethical Sensitivity and Managerial Decisionmaking." An argument for the use of experiments in public policy and management, and a review of relevant work, can be found in Bozeman and Scott, "Laboratory Experiments in Public Policy and Management." A more general argument for the use of experiments in assessing psychological behavior can be found in Mook, "In Defense of External Invalidity."

38. This scoring is consistent with other quantitative analyses of PART, such as Gilmour and Lewis, "Does Performance Budgeting Work?"; Gilmour and Lewis, "Assessing Performance Budgeting at the OMB." It is also consistent with the perspectives of agency staff, who consider the "results not demonstrated" rating as "the absolute wors[t] one a program could receive under the PART—far worse than an 'ineffective' rating"; see Hughes, *Testimony to the Senate,* 2006, 10.

39. However, for one of the budget recommendation decisions in question, the rater asked for greater information and expressed doubt that the committee should commit to the increase recommended by the OMB based on the evidence presented. On this basis, I consider it reasonable to assume that this budget recommendation indicates disagreement with the OMB recommendation and essentially calls for lower funding.

40. In part, this variance between levels of agreement about funding and allocation decisions is because the limited PART evaluation scale encourages raters to move from the initial evaluation score only if they experience a high level of disagreement, whereas students who did not feel deep disagreement might have kept the same rating measure but added or subtracted an incremental sum from the president's recommended sum (this happened twenty-eight times).

41. To control for the role of outliers, I converted the variables into a simplified disagreement scale, where students evaluating the program higher than the OMB is scored at -1, evaluating the program lower is 1, no disagreement is 0; students recommending higher budgets than the OMB is -1, recommending a lower score is 1, and no disagreement is zero.

42. March and Olsen, *Rediscovering Institutions*.

43. A dummy variable representing being a Wisconsin student was positively correlated with willingness to disagree with OMB officials on PART assessments at 0.325 (significant at 0.001) and positively correlated with disagreeing with OMB budget assessments at 0.288 (significant at 0.01). Being a Wisconsin student was positively correlated with proposing a higher PART rating than OMB officials at 0.321 (significant at 0.001) and with proposing a higher budget at 0.381 (significant at 0.001).

44. U.S. Government Accountability Office, *Performance Budgeting: PART Focuses Attention on Program Performance*, 7.

45. More examples of how students used these rationales can be found in Moynihan, "What Do We Talk about When We Talk about Performance?"

46. Wildavsky and Caiden, *The New Politics of the Budgetary Process*, 5th ed.

47. Gilmour and Lewis, "Does Performance Budgeting Work?"; Gilmour and Lewis, "Assessing Performance Budgeting at the OMB."

48. Hughes, *Testimony to the Senate*, 2006. One seemingly perverse implication of this approach is that agencies can be punished for simply following the rules of their program design.

49. Thurmaier and Willoughby, *Policy and Politics in State Budgeting*.

50. Nathan, "Presidential Address."

9

Dialogue Routines and Learning Forums

Even if elected officials rarely use performance information, performance management advocates hope that managers use this data. Chapter 5 found that agency managers did use performance information, although not always predicted by performance management doctrine. Having introduced the interactive dialogue model, this chapter revisits the states to examine how agency managers use information.[1] The interactive dialogue model suggests that the potential for goal-based learning routines is higher within agencies than in other settings because they contain a relatively homogenous group of decision makers who share similar goals. In two of the three states examined, managers used dialogue routines to improve organizational capacity and reframe the basic goals of the organization. These uses of performance management were fostered by organizational characteristics that led to different types of learning. Learning was used both for internal management purposes, in the cases of Virginia and Vermont, and also to shape the external policy environment in Vermont.

The Interactive Dialogue Model in Management

A basic premise of the interactive dialogue model is that ambiguity is inherent in the development and use of performance information. The interactive dialogue model also points to the subjectivity of performance information and how this subjectivity increases as advocates represent their interests. The evidence presented thus far suggests the difficulty of fostering productive dialogue because of disagreements and mutual suspicion. We have little evidence of performance being discussed in the legislature or among elected officials. The experience of PART and other performance budgeting initiatives suggests the difficulty of fostering constructive dialogue across institutions designed to check one another. In these settings, agencies have little incentive to participate in dialogue routines other than to defend their record of effectiveness and win resources.

The prospects for solution-seeking dialogue routines should be better within agencies, the venue in which we expect to see management innovations and improvements occur. Agencies are subject to the tensions of political struggles, and their organizational design and strategic goals often reflect compromises between factions with different ideas of what the organization should be doing.[2] However, agencies and their members have characteristics that can help them reduce political tensions in decisions. They are more homogenous than the body politic. They fall under a hierarchy where a leader has authority to direct employees. They are more likely to agree on shared goals. They are more concerned with issues of implementation than other actors in the governance process, focused on the processes that convert inputs to outputs and outcomes and form the black box of management that remains largely opaque to outsiders. Finally, the organizational culture and standard operating procedures shape how members think and act.

Together, these factors help reduce the potential for different perspectives between actors within the same organization. In turn, this reduces the potential for rival and irreconcilable interpretations of performance information to emerge. Because of individual differences and organizational politics, different perspectives will inevitably exist within organizations.[3] But these differences are less pronounced than in dialogue routines that cut across institutional settings. The common bonds within organizations, and basic imperative to cooperate toward shared goals, increase the potential for dialogue routines to generate clear direction for management purposes.

When dialogue no longer bears the weight of institutional interests, there is greater likelihood of fostering consensus or, if not consensus, adopting some decisive course of action. This chapter provides examples of agencies using dialogue to foster organizational changes. In doing so, these agencies created, interpreted, and re-created strategic goals and performance measures. In short, these agencies used dialogue routines to enable learning. Since there exists a well-established literature on organizational learning, I use this theoretical lens and language to increase our understanding of how dialogue can foster performance management.[4]

Performance management doctrine is based on what is essentially a theory of learning. Decision makers are expected to learn from performance information, leading to better-informed decisions and improved government performance. However, performance management doctrine has been relatively weak in identifying routes to learning. The organizational learning literature is helpful in understanding how interactive dialogue fosters performance management in three ways:

- Identifying the types of learning that organizations can engage in
- Identifying different routes towards learning

- Identifying the characteristics of forums where dialogue can foster learning

Each of these benefits is examined in turn, using case evidence from Virginia and Vermont.

Types of Learning through Dialogue Routines

The work done by Chris Argyris and Donald Schön has been instrumental in developing the concept of organizational learning and identifying different types of learning.[5] Single-loop learning is "instrumental learning that leads to improvement in the performance of organizational tasks" and that "changes strategies of actions or assumptions underlying strategies in ways that leave the values of a theory unchanged."[6] In the context of governance, single-loop learning is appropriate for routine, repetitive operations, when public sector goals are clear and widely accepted. In terms of performance management, it implies specifying goals to the point where they are measurable; tracking achievement of goals; and judging these results in the context of a point of comparison, whether it be preset targets, previous performance, the performance of other organizations, or other parts of the same organization. Such comparison prompts a dialogue that analyzes the factors and processes that underpin performance, and how they might be changed. In short, single-loop learning allows organizations to do the same things better.

Double-loop learning is "learning that results in a change in the values of theory-in-use, as well as in its strategies and assumptions. . . . Strategies and assumptions may change concurrently with, or as a consequence of, change in values."[7] Double-loop learning occurs when public actors test and change the basic assumptions that underpin their mission and key policies. It is more relevant for complex, nonprogrammable issues important to the survival of the organization rather than short-term efficiency. Double-loop learning means questioning the goals of a program, asking whether the program is worth pursuing, or if so, whether it should be pursued in the public sector. In the context of performance management, it implies a willingness to revisit the basic organizational mission, goals, and strategies.

Performance management has largely neglected the possibility of double-loop learning. Nathan comments, "the preponderance of attention and literature on managerial oversight in government has focused on rigid numeric goal setting."[8] Single-loop learning appears to be the only type of learning promoted in performance management doctrine recommended to practitioners and realized in mandates: Bureaucrats will figure out ways to achieve organizational goals more efficiently, not challenge these goals.[9] The policymaking aspect of strategic planning is rarely discussed and can be conveniently overlooked if we assume that bureaucrats will use the process only to clarify, not challenge, preexisting goals and that the adoption of new goals will be at the behest of elected officials and stakeholders. Occasionally there is an acknowledgment that data can contribute to double-loop learning, but this is usually in such narrow terms—should government be charged with providing a service, or is it more cheaply provided by another sector?—that it does not appear to be a substantial departure from single-loop learning.

What explains this oversight? To a large degree it reflects the constraints of normative assumptions about decision making in the public sector, that is, the hoary politics/administration dichotomy. As a reform, performance management harkens to the concept of the neutral administrator seeking to most efficiently implement the goals handed down by elected officials. Performance management certainly does not promise to empower bureaucrats with policymaking authority or to question the nature of the goal they pursue.[10] While the dichotomy has suffered many a battering, no reform has ever enhanced its potential for adoption by explicitly rejecting its existence. The widespread success of performance management reforms is due in part to the willingness to reaffirm the dichotomy and overlook how performance management can potentially violate it. Performance management advertises itself as a way in which elected officials can reassert control over administrators by virtue of setting goals in the strategic planning stage and closely overseeing outputs. If double-loop learning is to occur at all, it is the presumed province of elected officials, not bureaucrats.

Structural and Cultural Routes to Learning

The organizational learning literature emphasizes the importance of organizational culture to learning. Learning is based on shared experiences, norms, and understandings that foster intelligent behavior.[11] Characteristics of a learning culture include high employee empowerment, participation, and discretion.[12] Lipshitz, Popper, and Oz criticize the abstract nature of this cultural approach to learning.[13] They argue that learning can be better studied and promoted by undertaking a structural approach, what they call organizational learning mechanisms (OLM): "institutionalized structural and procedural arrangements that allow organizations to systematically collect, analyze, store, disseminate, and use information that is relevant to the effectiveness of the organization."[14] While a cultural approach emphasizes creating shared and functional norms among workers, the structural approach denotes a reliance on formal rules and procedures to enable learning.

A structural approach to learning is attractive to reformers, since structure and procedure are aspects of the organization that can be changed through formal mandates. A structural approach is also consistent with rational—analytic theories of learning that emphasize collecting, storing, and distributing data.[15] It is clear that performance management, as currently implemented, is closer to a structural rather than a cultural approach to learning. The structure comes from legislative and administrative mandates that create formal rules and procedures to generate, collect, and disseminate performance information. These mandates largely ignore the role organizational culture plays in enabling the use of performance data but, as shown in chapter 4, makes sense to elected officials. They are clear and specific reforms that elected officials can adopt to demonstrate that they care about results-based government. In contrast, cultural reform is slow, difficult, hard to observe, and largely shaped at the agency level.

A focus on structure is not the only characteristic shared by OLMs and performance management. Both approaches share the assumption that information forms the basis for improved decision making. Both assume that routines of information collection and dissemination are followed by routines of information use. The weakness of most state performance management systems therefore lies between the point of dissemination of data (which is done well) and use (the ultimate purpose, which is done poorly).

The gap between dissemination and use occurs in part because of an absence of routines where data is examined and interpreted—learning forums. While dialogue routines are any routine where performance information is exchanged, learning forums are dialogue routines specifically focused on solution seeking, where actors collectively examine information, consider its significance, and decide how it will affect action. Such routines are unlikely to occur as an organic reaction to the simple provision of quantitative information. Managers prefer to spend their time interacting with people and collecting oral data, not contemplating quantitative data.[16]

Routines are the critical lever by which behavior can be adjusted in organizations.[17] However, whether and how organizational actors decide to create and participate in routines depends on what they consider appropriate to their organization. This returns us to the issue of culture. Actors will learn if they have the information to learn but also if the organizational culture portrays routines of data consideration as appropriate organizational behavior. Structural approaches that ignore cultural aspects are therefore weakened.

Culture and structure interact in other ways, too. The organizational learning literature sees high employee empowerment, participation, and discretion as conducive to learning. In contrast, punishment-oriented control systems tend to discourage learning and lead to defensive reactions.[18] Centralized structures reinforce past behaviors and make new learning more difficult. The public sector has traditionally relied on centralized controls on behavior, human and financial resources, and decision making. Even with the introduction of new rules and procedures designed to encourage learning, the failure to remove the old rules will thwart change. Individuals need to "unlearn" behaviors before new learning can take place.[19] The ability to unlearn is most at risk when old cognitive frameworks are in contradiction with ways of thinking. Chapter 3 showed that while state governments have enthusiastically implemented strategic planning and performance measurement, they have been much slower to remove central controls on financial and human resources.

Single-Loop Learning in Virginia

The state case studies illustrate the problems and possibility of learning in the context of performance management. As discussed previously, Alabama's performance management process was weakened by lack of resources and support, and there was little evidence that performance management led to any type of useful learning. I therefore discuss Alabama only to the extent that it provides inferences about failure to induce learning, and I focus the analysis on Virginia and Vermont. The characteristics and case outcomes for these two states are summarized in table 9.1.

Does performance management promote single-loop learning at the agency level? All three states had established performance information systems that provided the data necessary for such learning. All three corrections departments had strategic goals and matching performance targets; all reported actual performance on a regular basis. However, there was little evidence that they regularly evaluated this knowledge in the search for improved alternative organizational processes, thereby crystallizing the potential lessons of single-loop learning. A common weakness was the failure to develop regular learning forums among target users of performance data.

The DOC in Virginia provides the strongest example of where learning forums led to single-loop learning. A series of 1996 strategic planning meetings among senior managers used performance information to draw attention to critical organizational issues and to provide a metric by which to judge and compare alternative processes. Staff embarked on benchmarking exercises, creating teams that searched for ideas about ways to deal with these issues from other organizations regarded as national leaders or from their own employees. The experience resulted in changed practices in the critical areas, changes that Virginia DOC managers regarded as successful in terms of cost and performance.

Chapter 5 detailed a number of examples of learning for the purposes of improving capacity in the Virginia DOC, such as cultivating a new generation of organizational leaders, improvements in interorganizational communication, the

Table 9.1   Case characteristics and outcomes

Case outcomes	Virginia	Vermont
Single-loop learning	Occurred in a number of instances and among a variety of organizational actors.	Occurred to a limited degree, but without frequency.
Double-loop learning	Did not occur.	Occurred among agency leadership, who successfully promoted dramatic policy change.
View of performance management	As a management tool to promote and demonstrate performance improvement.	As a "learning metaphor" to understand and communicate policy choices and outcomes.
Learning forums	Used throughout the organization, e.g., benchmarking teams; promoted by performance management requirements but without formal routine or structure; focused on capacity improvements and process change.	Used infrequently by high-level actors on major strategic decisions (strategic visioning) and on an annual basis on programmatic decisions.
Role of culture	Tied performance improvement to creating an employee-centered mission-based culture.	Open and experimental culture among leadership; challenged institutional culture of staff.
Major challenge	Further formalizing performance improvement efforts.	Gaining buy-in from institutional staff on new policy goals.

Source: Adapted from Moynihan, "Goal-Based Learning and the Future of Performance Management."

decision to build an organizational culture that was both employee centered and mission based, and to increase the involvement of employees in strategic planning decisions. At a time when managers are exhorted to focus on outputs, or preferably outcomes, there is a potential for them to overlook improvements that do not immediately improve some measurable aspect of performance. Experienced managers know that capacity links to performance and so solving such problems will increase program outputs and outcomes over time. The importance of such changes should not be discounted, as they are essential for ensuring long-term capacity to perform difficult tasks.

Performance management requirements did promote single-loop learning in Virginia, but these requirements were helped by committed organizational leadership and parallel efforts to build a mission-based organizational culture. Department leadership decided to institutionalize performance management and other organizational improvement techniques through a revitalized management-training program. Managers report that the training helped to reshape the organizational culture by leading to a shared ethos of organizational improvement and a willingness to examine existing procedures to seek more effective ways of doing things. Frequently the change efforts that resulted did not employ rigorous benchmarking of cost and performance data but were based on the logical advantages of a new procedure and the experience and reputation of the source of the innovation. The 125 most senior managers continued to meet annually, sharing stories about organizational successes in achieving strategic goals, and institutional staff reported monthly meetings where performance data is discussed. On an informal basis, employees found time to share ideas, and they reported that suggestions are frequently adopted as organizational standard operating procedures.

Such learning forums foster process change through the dissemination of innovations, taking advantage of the knowledge on the part of the change agent and the audience. Such knowledge is difficult to encode into a purely quantitative benchmarking exercise, which might neglect implicit standards that employees are constantly aware of, such as staff safety. The change agent is likely to have experimented with different options before coming to the one that he or she regards as innovative enough to promote. The recipients also have a knowledge base has that allows them to consider how an innovation fits in their organizational environment.

Double-Loop Learning in Vermont

Despite its relative success, performance management in the Virginia DOC did not induce double-loop learning. The initial round of strategic planning in 1996 did not challenge existing organizational goals and values. Instead, it reinforced traditional values of safety and incarceration while emphasizing the key role of employees. In Vermont, by contrast, the primary benefit of performance management was double-loop learning: questioning the basic outcomes of corrections and persuading the external environment as to the benefits of an alternative approach. How did this come about? In November 1991, shortly after John Gorczyk became commissioner, the Vermont DOC published a twenty-year plan that outlined many of the principles that formed the basis of policy documents, presentations, budget requests, and strategic plans over the following decade.

The principles were the result of a decade of searching for a guiding philosophy within the Vermont DOC. Gorczyk and other senior managers had been involved in this search, which was framed in the context of the previous correction policies in Vermont and the prevailing trend toward a more punitive approach. In the late 1960s and 1970s the Vermont DOC had focused on community treatment, with a minimal emphasis on incarceration and a strong faith in rehabilitation. This approach came under criticism because it ignored the real dangers posed by violent offenders who repeated their behaviors. It also ignored the politics of public safety. During the 1980s and 1990s legislators in Vermont and across the nation reacted to public safety concerns through tougher sentencing, a punitive approach. Department leadership recognized the failings of the purely rehabilitative approach, but corrections research and their own analysis led them to believe that increased incarceration had negative outcomes for the majority of the corrections population and simply cost too much to be a practical long-term policy.

The 1991 plan outlined a series of principles that incorporated elements of both the rehabilitative and the punitive models, as well as some new ideas that became known as restorative justice. Restorative justice provided the Vermont DOC with a coherent philosophy, with its own language, values, and outcomes: victim-based rather than offender-based, restorative rather than retributive or rehabilitative. The concept of restorative justice did not originate in Vermont; variations of the idea were occurring in many places during the 1980s.[20] These ideas appealed to managers in Vermont, but their own learning process also led them to emphasize other elements of the justice system not associated with the restorative justice movement, including the focus on punishing violent offenders and the use of alternative sentencing. Consistent with the interactive dialogue model, members of the Vermont DOC created strategic goals based on an alternative interpretation of existing information, based partly on the background of the actors involved, partly on the information they collected, and partly on the learning forums they developed to process that information.

In searching for an alternative philosophy, the Vermont DOC undertook what it called "market research," surveys and focus groups of the public and individual stakeholders in 1993. The results found opposition to some aspects of existing corrections policy, support for others, and guidance for new ways of thinking about corrections. The market research found that people wanted a criminal justice system that

- increased safety but did not inflict needless harshness or deprivation,
- offered treatment when it was likely to work,
- held offenders accountable for their actions, making them repair the damage they had caused,
- returned value to the victim and community,
- avoided spending money on incarcerating those who offered little threat to society, and
- offered greater opportunity for public involvement in the criminal justice process.

While one part of market research was based on finding out what "customers" wanted, another part was in better categorizing its inputs and outputs. The Vermont DOC began tracking in great detail different aspects of corrections and the wider criminal justice system: crime rates, sentencing, differentiating prisoners by type of crime and individual characteristics. With these findings, the DOC identified a mandate to reshape its own operations and, to the extent possible, the wider criminal justice system. Since the early 1990s the DOC has used this philosophy as the basis for a number of innovative criminal justice programs.

It is too simplistic to suggest that strategic planning and performance measurement were *the* factor that enabled double-loop learning. Clearly, other factors were at work, most prominently the agnostic predisposition of the Vermont DOC leadership toward the traditional and prevailing corrections model, in part because of the social science rather than criminal justice training of many of the senior managers.[21] This culture of openness to new ideas among the leadership led to a willingness (and need, given limited resources) to search for alternative goals and policies. It is not too much, however, to suggest that performance information both shaped the policy outcomes that emerged and allowed the Vermont DOC to convince others of the legitimacy of these outcomes. Commissioner Gorczyk is more assertive than this: "It's [performance management] enabled us to significantly change the nature of the delivery of correctional services in Vermont. Without strategic planning I don't believe in any way we could have gotten there."

Learning Metaphors

What the DOC leaders in Vermont needed was a tool to help them structure their questions, their search for solutions, and ultimately their ability to persuasively communicate these solutions. What they employed were a series of "metaphors," of which performance management was just one.[22] These metaphors provided a means by which the Vermont DOC staff and their stakeholders were offered a credible alternative perspective to challenge the otherwise dominant "mental model" about the corrections function.[23] The credibility of a metaphor comes from being associated with a respected body of knowledge or way of thinking/operating. The insights derived from the use of metaphors are more likely to be accepted by an audience that places a value on the associated body of knowledge. Such insights cannot be classified as simply ideological or radical, the likely reception that the restorative justice philosophy would have received if it had been presented in the absence of a narrative that included the use of metaphors.

The use of metaphors facilitated the questioning of existing technologies and purposes of corrections, and it allowed the Vermont DOC to classify these technologies as ineffective and traditional corrections outcomes as ideological and counterproductive. For instance, a departmental analysis showed that the punitive approach to incarceration, in aggregate, led to reduced public safety, as those who entered institutions were more likely to recidivate than those placed into alternatives to incarceration, even when controlling for the risk profile of prisoners.[24] A manager contrasted this with the previous rehabilitative approach, which was "based on their [previous DOC staff] belief, not science, that prisons were bad and that people could grow and learn if they were instituted in the community and treatment was provided."

Performance management was not the only metaphor used. Business and science were also used in conjunction with performance management. The business metaphor was particularly appropriate for communication purposes during a time when the state was searching for more businesslike ways of government. This metaphor described the criminal justice system as a marketplace, where demand for services was growing without an equivalent increase in resources. By identifying and interviewing the "customers"—the public and corrections stakeholders—of the criminal justice system, the Vermont DOC argued that this demand was artificially created by legislators and did not reflect what customers actually wanted or were willing to pay for. The market research essentially told legislators: "We have talked to the people, and what they want is different from what you are giving them."

The metaphors employed the idea of logical, rational, nonideological judgment of performance based on empirical analysis. Strategic visioning—identifying the mission, vision, and principles of the organization—was used as a forum in which information could be codified into a set of philosophical statements. In these forums, participants make sense of the information derived from the knowledge metaphors and relate it to how the organization should operate and what goals it should pursue. As a process, strategic visioning occurred on a fairly frequent basis in the 1980s and the 1990s, involving senior staff and was the subject of intensive debate. As time passed, consensus developed on high-level strategic goals. The focus of debate became specific programmatic planning and the reporting of goals and performance measures, which occur on an annual basis as part of performance budgeting requirements.

Double-Loop Learning and Policy Shaping

How did the process of double-loop learning lead to new policies? Prompted by the new departmental vision, the Vermont DOC leaders developed a set of new policies that sought to divert nonviolent offenders from incarceration and convinced the political environment to adopt these policies. Departmental analysis found that more punitive sentencing was the primary factor behind the increased inflow of offenders into the criminal justice system.[25] One option to deal with prison overcrowding was to find ways to put offenders back into the community more quickly or to divert them completely from prisons in the first place. The Vermont DOC pursued these options in a number of ways. Probation and furlough jumped dramatically from the early 1990s. In 1994, the DOC created other intermediate and community-based sentencing alternatives to incarceration. These options were more intrusive and expensive than probation, offering less due process for misbehavior, but were less expensive than prison. Intermediate sentencing options have been increasingly relied upon as an alternative to incarceration and as a way of controlling the size of the prison population. Between 1994 and 1999 the population under corrections control expanded from 7,511 to 12,386. During this time the percentage incarcerated stayed relatively steady, dropping from 12.3 percent to 11.6 percent of the total offender population. The percentage of those on probation also dropped from 77 percent to 74 percent. The difference was largely made up through the introduction of intermediate sanctions, accounting for 4.8 percent of the corrections population in 1999.[26]

As new and traditional sentencing alternatives to incarceration reduced the demand for prison beds, the Vermont DOC developed techniques and programs to differentiate the corrections population based on the severity of the crime and potential to reoffend. The Vermont DOC dubbed this a "risk management" approach, where the most expensive service, incarceration, is reserved for offenders who pose the most threat to society. The approach is based on the assumption that it is possible to classify offenders by their threat to society, where threat is calculated by multiplying the severity of offense by the likelihood of reoffending. According to the threat level each offender reaches, there is a logical response for how the offender should be treated by the criminal justice system.

This risk management employs the metaphor of science, portrayed as "the pragmatic judgment of whether the offender can safely reenter society and be a productive citizen without intensive State intervention. The judgment combines both the science of risk assessment and the experience of the corrections professional."[27] The risk-management approach also has the virtue of being cost-efficient, offering a means to safely reduce the expenses of incarceration. The department claims that the development of intermediate sanctions prevented the creation of an additional one thousand bed spaces, which would have cost an additional $21.5 million per year.[28]

Another policy innovation consistent with the restorative justice approach was the introduction of reparative boards in 1994. The program began by targeting low-risk, low-severity offenders who had pleaded guilty and received court sentencing for nonviolent crimes, such as DUIs, petty thefts, or disturbing the peace. Reparative boards are made up of community volunteers appointed by the Vermont DOC. The idea of such involvement fits well with Vermont's tradition of citizen involvement in governing (see appendix B). Board members encourage offenders to accept responsibility for their crimes. Offenders first tell their story, and the boards frequently organize meetings between offenders and victims. Contracts are created where the offender and board members agree on appropriate reparations to the community and victims. Offenders who fulfill their contracts to the satisfaction of the boards are recommended for termination of probation.

Sixty-seven reparative boards operate in dozens of Vermont communities, involving hundreds of citizens. The recidivism rate is lower for offenders in the program than for those on probation for similar offenses, and a portion of those who go before reparative boards would otherwise be incarcerated. In terms of the overall corrections population, reparative boards represent a small, albeit growing fraction. However, the Vermont DOC has devoted a high amount of energy in creating and expanding the boards, viewing them as the most tangible representation of the restorative justice philosophy. The Vermont DOC strategic plan states: "Restorative justice focuses on the restoration of the victim, the repair of the community, and the reintegration of the offender as a productive citizen who has acknowledged responsibility for his offenses, made amends and repaired the damage. The restoration is done by the community, in the community, with the victim as partner."[29]

The success of the original reparative boards enabled the Vermont DOC to extend such policies. A 1999–2000 wave of market research found public support for a subsequent expansion of the program to include all types of violent offenders, particularly sex offenders, who had participated in treatment programs. The research found that the public wanted to be involved in these decisions, but people also wanted the expertise of traditional governmental actors as a support, particularly law enforcement officials and community-based social services. To meet this demand, the Vermont DOC established community restorative justice centers in major towns and restorative programs in smaller communities, and offered training to volunteers. The centers provide a venue for reparative boards, conflict resolution, and neighborhood forums. Neighbors and officials can more easily come together, identify their particular capacity and concerns, and build partnership solutions. For example, a center in Burlington created a program for volunteers to help victims of property crime and vandalism.

Performance Management in Shaping the Organizational Environment

The Vermont case illustrates an organization that has been highly successful in controlling and shaping its external environment. The Vermont DOC enjoyed increased resources as the offender population rose, and it reshaped sentencing and release policies in ways at odds with the stated preferences of elected officials. In arguing for restorative justice, the Vermont DOC developed a standard narrative that pointed to the problems of overcrowding and excess demand on corrections, the causes of this problem, and the benefits of the innovative, pragmatic, and cost-effective options inspired by a restorative justice approach. In making its case the Vermont DOC relied heavily on different aspects of performance management—public surveys, strategic goal-setting, population trends, performance data and targets, and charts—to make these policy preferences appear logical, cost-conscious, pragmatic, and nonideological. A senior manager admitted that "data has allowed us to establish significant credibility with the legislature and . . . have more influence on the overall criminal justice system and its practices than we would have absent that information." The narrative was calculated to demonstrate that the Vermont DOC had thought long and hard about corrections—carefully and rationally investigating its every aspect, relying on facts rather than ideology—and developed solutions with demonstrably positive outcomes.

The Vermont DOC had a high degree of success in convincing the three branches of the state government and the public that a punitive approach to corrections is wrong, that incarceration is largely wasteful and counterproductive for most offenders, and that rehabilitation is sometimes possible and should be pursued. These arguments ran counter to the prevailing criminal justice policy trends in corrections throughout the country and in Vermont itself. Proponents of these arguments have had limited success elsewhere, seen as soft on crime. Corrections officials in Vermont were largely able to avoid this characterization by emphasizing public safety and arguing for increased incarceration for violent offenders.

The Vermont DOC also argued for community involvement to reduce the distance between citizens and the justice system, a move that helped it to build wider and deeper public support for its mission throughout the 1990s. In Vermont, as elsewhere, corrections was an unpopular function. The only groups that cared about it deeply—offenders and their families—were not politically influential. Surveys of the public and particular focus groups provided the basis for building a constituency, by finding out how the Vermont DOC could improve the public perception of corrections. The emphasis on public safety, reparative boards, and the wider restorative justice movement proved popular with Vermont residents. Between 1994 and 1999 surveys that the department administered to the public found the department's approval rating jumped from 37 to 44 percent. In addition, the Vermont DOC built strong support from stakeholders with high political legitimacy, such as victims' groups and a constituency that the department actually created, the members of the reparative boards. A central agency official put it this way:

> At some point the Department of Corrections here in Vermont became very creative. They wanted to be more of a service-delivery type of organization and

provide services. Then the question became, Who we are providing services to? It's an agency that provides services to a number of different customer bases. One of them was the offender. But another one was clearly the victim, across the board. And another one just became the community itself, the families in Vermont. When they started to look at that, they started asking what kind of services can we provide to these different groups and how can we provide those services in such a way that satisfies everyone concerned? . . . And when they got engaged and got a new dialogue out of it, it meant that you had to now start measuring the services to the constituents.

As the Vermont DOC developed new principles and goals, it created performance measures to reflect these changes. Most of the traditional performance measures of corrections—recidivism, escapes, disciplinary infractions—are negative outcomes, that is, outcomes where improved performance means reducing the incidence of the measure. Negative outcomes, by their very nature, do not gain public or elected official attention unless they are moving in the wrong direction. The public does not cheer when zero escapes occur, but people become upset if many prisoners escape. Department officials believed that positive measures would help to convince the public and the legislature of the importance and benefits of corrections, for example, post-incarceration employment, hours, or dollar-value returned to the community.

The support of the public and stakeholders has been critical in winning over elected officials. In 2000, the legislature added the principles of restorative justice to criminal justice policy: "It is the policy of this State that principles of Restorative Justice be included in shaping how the criminal justice system responds to persons charged with or convicted of criminal offenses. The policy goal is a community response to a person's wrongdoing at its earliest onset and a type and intensity of sanction tailored to each instance of wrongdoing" (2000, 28 V.S.A. Sec 2a). This followed a four-year period where a special legislative committee had been created to determine the future of the corrections system. The Vermont DOC targeted the committee, providing it with the standard narrative about corrections and the reasons why the restorative philosophy worked.

The Vermont experience underlines that double-loop learning, whether it occurs among elected officials, political appointees, or bureaucrats, is the divination of dramatic policy alternatives. It is a political act. It requires value judgments. Transforming such learning into a reality requires political skills. The Vermont DOC leaders had such skills, creating a convincing narrative about how traditional correctional policies were failing and the need for alternatives. They cultivated support from stakeholders and the public, and they expanded the traditional corrections constituency.

The Vermont DOC leadership was also fortunate. Their narrative may have been persuasive, but they were lucky in finding elected officials willing to listen and willing to move from the punitive approach. They benefited also from the long-term continuity of a group of reform-minded individuals among senior managers and from Commissioner Gorczyk leading the organization from 1991 to 2001. Continuity allowed the development and promotion of a distinct vision. Such continuity is rare, and it is even more rarely combined with a willingness to engage in dramatic change. Such continuity of leadership is important because of the difficulty in overcoming agreed-upon organizational goals and understandings and because organizational interpretation is shaped by senior-level managers and then transferred to the rest of the organization.[30]

Dialogue in Learning Forums

Designers of performance management systems need to take routines to consider and discuss data as seriously as they do the routines to collect and disseminate data. Without learning forums, performance management is an insufficiently specified structural approach to learning. As an OLM, performance management has been widely, if imperfectly, adopted. Almost all states have similar procedures in place that guarantee the collection and reporting of performance data, but they have struggled to establish new routines that ensure data is carefully evaluated. Even in Virginia, the primary learning forums are a by-product of strategic planning procedures and training, not the conscious effort of organizational design. Strategic planning is an opportunity to contemplate the goals and performance of the past, but it has disadvantages as a learning forum. First, the primary purpose of strategic planning is goal setting, not process change. Strategic planning further limits single-loop learning by frequently excluding lower-level managers whose input can inform process change. Virginia partially overcame these problems by building process-review elements into its departmental strategic planning and by encouraging lower-level strategic planning at the regional and institutional level. Does strategic planning work as a double-loop learning forum? It should, but instances such as Vermont are rare. Even in setting goals, most organizations limit their potential to learn by implicitly or explicitly making any direct challenge to existing organizational goals a taboo and inappropriate action.

The organizational learning literature and the case studies offer insights in terms of what factors move interactive dialogue to learning in management, in terms of the nature of the forum, who is involved, how participants relate to one another, and the role of performance information. These insights are summarized in box 9.1.

Box 9.1   Elements of learning forums

- Routine event.
- Facilitation and ground rules to structure dialogue.
- Nonconfrontational approach to avoid defensive reactions.
- Collegiality among participants.
- Diverse set of organizational actors responsible for producing the outcomes under review.
- Dialogue centered, with dialogue focused on organizational goals.
- Identify, examine, and suspend basic assumptions (especially for double-loop learning).
- Employ quantitative knowledge that identifies success and failure, including goals, targets, outcomes, and points of comparison.
- Employ experiential knowledge of process and work conditions that explain success, failure, and the possibility of innovation.

Source: Adapted from Moynihan, "Goal-Based Learning and the Future of Performance Management."

Learning forums are more likely to succeed if they are an organizational routine rather than an extraordinary event.[31] The key characteristic of such forums will be to exchange dialogue as a precursor to learning. Managers often live in "psychic prisons," limited by norms and habits that lead them to view their organization and its problems from a single frame.[32] Dialogue allows participants to examine their own thinking, look at old problems in new ways by experimenting with multiple frames, and create common meaning. Dialogue gives managers an opportunity to "practice," experimenting with decision styles in a way not feasible in real life. Commitments given in front of peers are taken seriously and usually prove binding.[33]

Senge suggests that the necessary aspects of a successful dialogue include the suspension of assumptions, facilitation that explains and enforces the ground rules for dialogue, active involvement of members, collegiality among participants, and a willingness for members to raise the most pressing organizational issues.[34] These standards are similar to the advice given by argumentation theory on appropriate standards for structuring conversations. In facilitating a critical discussion, all participants must be willing to clearly discuss their viewpoints; willing to accept, on a provisional basis, the presumptions of others; and cooperate with one another in evaluating the relative plausibility of inferences drawn from such presumptions.[35]

Performance data highlights relative success or failure of a unit or process, but only a dialogue can help identify and disseminate the reasons *why* success occurs. Interviewees from Virginia and Vermont noted that a sense of professional pride is at least as strong a motivator as high-level demands for performance. Mintzberg argues that forum participants should be the decision makers that reformers hope will use performance information, and not central planners who produce formal policy evaluations removed from managerial realities.[36] For single-loop learning this means lower-level employees who oversee organizational processes; for double-loop learning it means more senior-level employees who understand the entire organization and its environment. Kaplan and Norton argue that diversity of expertise improves the potential for team learning. They advocate that teams be cross functional and mix senior and operational managers, as Virginia did. This makes sense because it overcomes a classic bureaucratic malady—"those who have the necessary information do not have the power to decide, and those who have the power to decide cannot get the necessary information."[37] Bringing together lower-level managers with senior officials joins operational knowledge with the authority to change processes.

Kaplan and Norton also emphasize linking dialogue to critical organizational goals. Learning is enabled by "a team problem-solving process that analyzes and learns from the performance data and then adapts the strategy to emerging conditions and issues."[38] Such analyses should be open to both quantitative and qualitative evidence, including correlations between process changes and intended outcomes, in-depth management gaming/scenario analysis, anecdotal evidence, interim review of the progress of process changes, and peer review of performance. In both the Virginia and Vermont cases, managers brought different types of information to the table, sometimes quantitative data, but sometimes experiential information or new policy ideas. Dialogue among peers subjected all types of information to questioning and review.

Most organizations struggle to create learning forums because the concept is foreign. The idea of setting aside time to collectively consider performance data appears odd or brings to mind images of pointless office retreats that distract employees from their real work. The characteristics of learning forums are also unfamiliar. Hierarchical structures make some actors more powerful than others and foster a presumption among higher-level officials that they hold superior knowledge to lower-level actors, who must be monitored to avoid shirking. All organizations, except those which are new or in crisis, have little incentive to question the norms and values that ushered them into existence and have accompanied their survival. Setting aside these ways of thinking is remarkably difficult. In the examples from Virginia and Vermont, a great deal of credit rested with the organizational leadership in setting the tone.

The Balance between Accountability and Defensiveness

The literature of organizational learning suggests that confrontational uses of data lead to defensive reactions rather than learning, so an open and nonconfrontational approach among colleagues is preferable to a top-down analysis of failure.[39] Lipshitz, Popper, and Oz point out the benefit of an equal footing for all members of a learning forum.[40] Collegiality not only defuses defensive reactions, but it also encourages the sharing of information about successes. Heinrich cites an example of such learning in North Carolina, where city government officials share financial and performance information on a range of services. They come together to talk about why performance is going well or poorly, and the simple process of discussing performance is motivational and provides information. The cities involved have no authority over one another, so the process is motivated by solution-seeking and characterized by equality among participants.[41]

In the absence of equality among participants, a top-down political pressure to perform may encourage learning. A top-down pressure to perform has been associated with the use of performance data to improve organizational performance both in managed competition initiatives and in the growing "stat" approach to performance management. The original CompStat program for New York police operations has spawned many followers, including the CitiStat program in Baltimore and the PowerTrac approach to policing in Broward County, Florida.[42] CitiStat put real-time information on the performance of a variety of public programs on maps available on the city website. CitiStat has prompted single-loop learning that has led to improved processes and cost reductions.[43] While the quality and sophistication of the CitiStat performance information has drawn attention, this data would have had limited impact without the use of learning forums. Performance data is reported for every two weeks by agencies to the CitiStat team in the Mayor's Office, which enters the information into tables for presentation and onto a map of incidents and activities. Agency and bureau heads meet every two weeks with the mayor, chief of staff, deputy mayor, and cabinet. At the meeting there is discussion of performance, why problems are occurring, and what resources and strategies are needed to improve performance.

Many of the characteristics of learning forums exist in the CitiStat case. There are frequent meetings to discuss performance, wide participation ranging from senior officials to operational staff, a reliance on quantitative measures and experience, and a discussion of the variables that affect performance. But CitiStat and similar approaches vary from the learning forums described above in terms of the unequal footing of participants and the sometimes confrontational approach employed. The meetings create a pressure to perform, tying responsibility to perform on agency heads rather than discovering improvement as a collective experience.

Top-down learning forums such as CitiStat, CompStat, and PowerTrac seek both accountability and problem solving. Agency officials are expected to have answers to tough questions, implying the need for learning to occur within the agency before or after meetings with the mayor, rather than at the meeting itself.

For example, as CompStat meetings became ingrained in the organizational culture, lower levels of the NYPD started to employ "mini-CompStats" to consider crime statistics and strategies. One CompStat participant noted, "It became a trickle-down process of thinking because nobody wanted to be embarrassed at the big show."[44] Similarly, in Baltimore, CitiStat meetings have spawned their own "agencystat" meetings to prepare for the grilling they receive.[45] While the top-level meeting focuses the attention of senior managers, it is through considerations of data and processes at the agency and subagency levels that learning within a unit or agency takes place. The top-level meetings have three particular advantages over agency-level learning forums. First, they offer a forum to diffuse the lessons that have been developed at lower levels. Second, the inclusion of senior elected officials signals that performance is a serious issue and motivates agency heads. Finally, decisions that significantly affect resources, strategies, and policy can be made quickly because the key players are together.

However, much depends on the dedication of senior-level political officials and their willingness to ask management questions. In the absence of political involvement, top-down learning forums such as CitiStat will struggle. In addition, at some point, top-down pressure in the name of accountability will foster defensive reactions, which ultimately weaken a common focus on problem solving and encourage agency staff to circumvent or discredit performance information systems.[46] The existence of performance information does not eliminate information asymmetry, as agency staff still have information advantages about how the information was collected and its meaning. To be successful, therefore, the dialogue must retain a basic level of legitimacy.

If agency staff see learning forums as exercises in political blame assignment rather than solution seeking, they become disillusioned. The tone of the dialogue shifts from solution seeking to strategic advantage, turning learning forums into sessions where different sides seek to present conflicting accounts of the meaning of performance information. PowerTrac struggled when senior officials sought to use the forums to uncover performance problems, preparing prescribed questions and evidence to embarrass agency staff. As the legitimacy of the dialogue declined, middle- and lower-level managers viewed it as acceptable to collude in evading performance management controls. DeHaven-Smith and Jenne warn:

> To the extent that administrative discourse is seen as a game of " gotcha, " it will reinforce rather than expose and dissolve defensive thinking, and the communicative weakness of performance management will be amplified rather than corrected. Hence, it is essential that inquirement processes be carefully structured to facilitate discursive problem solving, discourage heavy-handed questioning, and respect the dignity of all participants.[47]

Another way to raise agency defenses is to tie performance assessments closely to budget rewards. This is a key risk for PART. PART offers multiple opportunities for learning forums. It can prompt agencies that receive PART scores to perform a self-evaluation. It can push Congress to consider program quality. However, the only learning forum that the OMB can actually structure is the interaction between the OMB budget examiner and agency representatives. However, because the OMB has the final say on the PART assessment, and there are potentially large consequences arising from the accompanying budget recommendation, there is little possibility of fostering a sense of equality between participants. As the budget process becomes the backdrop of dialogue routines about performance information, this increases the incentive for managers to lose their sense of purpose and to act strategically. Agencies may feel forced to agree with OMB recommendations because they fear reduced budgets and, in turn, may not truly buy into management recommendations, completing those that are easy or with which they agree, while doing little with the others. They will point to results that paint a positive portrait of their programs while discounting, ignoring, and even manipulating other data.[48] A GAO observer of the PART process warns that "an overly instrumental view of performance can be problematic. Performance information becomes a gun pointed at people's head. The integrity of that information becomes questioned and debated. Performance information is not as useful for budget decisions because of all the interests involved and because of the high stakes of the budget process." The irony is that GPRA, criticized by the OMB for being disconnected from budget decisions, may have been more likely to foster bottom-up learning for that very reason.[49]

An example of this comes from an effort to use PART to analyze overlapping community and economic development programs. These eighteen programs were featured in five different agencies, but the largest was the Community Development Block Grant in Housing and Urban Development. OMB examiners convened a set of interagency meetings in 2004. A number of agencies participated, and the meetings were characterized by a focus on improving shared goals by increasing collaboration, sharing insights from previous experience, suggesting how to make programs more effective, and developing new proposals. In most respects, the meetings were effective interagency learning forums. As senior OMB staff learned about the meetings, they saw an opportunity to do a crosscutting analysis that led to a proposed consolidation of the programs into the Department of Commerce and an overall reduction in resources assigned to the program. Not surprisingly, program staff were upset when they found out about the consolidation plan. Congress ultimately did not support the consolidation plan, but the Community Development Block Grant has seen significant reductions in resources. The interagency meetings stopped, and working relationships between the program staff and OMB examiners became strained. A participant at the meetings noted,

"What incentives do agencies have to participate in these meetings when they see this happening? Crosscuts become code for budget cuts." More broadly, the concept of interagency collaboration became associated with possible consolidation and reductions.

The Inescapable Role of Culture and the Language of Performance

The cases make clear that the success of structural learning procedures is inextricably bound to the culture of the organization. Research on previous reforms designed to foster learning and process change through employee participation, such as strategic management and the Total Quality Management movement, have made this point.[50] The DOC in Alabama sought to implement performance management without changing any other aspect of the organization. As a result, performance management was simply considered a reporting mechanism and not a mechanism to learn. The performance improvement ethic in Virginia found its way to lower-level supervisors in institutions. Because such supervisors considered it a shared norm of expected behavior, they followed the logic of appropriateness established in their culture. In Vermont, the departmental leadership was able to engage in double-loop learning because of a culture of openness and experimentation. However, the department struggled to gain the degree of buy-in among institutional staff that Virginia enjoyed. To a large degree this was because the Vermont DOC undertook a more ambitious task, seeking to challenge the existing goals of the organization and emphasizing nonincarceration programs. Understandably, this was met with some resistance by prison officers, whose daily existence is shaped by the demands of keeping prisoners safely incarcerated.[51] In contrast, Virginia did not seek to change its organizational goals; rather it tried to increase effectiveness toward goals that staff were familiar with and supported.

Another factor limiting the degree of buy-in in Vermont was that the actors involved in the learning forums were senior staff, not prison staff. This helps to further explain the disjunction between the department philosophy and the culture of institutions. Having not undergone the same process of learning, prison staff were less accepting of the philosophy developed by senior managers. Greater emphasis on communication may overcome this issue to some extent, but it cannot replicate the process of learning for the institutional staff.

The ultimate measure of whether performance management is shaping organizational culture is if it shapes dialogue outside of learning forums and in everyday interactions. An example is agency budget preparation and execution. Officials seeking more resources become adept at discussing their needs in the context of performance goals. For instance, a corrections official involved in education programs in Vermont made the following point:

> [What] we're beginning to realize is that with all of these outcome measures, what you count is what you get. They become the central focus of the organization. It is also what you start signaling through your budgeting decisions. Even this morning, for example, a guy called me up and wanted a new piece of equipment for his automotive program. So I said to him, What difference are we going to see in outcomes for this $30,000 investment? We have been engaged in the process long enough that I really don't have to ask the question. They are already coming to me with "if you give us this equipment for the automotive program next September we're going to be able to get so many different more guys, and you will have this many more credits, and you will have this many more students." They have learned the language of how to support their budgets.

Adopting the language of performance is a major achievement for agencies. It requires that agencies move away from a focus on rules and ensures that mission becomes intrinsic to organizational culture and daily interactions. To reach this level of dialogue, managers, budgeteers, and staff in the agency learn how to ask and answer questions, make presentations, write memos, and motivate others in terms of performance. As with any cultural shift, and as demonstrated by case evidence, the leadership of an agency has a critical role in institutionalizing the language of performance.

Conclusion: The Effect of Performance Reporting Mandates

Performance management reforms have been interpreted and implemented without consideration of factors that will enable learning—and therefore more efficient and effective government—to occur. As an OLM, these reforms have failed to structure learning forums that allow for consideration of performance data among its target users. The highly structural bias of these reforms also ignores the role of leadership and the logic of appropriateness in learning. Goal-based learning is likely to occur only when the design of results-based reforms takes these factors into account. Otherwise, performance reporting mandates are likely to lead to little more than compliance, as was the case in Alabama.

The good news is that performance reporting mandates can help learning, if they interact with the right organizational conditions. In Vermont and Virginia, both DOCs enjoyed organizational resources that were used to support performance management with training programs and specialized staff support. Both

DOCs were led by managers who saw performance management mandates as an opportunity to further the organizational agenda they were pursuing. Statewide performance management mandates may therefore aid managers already intent on pursuing change. In Vermont and Virginia, performance management provided a tool to engage in interpretation and disseminate the results.

Learning is possible, and agencies can pursue either single- or double-loop learning. There is a trade-off between the exploration of new possibilities and the exploitation of old certainties. Both types of learning compete for resources and attention. Ultimately, argues March, the long-term capacity of the organization demands a balance between the two approaches: "Adaptiveness requires both exploitation and exploration. A system that specializes in exploitation will discover itself becoming better and better at an increasingly obsolescent technology. A system that specializes in exploration will never realize the advantages of its discovery."[52]

Notes

1. Portions of this chapter previously appeared in Moynihan, "Goal-Based Learning and the Future of Performance Management."

2. Moe, "The Politics of Bureaucratic Structure."

3. Mahler, "Influences of Organizational Culture in Learning in Public Agencies."

4. Argyris points out that the learning literature tends to be divided into two subsets: the learning organization and organizational learning literatures. The learning organization approach emphasizes the adaptability of organizations, has a positive action bias, and is associated with consultants and practitioners. Organizational learning, by contrast, tends to be more academic and theoretical, focusing on barriers to and difficulties of learning. It points out that learning can occur only through individual members of the organization and therefore depends on the limits and weaknesses of human cognition and the potential for coordination. Learning organization writers are prescriptive, assuming the ability of organizations to perform heroic feats of adaptability. The organizational learning approach treats "observed impediments as unalterable facts of organizational life." This chapter attempts to straddle the two literatures, looking at deliberate efforts to foster organizational learning, pointing out its failings and its possibilities. See Argyris, On Organizational Learning, 2nd ed., 14.

5. Argyris and Schön, Organizational Learning.

6. Ibid., 20.

7. Ibid., 21.

8. Nathan, "Presidential Address," 207–15.

9. Barnow, "The Effects of Performance Standards"; Liner et al., Making Results-Based State Government Work, 91–96.

10. Koteen, Strategic Management in Public and Nonprofit Organizations.

11. Senge, The Fifth Discipline.

12. Argyris and Schön, Organizational Learning; Fiol and Lyles, "Organizational Learning."

13. Lipshitz, Popper, and Oz, "Building Learning Organizations."

14. Ibid., 293.

15. Mahler, "Influences of Organizational Culture."

16. Mintzberg, *The Nature of Managerial Work.*

17. Levitt and March, *Organization Theory.*

18. Argyris and Schön, *Organizational Learning.*

19. Hedberg, "How Organizations Learn and Unlearn."

20. Lemley, "Designing Restorative Justice Policy."

21. Simon (1991) observes that organizations themselves do not learn but that learning occurs within organizations via their individual members. Therefore, new organizational learning can occur only if existing members acquire new knowledge or if the organization hires new members with a different variety of knowledge. The latter mechanism was clearly at work in the case of Vermont, and the educational background of its senior managers. See Simon, "Bounded Rationality and Organizational Learning."

22. A senior manager closely involved in the search for knowledge used the term *metaphor.* Describing the "business" approach to corrections, he stopped to emphasize that he viewed business as a metaphor for operating, not as a literal model that the public sector should adopt. It is also worth noting that Lipshitz, Popper, and Oz also use the term *metaphor* to describe the cultural approach to learning. Lipshitz, Popper, and Oz, "Building Learning Organizations."

23. Senge, *The Fifth Discipline.*

24. Vermont Department of Corrections, *Corrections in Vermont,* 21.

25. Ibid.

26. Vermont Department of Corrections, *Facts and Figures FY 1999,* 3.

27. Vermont Department of Corrections, *Corrections in Vermont,* 18.

28. Ibid.

29. Ibid., 44.

30. Weick, *Making Sense of the Organization.*

31. Levitt and March, "Chester I. Barnard and the Intelligence of Learning."

32. Bolman and Deal, *Reframing Organizations.*

33. DeHaven-Smith and Jenne, "Management by Inquiry."

34. Senge, *The Fifth Discipline.*

35. Walton, *Plausible Reasoning in Everyday Conversation.*

36. Mintzberg, "The Fall and Rise of Strategic Planning."

37. Crozier, *The Bureaucratic Phenomenon,* 51.

38. Kaplan and Norton, *The Balanced Scorecard,* 252.

39. Argyris and Schön, *Organizational Learning.*

40. Lipshitz, Popper, and Oz, "Building Learning Organizations."

41. Heinrich, "Measuring Public Sector Performance and Effectiveness."

42. Henderson, "The Baltimore CitiStat Program: Performance and Accountability"; deHaven-Smith and Jenne, "Management by Inquiry."

43. Henderson, "The Baltimore CitiStat Program."

44. Chetkovich, *The NYPD Takes on Crime.*

45. Behn, "The Varieties of CitiStat."

46. DeHaven-Smith and Jenne, "Management by Inquiry," 69.

47. Ibid., 72.

48. Nathan, "Presidential Address," 210.

49. One example of the potential of GPRA for learning comes from the Department of Health and Human Services, where the GPRA process was characterized by a bottom-up dialogue among staff rather than the top-down approach that has characterized both the departmental strategic planning process and the development of PART; see Radin, *The Accountable Juggler.*

50. Nyhan and Marlowe, "Performance Measurement in the Public Sector: Challenges and Opportunities"; Poister and Streib, "Strategic Management in the Public Sector."

51. Shtull, *Assessment of the Vermont Department of Corrections Vision, Mission, and Values, and Principles.*

52. March, *The Pursuit of Organizational Intelligence.*

Rethinking
Performance Management

This evidence presented in this book falls between two traditional perspectives on performance management. The first view is that performance management is an unambiguously good idea with clear benefits. The second is that it has little real impact, engendering little other than compliance as bureaucrats wait for the next wave of reforms. The current approach to performance management in the United States is problematic but fostering some benefits. Efforts to create governmentwide performance information systems certainly have not lived up to the standards of advocates and have done little to change how senior public officials make decisions. On the other hand, agency managers have found ways to make these reforms work in some cases. Ultimately, while there is promise in the future of performance management, its potential will best be achieved if governments rethink what it means, offer realistic expectations rather than hyperbole, and focus on the agency-level factors that induce performance success rather than governmentwide systems.

Another theme to emerge from the previous chapters is the multiple ways in which politics interacts with performance management. There is a politics of performance management adoption, and chapter 4 detailed the importance of symbolism in making reforms valuable. Chapter 7 illustrated how a reform idea, in this case PART, can become perceived as a partisan cause, weakening the potential for bipartisan support that is essential to continuity and influence. There is a politics of implementing reforms, important because it empowers some actors, often at the expense of others. In chapter 5 we saw how agency leaders pursued performance management reform to the extent that it helped their organizational agenda. In chapters 7 and 8 we saw how the OMB created a new type of performance management reform that gave it considerable new influence in terms of defining the meaning of performance. There are the politics of political institutions. At both the state and federal levels legislatures largely declined to use performance information produced by the executive branch, preferring instead to rely on their own judgment, even when

> **Box 10.1**   Ten ways to rethink performance management
>
> 1. Performance information systems are not performance management.
> 2. The symbolic motivations for adopting performance management do not (necessarily) spell doom.
> 3. Performance information is not objective.
> 4. The key challenge for performance management is fostering performance information use.
> 5. Change our expectations about how performance information succeeds.
> 6. Use of performance information occurs mainly at the agency level.
> 7. Build agency-centered systems of performance management.
> 8. Performance management gives agencies a tool to engage in policy change.
> 9. Performance management is less important to performance than many other organizational factors.
> 10. Performance management depends on other organizational factors to succeed.

they were of the same party as the executive branch. There is a politics of program advocacy. Agency staff use performance information to promote arguments in their political environment on the worth of their efforts, most successfully in the case of the Vermont DOC in chapter 9. More fundamentally, there is a basic politics of performance information use. The interactive dialogue model has proposed that the creation, presentation, and use of performance data in the public sphere will reflect the values of those involved, be they partisan, organizational, institutional, ideological, or other.

Throughout this book I have applied a variety of theoretical perspectives, most notably the interactive dialogue model, to actual cases. Based on these findings, an empirical literature on public sector performance, and previous research on performance management, I offer a list of ten ways in which scholars and practitioners might rethink how we approach performance management. It is worth noting that these insights arise from the study of performance management primarily from the federal and state levels, and should be applied only to those levels of government.

Performance Information Systems Are Not Performance Management

Everyone is doing performance management. Just ask them. There is not a state in the union that does not claim to be using performance management, performance budgeting, or both. But what they mean by performance management is different from what one might expect. As evidence of their performance management initiatives, government officials point to documents. Within those documents are lists of requirements, either from the legislature or the central budget office, that agencies produce performance data. These requirements beget more documents: strategic plans, performance plans, performance reports, and performance budgets. And these documents are also cited as evidence that performance management is taking place.

What do these documents amount to? They provide some measure of transparency, which is laudable. They suggest that elected officials are excited about the prospect of results-based reform, while telling us little about their motivations. They also tell us little about management. We can try to plan for better management, but management is ultimately about action rather than documents. We can have formal controls to induce compliance among managers, but such controls do not work terribly well for performance management. The requirements foster compliance in the supply of information, but they cannot force the use of that information.

The use of information cannot be rendered by rules, since it is an action that requires some measure of innovation. Flesh-and-blood managers are the essential ingredient in developing creative solutions to foster process change and performance improvement. Such creative innovation is difficult to observe or at least more difficult than legislative or executive requirements.

We can say with some certainty that an extended period of creating performance reporting requirements has given rise to performance information systems and mounds of data. The cross-state evidence presented in chapter 3 provided evidence that all states are in the business of producing performance information. We have weak and usually anecdotal evidence that the information is being used. The weakest evidence of use comes from the elected officials who asked for the information. In none of the three states studied, or at the federal level, do we see evidence that elected officials are frequent or systematic users of performance information. Their responses are sometimes characterized by indifference—Alabama stopped printing performance information in its budget because it was not worth the bother—and sometimes by hostility—some federal appropriations subcommittees have told the OMB to reduce the emphasis on performance information provided in budget submissions. Performance information systems are essentially badges for performance management, but not the real thing. We know that useful performance information is a precondition for effective performance management, but it is not clear if the current format of performance information systems is in any way predictive of use.

If an agency reports performance information, and nobody uses it, should anyone care? Well, only those who expect that the performance of government is weak and can be improved—most of our citizens and elected officials—and those who are affected by results-based reforms, which encompasses all our public managers.

The Symbolic Motivations for Adopting Performance Management Do Not (Necessarily) Spell Doom

Performance management is a classic good government reform. Once the cause finds a champion in the central budget office, the Governor's Office, or the legislature, its prospects for passage are good. It is hard to be against requirements that promise to make the government more transparent and performance oriented. Support for government reform tends to be a "mile wide and an inch deep."[1] There are not strong political gains to be made with good government reforms, but it does have symbolic value for elected officials who are perceived as battling government waste. With formal requirements, elected officials can point to winning a battle for results-based management, declare victory in the war on government inefficiency, and go home (at least until the war is revisited once a suitable period has elapsed). As long as the reform does not appear to benefit one party over the other and is tailored to avoid offending key constituencies such as public service unions (which care more about employee protections than reporting requirements), it should succeed. The political benefits of performance management were apparent in the state governments studied. Virginia has taken a great deal of pride in being viewed as one of the best managed states in the country. In Alabama, a governor thought—incorrectly—that performance management might help to convince citizens that government could be trusted with their money.

If we resign ourselves to the glum fact that performance management reforms do not arise out of pure intentions, does this mean that the design of these reforms guarantees failure? It is tempting to think so. Performance management requirements create a large reporting burden without consideration of use, and the history of performance management reform is replete with failure. It is natural for cynical reactions generated by the motivations for adoption to shape our evaluation of the potential success of the reform. However, while it is possible to design smarter reforms (see the fifth point on box 10.1), the interest of the political class in performance management is, on balance, a good thing for managers in government who care about such things.

Performance management reforms give motivated managers a license, even if it is largely a rhetorical one, to pursue organizational change and actual performance improvement. Agency managers can blame the burden of reporting requirements on political actors or the central budget office. The external imposition of these requirements can be used to overcome reactionary internal resistance to change. What matters is how managers use these requirements to build internal change. For example, chapter 9 discusses how the DOC in Virginia used a basic requirement for strategic planning to bring staff together, develop benchmarking teams, consider future leadership needs, reshape the organizational culture, and improve communication. Such benefits do not automatically accrue from these require-ments. A similar reform in Alabama led to the production of performance infor-mation and little else. Performance reporting requirements do not, therefore, spell doom for actual performance management. In some cases they can be helpful, but much depends on leadership and other organizational factors.

Performance Information Is Not Objective

The interactive dialogue model advanced in this book argues that performance in-formation is not objective and has characteristics of ambiguity. Chapter 8 pro-vided an illustration of this point based on an experiment where graduate students in public affairs programs assessed OMB PART analyses, and sometimes offered contradictory, though logical assessments. Different actors can take the same piece of performance information and interpret its meaning differently, depending on their individual personality, their understanding of the context of programs, and their institutional affiliation. It is through such actors that performance informa-tion is selected, measured, and presented to the world.

We should put aside notions that performance data is neutral, scientific, or de-finitive, but assume instead that it represents the interests of an advocate seeking to persuade. Such a realization prompts us to ask probing questions rather than ac-cept performance information at face value: Who collected the information? How was it measured? What alternative measures exist? What is the context of per-formance? To some extent this already happens, reflected by both the requirements in some states that agencies provide detailed records of how performance data is created and by the norm in most states that data can be audited by a third party. It is also likely to happen when actors from different institutions engage in a dia-logue and question the interpretations of the other.

Even with the role of auditors, the basic problem for the principal agent remains in performance information creation and diffusion. Agents have an advantage in terms of creating and diffusing the information that reflects their preferences, and they are in the best position to offer credible explanation as to the meaning of the performance data and what it tells us about future action, for example, "performance was lower than expected because we lacked staff at critical points—more resources will remedy this problem." Performance data was selected at the agency level in the three states studied, and the Vermont DOC was particularly adept at using per-formance information to present a narrative to support its policy preferences.

It is not surprising that legislators in many states report skepticism of perfor-mance data produced by agencies. They assume that it reflects the interests of the executive branch rather than what they consider to be a "true" rendering of performance. At the federal level, for similar reasons, Congress and many agency staff have resisted the use of PART information and a stronger performance budget format because of a suspicion that these tools reflect the interests of the OMB and the White House and because of a preference for traditional forms of information Congress is used to. Congress has also shown a tendency, in appropriations bills, to try to exert its own preferences in performance measurement by asking agencies to collect certain types of information on specific programs.

The interactive dialogue model suggests that performance information is not likely to easily solve policy disagreements, especially those that revolve around values. Having performance data about a policy problem often simply adds to the realm of information that different sides can shape for different purposes. In some instances, the performance information may clearly demonstrate that one side is correct. Even when this occurs, we can expect the defeated to reject the performance measures as invalid or inappropriate.

The Key Challenge for Performance Management Is Fostering Performance Information Use

Governments have shown a capacity to construct performance information systems, but the key challenge is ensuring that this information is used by decision makers. The use of performance information means that decision makers consistently take it into account and that the language of performance becomes part of the dialogue of decisions, characterized by a fluency in describing inputs and processes in relation to outputs and outcomes. The clearest evidence of this comes from the three states studied. All three states had performance information systems. But tangible evidence of performance information use could be found only in the Virginia DOC and Vermont DOC. The Alabama DOC had the costs of a performance information system but none of the benefits because the information produced was not being used.

Performance information use remains the basic challenge for performance management because it is the most difficult and important aspect of it. It requires individuals to change their behavior and decision styles by widening the scope of information they consider. This is difficult because decision patterns are usually deeply entrenched in both individuals and institutions. In budgeting, there is a traditional tendency not to consider performance (at least in quantitative terms) and to rely on heuristics such as incrementalism and political priorities to make budget decisions. Among managers, the repetitive nature of public funding and lack of competition creates incentive for little other than following the status quo of operations. Both traditional stances must be changed if performance information is to be used.

This book has portrayed performance information use as an interactive dialogue between interested actors. The actors might not always agree, but the possibility of learning exists. The nature of the dialogue can mirror the basic attributes of a pluralistic system, allowing those who care about an issue a chance to offer their perspectives. As the dialogue contains a greater variety of conflicting interests, this increases the ambiguity and subjectivity of performance information and reduces the prospects of consensus. If there are fewer interests, or little disagreement between interests, this increases the potential for agreement about what performance information means.

Within agencies there should be a relatively low potential for conflict about performance information because of the shared background and goals of the organizational members. Dialogue is perhaps most valuable at this juncture, since it forces members to think about performance data they might otherwise ignore, exchange ideas about what it means, learn new ideas about how to improve performance, and develop a coherent organizational strategy. There is, therefore, a relatively high prospect for goal-based learning within agencies, as shown by the examples in chapter 9. Vermont used learning forums to develop an alternative philosophy of corrections, which gradually reshaped the operations of the corrections department. In Virginia, the department used learning forums to examine basic concerns that had real, though not immediate, consequences for the DOC: agency leadership, training, communication, and an employee-based culture. These issues were not of interest to actors outside the Virginia DOC, and within the department, the agency was able to build consensus on what to do.

What encourages the use of performance information? Surveys of public officials suggest the importance of available resources, the existence of an external demand for information and performance among citizens and interest groups, and a commitment to performance among political and agency leaders.[2] Managers can also increase the chances of learning (a) by encouraging a culture that values learning and (b) by establishing routines where performance information and other data are regularly considered. Learning forums work best when

- they are not confrontational,
- they include a wide array of perspectives from within the organization,
- there is a sense of collegiality among the participants, and
- they employ a range of different types of information, both quantitative and qualitative.

Organizations are not accustomed to slowing down to take time to consider what performance data means, and they may have trouble structuring many of the characteristics of learning forums.

Change Our Expectations about How Performance Management Succeeds

Our expectation for performance management reforms should be that performance information is consistently used in decisions, not that performance information produces a consistent type of decision. Careful proponents of performance budgeting argue that performance data is only one type of information that is relevant to decision makers and that the relationship between performance information and results should not be mechanical. Decision makers can use a variety of rationales for treating performance information, but they may not use these rationales consistently. This creates a perception that performance information is not being used in a systematic way, which risks offending a sense of fair play: "Why is my program cut for poor performance when a program with a similar record received more money?" Such decisions will be deemed political (in a pejorative sense), and if the use of performance data consistently favors one party over another, or attacks particular types of programs, it will lose credibility.

Such decisions should be political. We expect our elected representatives and experts in government to exercise discretion and judgment. The ambiguity of performance information calls for dialogue and engagement, not for demanding that performance information be the only factor in shaping decisions and that it shape decisions in a consistent way. A mechanical link between performance and decisions means that all programs would work like an entitlement with a performance contract. Once a program maintained performance targets, it would continue to receive funding regardless of whether it had fulfilled its purpose or matched the political preferences of our elected officials.

In management we also need to change our expectation of how performance information matters. The standard use of performance information is as a spur and benchmark to prompt innovation in processes, resulting in an increase in some measurable aspect of technical efficiency. However, performance information can be used for a variety of other purposes that improve organizational capacity and ultimately should make a difference to performance, although the causal link is not clear. The case studies of Virginia DOC and Vermont DOC illustrate this point. If we judged simply by the doctrinal expectations of performance management, neither case would have looked terribly impressive. However, performance management helped the Vermont DOC to create an alternative philosophy of corrections and improve external communication, and it helped the Virginia DOC consider leadership planning, improve internal communication, place a new emphasis on training, and change the nature of the organizational culture. For each of these examples, managers considered the changes to be beneficial to the organization and the programs provided, although it would have been difficult to come up with a metric that verified improvements had taken place.

In judging whether performance management makes a difference, we should look for some of these unexpected benefits, relying on the perspective of managers. For researchers, this poses a challenge, requiring carefully constructed case studies that trace the causal effect of performance management, take into account context factors, and rely on the testimony of multiple actors to develop a coherent narrative.

Use of Performance Information Occurs Mainly at the Agency Level

The state case studies in this book showed evidence of performance information being used at the agency level in Vermont and Virginia, and of little use anywhere else. There is a basic logic for why agency-level actors are more likely than others to use performance information. Central budget officials and legislators, even if they specialize in particular functions, usually have a relatively broad degree of oversight, with less time and expertise to consider what the performance information means, develop a narrative around the information, and identify next steps as a result of the data. Agency actors are more specialized and more homogenous, making them more likely to focus on relevant performance information and engage in learning.

Agency actors also have a great deal more at stake. They are in the business of delivering programs, either directly or through third parties. Using performance information for external communication may help (even if only at the margins) to protect programs from criticism and maintain resources. Using performance information to improve performance and organizational capacity strengthens agency programs and helps agency leaders to bring about changes consistent with their vision of the organization. The organizational environment shapes the motivation of agency leaders. In resource-poor Alabama, the leadership focused on limiting the costs of performance reporting requirements that they felt offered little real chance of improving efficiency or a better resource base. In Vermont and Virginia, agencies used similar requirements to foster change, driven by a leadership agenda that was informed by organizational and environmental constraints.

With the PART process, budget examiners from the OMB assess agency performance data and develop management recommendations. This appears to be an exception to the logic that agency-level actors are the natural users of performance information, but closer inspection suggests that the experience is not inconsistent. Many have remarked on the enormous workload this task entails for the OMB, in part because it is essentially the type of detailed management assessment we expect that agency managers themselves should be doing. Agency staff are wary of OMB budget examiners making judgments about their programs and offering budget recommendations. OMB staff speak of the desirability of agencies becoming inculcated with the values of PART. The OMB would turn the work of PART over to agencies if it believed the underlying values of the tool would be maintained. The OMB sees PART as primarily a management activity that is being undertaken by a central agency because agencies have failed to fully exploit performance data under GPRA. In short, PART is an exception to the rule that agency staff are the natural users of performance information and are recognized as such by all involved.

Build Agency-Centered Systems of Performance Management

The benefits of performance management achieved in all three states were concentrated at the agency level, were partly unexpected, and came about when performance management was greeted as an organizational tool rather than a compliance burden. Agency managers can better identify the potential positive uses of performance management for their organizations, and the agency is the most appropriate venue to create learning forums for management purposes. Agency actors consider the costs and benefits of a reform as they consider how to use it. An agency-centered approach to performance management would seek to expand agency benefits, without creating time-consuming statewide performance management systems with little additional marginal utility. An agency-based approach implies voluntary strategic planning and performance measurement at the agency level, allowing managers to discover the main benefits of performance management for their own organization, but with guidance and encouragement provided by central management agencies.

Central agencies are currently attempting to ensure the compliance of agencies to performance information requirements, as well as collect and ensure the validity of vast amounts of information from agencies, with little evidence of positive use. An alternative role for central agencies is to support agency-driven changes to the internal management systems of individual agencies, offering advice, disseminating learning, and providing some form of accreditation to motivate agency implementation or reforms such as performance management.

An agency-centered approach calls for tearing down much of the architecture associated with performance management reforms on the grounds that it lacks adequate instrumental benefits. The agency-centered model suggested is less ostentatious in form, more modest in expectation. Instead of assuming a fundamental shift in governing and the achievement of highly ambitious claims, it seeks simply to provide more information about how government is run, assuming that active agency managers will make better use of this tool than elected officials and central agencies. More concretely, an agency-centered approach would include the following components:

- Reduce emphasis on statewide performance information systems; create performance information for statewide decision making on an "as needs" basis rather than creating books of information that go unread.
- Redefine the role of central agencies so that they no longer seek compliance with reporting mandates, but instead they would develop standards for what a desirable agency performance management system would look like; encourage agencies to adopt these standards; and tailor them to their own situation.
- Encourage the creation of learning forums at the agency level.
- Ask agency leaders to envision what the potential benefits of performance management will be and give agencies control over how information is used.
- Offer positive incentives for performance management, recognizing and distributing success stories; provide formal recognition of high-quality agency performance management systems.
- Use elected officials and senior appointees to lend encouragement, public support, and administrative resources to performance management. A critical resource for every agency would be the creation of a new position focused on promoting the use of performance information, rather than appointing an existing budget person to police performance reporting.

The ultimate goal of such changes is to transfer to agencies the positive possibilities of performance management but avoid the negative pathologies that emerge from creating a sense of compliance. These reforms clearly require a great deal of trust in agencies, the antithesis of the distrust in bureaucracy that has fueled many of the underlying schools of thought behind performance management. It also requires the careful selection of energetic professionals who can define and implement an agency vision.

The greater modesty in expectation reduces, but does not eliminate, the potential political visibility and appeal of performance management as a policy option. However, the benefit of this approach is that it accepts that elected officials are unlikely to fundamentally reform traditional managerial controls. It also seeks to improve the ratio of time and energy spent implementing performance management to its positive benefits by reducing time and energy poured into reporting activities that do not generate any clear benefits. This means that fewer agencies would attempt strategic planning and performance measurement, but those that did would be more likely to use it. If an agency-centered approach were in place in Alabama, it is unlikely the DOC would have bothered to try to build a performance management system. The only real loss here would have been the time and effort lost to hiring consultants and creating and reporting the performance data. The Vermont and Virginia DOC would have been likely to pursue performance management in much the same way that they did.

An agency-centered approach is also consistent with the lessons we have learned from implementation theory, which leads to what Elmore has referred to as a "backward mapping" approach.[3] The logic of backward mapping is to entrust agency-level officials to figure out the best way to implement change management and design a reform around their insights. It is the opposite of the forward-mapping approach currently in place, where policymakers are designing reforms with little reference to the groups that are most affected. An agency-centered approach is also consistent with the insights of the interactive dialogue model, which proposes that dialogue routines across institutional settings will struggle to develop solutions while learning forums within agencies will foster performance information use.

Performance Management Gives Agencies a Tool to Engage in Policy Change

In some instances, agencies engaged in learning may come to the conclusion that the basic goals and underlying policies of an agency are flawed. Evidence of such double-loop learning can be found in Vermont, where over the course of two decades the DOC used strategic planning and performance measurement as a vehicle to develop a new philosophy of corrections, with new policies and new goals. In the private sector, such ambitious learning would be an unambiguous positive as long as it contributed to the bottom line, an example of companies engaged in the art of creative destruction. In the public sector, we are much more circumspect about the idea of double-loop learning on the part of agency staff, even when such staff can present measures to show that alternative policies are better. In a representative democracy, explicit policy change is presumed to be left to elected officials. Reforms such as performance management have never been proposed on the grounds that they will strengthen the policymaking power of bureaucracies. If anything, the opposite is true: Performance management doctrine has promised performance information as a way to control bureaucracies.

It is, therefore, an uncomfortable truth that performance management gives agencies a tool to engage in policy innovation. There are reasons to welcome this truth. First, legislators are less likely to use performance information than agency staff, and so the best hope for evidence-based development of policy within government lies with agency staff. The restorative justice philosophy in Vermont was a response to a failed rehabilitative approach and a nascent punitive approach, neither of which had strong evidentiary backing. However, the punitive approach had political support and would have dominated criminal justice policy without the influence of the DOC. Second, concerns about the loss of democratic control are overstated. Agencies depend on governments for funding tied to specific programs, and they cannot choose to ignore the legislature's instructions. To comprehensively change programs and implement new goals, they need legislative support. To gain this support they need to convince the legislature of the virtues of new ideas. While the budget process can be faulted for its failure to rigorously examine old programs, new areas of spending receive a great deal of attention. In Vermont, agency staff had to develop basic elements of their new philosophy, and some evidence of superior performance, before they could convince the legislature to support restorative justice programs. In doing so, they also built a constituency of supporters, through surveys, meetings, and ultimately coproduction of corrections outcomes. It is fair to say that the two decades that saw the evolution of restorative justice in Vermont saw a measure of greater legislative and public debate about justice than would have been the case if the agency had simply embarked on a more punitive course. While performance management fostered double-loop learning, and gave the Vermont DOC the material to advocate its case, it did not usurp decision-making authority from elected officials.

Performance Management Is Less Important to Performance Than Many Other Organizational Factors

Performance management is based on the premise that the creation of performance information will improve the nature of decisions, which in turn will lead to improved performance. The simple plausibility of the theory explains its appeal. However, the empirical evidence is not terribly convincing. Much of the research on performance management focuses on best-practice research, in other words, finding an agency or government that is doing something that appears new or successful and reporting that innovation. It is understandable that practitioners want to know what new ideas are out there, but best-practice research is by its very nature not reflective of the norm and does not tell us if the same practices will succeed or fail elsewhere. Other research applies survey techniques, but mostly to track the degree of adoption of performance management reform, and it cannot verify if this adoption is in fact fostering performance. Other case-based work, such as the research presented in this book, tries to make this connection by developing plausible links between reforms and

Box 10.2 Characteristics more important than performance management	
• Autonomy	• Worker beliefs
• Agency clientele and stakeholders	• Organizational culture
• Political context	• Leadership
• Nature of function	• Stability
• Resources	• Structure

performance and investigating if these links were achieved. This is useful for theory development and adds a level of pragmatic detail missing from other studies, but as with any case research, generalizability is difficult.

There is a developing empirical literature in public management that seeks to explain performance of different agencies, programs, or policies, primarily by analyzing quantitative datasets, but also through careful case study research. In recent years, this research has been on display in journals, collected volumes, symposiums, and a number of review articles. From these studies emerges a set of recurring factors that are more frequently associated with performance than with performance management reforms.

Autonomy matters for performance in two related ways. First, agencies with more autonomy tend to perform better.[4] Agencies that empower workers and decentralize controls also appear to perform better.[5] The logic for both agency and individual employee autonomy is similar. Those who are actually undertaking the task have the expertise to succeed, whereas external or higher-level oversight tends to create constraints based on goals that are not related to the organization's primary task.[6] Autonomy also allows an agency to best define its tasks and infuse a sense of mission among employees.[7]

Agency clientele affects the actual difficulties posed in making programs a success because of sociodemographic background, location, willingness to receive services, or other factors.[8] Clients also shape the perception of the value of the agency and its programs. Clients who are seen as social, responsible, and deserving enjoy greater political support.[9] Clients may enjoy political influence simply because of the political capacity created by size, organization, and resources. In general, clients with strong political support can help agencies gain autonomy and resources necessary to do their job.[10] There are two exceptions to this rule. Agencies with different sets of clients with conflicting goals are likely to lose goal clarity, while agencies with dominant clients are hostile to the goals of the agencies, as is the case with most regulatory agencies, may be provided with limited resources and autonomy.[11]

Factors such as autonomy and clientele point us more broadly to the concept of *political context*. Agencies with higher levels of political support tend to be higher performers, at least in part because political support translates into resources and autonomy.[12] Rainey and Steinbauer argue that high performers "will have oversight authorities that are supportive, delegative, and attentive to agency mission accomplishment."[13]

The *nature of the function* that agencies face makes some public jobs easier than others. For example, accurately mailing Social Security checks is easier than trying to rehabilitate prisoners. More contentious missions are more difficult to implement.[14] If the actions of employees and the results they produce are clearly observable and clearly related, agencies are more likely to be able to establish standard operating procedures that ensure efficient production.[15] Certain functions also foster task design that provides intrinsic and extrinsic rewards to employees, thereby motivating higher performance.[16]

The availability of *resources* is generally associated with higher performance, although this relationship sometimes varies. In some instances, such as education, it is unclear that more resources foster performance.[17] This tends to be true in situations where resources are quickly added, and managers have little sense of how to use them to improve performance. More resources should in almost all cases increase the outputs of an agency, but an influx may not improve efficiency. However, lack of sufficient resources dooms programs to an inability to provide basic services, as illustrated by the Alabama case. Boyne suggests that the benefits of financial resources are indirect and useful only to the extent that they purchase "real resources" that contribute to performance.[18] Real resources are the actual resources used in providing a service, and for most public services this means people who work at the frontline. The availability of staff, and their quality, have been connected to organizational performance.[19]

The *beliefs* of those who work for public agencies are also related to performance. High levels of professionalism and a strong sense of mission, task, and public service motivation are associated with higher performance.[20] Schick notes that the fundamental difference between the public sector in developed and developing countries is the sense of public service and integrity, which in turn shapes the ability of public organizations to undertake reform.[21] More broadly, *organizational culture* can act as both a barrier and an enabler to performance. Organizations with culture that is based around the mission and that encourage adaptability, risk taking, and entrepreneurship will support performance.[22] Cultures characterized by efficacy, meaningful/engaging work, teamwork, and concern for the public interest are also associated with higher performance.[23]

It is frequently asserted that effective *leadership* matters to performance.[24] However, like the concept of culture, leadership can matter in different ways. Leaders can exert a top-down pressure to perform, holding lower-level actors responsible for fostering effectiveness.[25] New leaders can bring about change by encouraging the adoption of innovation.[26] Effective leadership fosters stability, commitment to mission, effective goal setting, and an ability to manage political stakeholders.[27] Organizations that enjoy a basic measure of *stability* are expected to perform better relative to those that see frequent disruption in areas such as the flow of finances, employee continuity, oversight, goals, and reporting requirements. Meier and O'Toole have built a model of organizational effectiveness around the concept of stability, placing a priority on managerial actions that ensure continuity.[28]

The *structure* of an agency has been taken to mean a variety of things, including ownership, source of funding, degree of autonomy, rules, and constraints as well as the actual design that appears on an organizational chart. Although the understanding of structure varies, it is always used to indicate something that is critical to how the organization operates and how it performs.[29] For instance, O'Toole has urged that understanding how networks deliver services poses a major structural concern for the organizations that direct, or are members of, these networks.[30] Ownership of service provisions (public or private) and the degree of market competition have been found to affect performance, although the empirical evidence is mixed.[31]

All the factors listed in box 10.2 are better established predictors of organizational performance than performance management reforms, enjoying stronger empirical support derived from qualitative and, increasingly, quantitative research. But volume of political support for a reform is not necessarily based on the credibility of underlying evidence. Performance management and its many variants continue to be the reform that managers hear about the most, and it is the reform most likely to be adopted by elected officials. Why performance management and not these other factors listed in box 10.2? Chapter 4 helped to answer this question by pointing to the symbolic appeal and limited costs of performance management. Arguments for agency autonomy are frequent, but they mean a loss of certain types of controls by elected officials and central agencies, a loss that chapter 3 demonstrates they have not reconciled themselves to. The other factors are difficult to legislate (culture, leadership, worker beliefs, the nature of clients and stakeholders) involve significant costs (resources) or go against the grain of legislative behavior (stability, reducing conflict between stakeholders, agency autonomy).

Collectively, the factors listed in box 10.2 have little symbolic appeal, are more difficult to explain than the concept of performance management, and do not suggest the same frustration with perceived bureaucratic failure as does the language of performance management. The one exception is structure, which, like performance management, is a formal requirement that elected officials can pass in an effort to increase effectiveness. While structure is important to how agencies operate, simple structural realignment of bureaus—such as the creation of the Department of Homeland Security—may have little effect on performance, and it is tempting to see structural changes as an effort to foster policy control or demonstrate a symbolic effort to deal with a problem.[32]

Performance Management Depends on Other Organizational Factors to Succeed

Does the empirical literature of performance hold any room for performance management? Although not frequently tested, some aspects of performance management or related behaviors do appear to be positively and significantly related to performance. For instance, firefighters who perceive that they do effective performance assessments are more likely to be effective.[33] Based on a survey of federal employees, Brewer finds that performance management practices are associated with higher perceptions of performance.[34] Clearly defined mission and goals help performance.[35] One the other hand, Wolf finds that agencies with measured indicators of performance have historically been associated with poorer performance, a surprising finding that he explains by pointing to the tendency of organizations to measure goals not related to performance.[36]

However, one of the key points made by this book is that performance management does not succeed by itself; it is dependent on organizational factors. The organizational factors listed in box 10.2 are important to performance in their own right, but they are also important in shaping performance management reforms. Performance management doctrine makes a number of implicit assumptions about the possibility of organizational change, but the ability to successfully bring about performance-driven change will be tied to existing organizational factors.

One of the key interactions is between autonomy and performance management reform. As noted in chapter 2, performance management doctrine includes an assumption that managers will have autonomy to make use of performance data, although legislatures are generally reluctant to provide greater autonomy. There should also be consistency between goals and measures and the structure of responsibility. Otherwise, strategies remain detached from the functional organization of activities and finances.[37] Performance management can help foster clearly defined missions and goals, but goal clarity is more likely to occur in agencies without competing demands from stakeholders and complex functions.[38] Creating a mission-based culture helps performance, but changing a culture is much more difficult than producing performance information, and it depends upon how embedded the existing cultural norms are and whether they run contrary to performance. For example, Jennings and Haist hypothesize that performance measures that are consistent with the organizational culture are more likely to improve performance.[39]

More broadly, political context matters for reform. Chapter 4 identified the political motivations of elected officials to support reforms and how this shaped the nature of the reforms adopted. Political context also matters for the use of reform. Chapter 9 examined how the Vermont DOC used performance management to pursue specific policy goals. The results of the experiment reported in chapter 8 identified how the political context of an organization (in this case a relatively liberal and a conservative policy school) shaped the interpretation of performance information. This finding is consistent with research on the use of performance information in social services, which shows that more conservative regions react to the same performance information in different ways than their more liberal neighbors.[40]

The ability to find valid measurements of major activities depends on the function of the organization, as well as on pressure from stakeholders to measure what they consider to be important.[41] Chapter 5 examined the dependence of performance management efforts on both leadership and resources, which include human resources and the technological ability to collect and distribute reliable information in a timely manner. The actions and goals of DOC leaders in Virginia and Vermont were the key determinant how performance management was used there. A survey of state actors provides support for this finding, showing that performance information is likely to be used to direct agency activities if it is perceived that agency leaders view performance management as important. The same survey also found that senior executive branch decision makers are more likely to use performance information if they believe that the governor perceives performance management to be important.[42]

Organizational stability helps performance management for the same reason it contributes to performance: Managers are better able to implement and gradually improve operational tasks if they are not constantly changed, and creating feasible plans is most likely if the past provides a reliable basis upon which to extrapolate.[43] When managers deal with high levels of unpredictability, ad-hoc reactions rather than careful planning shape their operations. This was plainly demonstrated in the Alabama case, where managers were too busy coping with a constant sense of crisis created by chronic resource inadequacy to be able to operate proactively.

A key point of this book has been that performance management can help the public sector, but its potential for success is uncertain and dependent on numerous other factors. This realization should prompt a more realistic set of expectations about the difficulties involved and more modest expectations for success.

Conclusion

The purpose of this chapter is not to suggest that performance management does not and cannot work. Although much of the book has been critical of performance management, it has sought to offer evidence of where and how performance information might be profitably used. The purpose of the chapter, therefore, is to set realistic expectations. Performance management doctrine often appears to float away from reality, inflated by its value as a political symbol, the beguiling simplicity of theoretical models that exclude most of the realities of management in government, and best-practice stories related with breathless conviction. This is a pity. Government managers will recognize such hyperbole when they see it, especially if they have seen it multiple times, and many may decide to passively comply with the letter of the reforms while ignoring the spirit. Academics can evaluate the reforms and find—no surprise—the same failings they have found for decades. The political champions for performance management quietly move on to something else or lose office to see another would-be reformer make similar promises. The reform is ultimately deemed a failure by insiders and outsiders.

How much better, then, if performance management were based on more realistic expectations, with a clearer map of the difficulties and opportunities in implementation? As a symbol of reform, it would be less potent. As a practical tool for management improvement, it would carry greater credibility. And it would be more likely to succeed, in part because we would have defined success into the realm of the achievable.

Notes

1. Alan "Scotty" Campbell made this remark when discussing support for the Civil Service Reform Act of 1978. See Moynihan, "Protection versus Flexibility."

2. Bourdeaux, "Legislative Influences on Performance-Based Budgeting Reform"; de Lancer Julnes and Holzer, "Promoting the Utilization of Performance Measures in Public Organizations"; Moynihan and Ingraham, "Integrative Leadership in the Public Sector."

3. Elmore, "Backward Mapping."

4. Knott and Payne, "The Impact of State Governance Structures"; Wilson, *Bureaucracy;* Wolf, "A Case Survey of Bureaucratic Effectiveness in U.S. Cabinet Agencies."

5. Donahue, "The Influence of Management on the Cost of Fire Protection"; Moynihan and Pandey, "Testing How Management Matters."

6. Borins, *Innovating with Integrity.*

7. Wilson, *Bureaucracy.* Boyne points to empirical evidence to the contrary; see Boyne, "Sources of Public Improvement." Knott and Payne suggest that measures of performance consistent with agency preferences may be increased under decentralized structures, and central preferences may be furthered through more centralized controls; see Knott and Payne, "The Impact of State Governance Structures."

8. Heinrich and Fournier, "Dimensions of Publicness and Performance in Substance Abuse Treatment Programs"; Donahue, "The Influence of Management on the Cost of Fire Protection."

9. Hargrove and Glidewell, eds., *Impossible Jobs in Public Management.*

10. Meier, *Politics and the Bureaucracy;* Rainey and Steinbauer, "Galloping Elephants."

11. Meier, *Politics and the Bureaucracy.*

12. Moynihan and Pandey, "Testing How Management Matters"; Wolf, "A Case Survey of Bureaucratic Effectiveness."

13. Rainey and Steinbauer, "Galloping Elephants," 14.

14. Wolf, "A Case Survey of Bureaucratic Effectiveness."

15. Wilson, *Bureaucracy.*

16. Rainey and Steinbauer, "Galloping Elephants."

17. Chubb and Moe, *Politics, Markets, and America's Schools.*

18. Boyne, "Sources of Public Improvement."

19. Rainey and Steinbauer, "Galloping Elephants"; Donahue, Selden, and Ingraham, "Measuring Government Management Capacity."

20. Rainey and Steinbauer, "Galloping Elephants."

21. Schick, "Why Most Countries Should Not Try New Zealand's Reforms."

22. Boyne, "Sources of Public Improvement"; Moynihan and Pandey, "Testing How Management Matters"; Rainey and Steinbauer, "Galloping Elephants"; Wolf, "Why Must We Reinvent the Federal Government?"

23. Brewer and Selden, "Why Elephants Gallop"; Brewer, "In the Eye of the Storm."

24. Wolf, "A Case Survey of Bureaucratic Effectiveness"; Brewer and Selden, "Why Elephants Gallop"; Brewer, "In the Eye of the Storm"; Boyne and Dahya find that turnover in leadership reduces organizational performance: "Executive Succession and the Performance of Public Organizations."

25. Andrews and Moynihan, "Reforms Don't Always Have to Work to Succeed"; Henderson, "The Baltimore CitiStat Program."

26. Other paths to innovation identified by Borins were elected officials reacting to a crisis and midlevel and frontline workers tackling an organizational problem; see Borins, *Innovating with Integrity.*

27. Rainey and Steinbauer, "Galloping Elephants"; Wilson, *Bureaucracy.*

28. Meier and O'Toole, "Public Management and Organizational Performance."

29. Lynn, "Public Management."

30. O'Toole, "Treating Networks Seriously."

31. Boyne, "Sources of Public Improvement."

32. Moynihan, "Homeland Security and the U.S. Public Management Policy Agenda."

33. Donahue, "The Influence of Management."

34. Brewer, "In the Eye of the Storm."

35. Chun and Rainey, "Goal Ambiguity and Organizational Performance in U.S. Federal Agencies"; Moynihan and Pandey, "Testing How Management Matters"; Rainey and Steinbauer, "Galloping Elephants."

36. Wolf, "Why Must We Reinvent the Federal Government?"

37. Durant, "The Political Economy of Results-Oriented Management in the 'Neoadministrative State.'"

38. Chun and Rainey, "Goal Ambiguity and Organizational Performance in U.S. Federal Agencies."

39. Jennings and Haist, "Putting Performance Measurement in Context."

40. Fording, Schram, and Soss, "The Bottom-Line, the Business Model, and the Bogey."
41. Jennings and Haist, "Putting Performance Measurement in Context."
42. Moynihan and Ingraham, "Integrative Leadership in the Public Sector."
43. Mintzberg, "The Fall and Rise of Strategic Planning."

Interview Protocol for State Interviews

General Interview Protocol: Note that this protocol was adjusted and reordered depending on the position and expertise of the interviewee, and to fit the unfolding nature of the conversation.

I. Strategic Planning

- Can you describe the strategic planning process?
    Probe: How could it be improved?
- Who is involved?
    Probe: Level of involvement? How are members of the public or stakeholders involved in the strategic planning process?
        If not at all?
        Does consideration of the public affect how strategic goals are set?
- Can you talk about your involvement in the strategic planning process?
- Are strategic goals relevant to your work?
- Do strategic goals link to daily activities?
- Is there a lot of time and resources devoted to strategic planning?
- Who places the most value on the process?
- How well are strategic goals communicated in the DOC?
- Do you think most of your colleagues are aware of the strategic goals of the organization? Do you think your colleagues see the process as important?
- What do you think have been the main benefits of strategic planning?
- Do strategic goals link to measures?
- Do measures inform strategic planning, or are strategic goals set with little consideration of measures?

II. Performance Measures

- Is there a high awareness of the performance measures in the DOC?
- How do you get access to performance measures?

- Are up-to-date measures easily available?
- Are measures relevant (seen as important to mission)?
- What do you think have been the main benefits of performance measures?
- How could performance measurement be improved?
    Probe: Accuracy? Availability? Relevance?
- Do you think you have enough time to consider measures?
- Is there any group in the organization or government that is more enthusiastic about the use of measures?
- Do you perceive pressure to demonstrate you have used measures? Does this encourage you to actually use them?
- Are targets taken seriously?
- Is it worth the trouble of collecting/tracking measures in improving performance?
- Can you talk about your involvement in choosing performance measures?
    Probe: Is your level of involvement adequate? Prefer more?
- Do you think strategic goals/performance measures would look substantially different if the process gave you greater say over strategic goals/performance measures?
- Do you think performance measures are a pretty good reflection of the main issues in Corrections?
    Probe: Are there issues that are overlooked?
- How are performance measures used?
    Probe: How do you use them? Can you give me a recent example of how you used them or how they affected a decision?
    Examples of other uses?
- How do performance measures contribute to the following:
    Performance improvement—decisions directly focused on increasing administrative performance, for example, benchmarking, performance targets, process reengineering?
    Internal contracting—performance contracts between public employees and their organization?
    External contracting—performance contracts between the public organization and external service providers?
    Incentives/sanctions?
    Monitoring employees?
    Monitoring program performance?
    Motivating employees?
- Would decisions be made in the same way in the absence of measures?
- What are the most important factors in making decisions?
- Do you have any incentives to use measures?

- Are there some decisions in which you are less likely to use performance measures?

    Probe: What about setting policy—what is the role of performance measures there?
- If you have a fair degree of autonomy over decisions, will you usually take into account strategic goals or performance measures?
- Do other members of the state government find strategic planning or performance measurement useful?

    Probe: Who finds it useful? What do they do with this information?

III. Culture Questions

- Could you describe to me the general organizational environment here? Are there certain adjectives or metaphors that come to mind when someone asks you to describe where you work?
- What is the overall philosophy that underpins the type of corrections provided at this organization?
- When you started to work here, what was the most memorable event that happened to teach you "how things are done around here"?
- What is a typical interaction with your supervisor?

    Probe: Is this similar to other people's interactions with your supervisor?
- How do you think people you work with in your office perceive strategic planning efforts? Performance measurement? How do they respond when these reforms are implemented?

Appendix B

State Backgrounds—
Political Culture, Budgeting Practices,
Performance Management History,
and Corrections Policies

Alabama

Alabama's strongly conservative political culture is characterized by limited government and citizen suspicion of government generally. Democrats dominated the state until the 1960s, largely because of the political alignment of southern states against Republicans after the Civil War and Reconstruction. Since the 1960s, the state has generally sided with Republican candidates in congressional and presidential elections, although the first Republican governor was not elected until 1986. More than any single politician or even political party, the single most critical factor to understanding governance in Alabama is its state constitution.

Adopted in 1901, Alabama claims the oldest operating state constitution, and perhaps the most unwieldy. Given the frequency of amendment—over seven hundred times—it is not surprising that the constitution is long, complex, and difficult to understand, containing contradictory statements that engender conflict and litigation.[1] There are a number of ways that the state constitution has operated as a straitjacket on state government efficacy.[2] First, the constitution allows six executive branch department heads to be elected, weakening gubernatorial control and fostering executive branch conflict. Second, the governor's veto power is somewhat unclear and weaker than in other states, since a simple majority of the legislature can override a veto. In addition, the governor cannot veto any spending bills that are passed in the last five days of legislative session. This creates an incentive to delay spending bills until the very end of session, to the point that the legislative clock is often stopped before midnight on the last day of session to enable negotiations to continue. The contents of the negotiated bills are usually poorly understood because of the last-minute nature of the legislation.[3] A 1982 constitutional amendment tried to make appropriations the "paramount duty" of the legislature by preventing the passage of nonappropriations bills before appropriations bills unless these bills have the support of 60 percent of the legislature. This amendment did little to change the timing of appropriations bills. It simply made it harder to pass nonappropriations legislation. Third, many of the items usually found in statute—most notably aspects of the revenue system, including tax rates and earmarks—are contained in the constitution.

Most states earmark some portions of taxes to specific areas of spending, usually when there is a logical connection between tax and service, such as motor fuels tax and tolls for highway maintenance. While other states earmark about an average of one-quarter of revenues, Alabama earmarks almost 90 percent, mostly toward education. Earmarks have a number of negative affects on policy and administration. First, earmarks make it more difficult for new policy initiatives to be adopted, since it is unlikely that they can be funded. This limits the state's ability to respond to evolving policy needs.[4] Second, it reduces policy competition across departments, limiting the ability of elected officials to prioritize one area of spending over another. This in turn weakens the incentive to examine the efficacy of spending for programs that have guaranteed flows of resources. Third, legislators have exploited the predictable but nonspecific nature of earmarks for pork, a practice known as the "pass-through." Legislators will often specify that spending earmarked for a particular department be spent on the legislator's priorities, which may have no connection to the particular department the project has passed through. Finally, earmarks weaken the budget capacity of some departments but not others. In particular, departments that are unpopular, or have no obvious connection to a specific fee or tax, will spend their time fighting for a tiny portion of the budget, regardless of their needs. This is certainly true of corrections, and it helps to explain why budgeted resources in the state have not kept pace with incarceration rates.

Given the conservative nature of the state and the growing political competition of Republican candidates, it is not surprising that Alabama embraced the adoption of punitive sentencing since the early 1980s, leading to a dramatic growth in prisoners.[5] The state has one of the highest incarceration rates in the country, leading to significant overcrowding and a dangerously low number of corrections staff per prisoner.

The state tax system has many regressive characteristics—it has the lowest individual income threshold for taxation among the states, and it relies on sales taxes for more than half of state revenue.[6] The reliance on sales tax is necessary because of the reluctance to tax property. The state has the lowest property liability in the country, a policy that reflects the political influence of large landowners, such as timber interests.[7] The tax code is complex, with a high number of exemptions, and the determination to attract new employers has resulted in generous tax breaks for corporations.

The state desperately needs more money and discretion in spending to counter continuing poverty, poor educational rates, and low spending per capita. Many of the details of the revenue system, including tax rates, are specified in the state constitution, and so changing the system requires a constitutional amendment and referendum. The most recent effort to change the revenue system in the constitution was overwhelmingly rejected in 2003, despite a $675 million state deficit and the urgings of the Republican governor, Bob Riley. The proposed changes would have closed many tax loopholes, increased the income tax threshold for tax payments, increased property taxes, and other provisions that would have made the system more progressive. The governor's efforts were met with a well-organized coalition of conservatives, businesses, and landowners who argued that the change was effectively a tax increase. Their message succeeded because of a preexisting popular sentiment that the state is overtaxed. This is partly because of the dependency on more obvious consumption taxes and the regressive nature of the tax.[8] Another problem is the "popular distrust of politicians at allocating money" and the perception that the state does not use the money effectively.[9]

In Alabama the adoption of performance management efforts has been closely tied to constitutional reform efforts. This book detailed the failed efforts of Governor Siegelman to use performance management to change negative public perceptions about state government as a prelude to changing the constitution. His successor, Governor Riley, tried to change the constitution first and then ordered the creation of a performance budgeting system to prove the worth of state government. Governor Fob James (1979–83) also tried unsuccessfully to amend the constitution and introduced performance budgeting.

This faith in performance management seems unrealistic. The problems of the revenue system are plain enough. Successive governors have failed to convince voters that such a system needs to be changed and that such a change would benefit them in terms of a more progressive tax system and better state services. Why expect that the same voters will start to read state performance reports or log on to the state website to download performance data and come to change opinions on government effectiveness? The state faces a catch-22 situation. The constitution forms both an institutional straitjacket on effective government and a barrier to change. To really improve performance requires changing the constitution, but to change the constitution requires a more favorable perception of state effectiveness. Given this logic, it is understandable why different governors have put their hope in performance management: They have little else to turn to.

Vermont

Vermont is the opposite image of Alabama and Virginia in many respects. In the latter half of the twentieth century Vermont moved from being strongly Republican to a competitive, though liberal-leaning one.[10] The state consistently supported Republican presidential candidates until the early 1960s. This was New England Republicanism, reflecting the antislavery stance of the GOP since the Civil War. Vermont elected its first non-Republican governor in over one hundred years in 1962. Democrats won a Senate seat for the first time in 1972, and they shared control of the legislature in the late 1970s and 1980s. Successful Republicans must be moderates to be competitive in the state. The growing influx of out-of-staters is another measure of change since the 1960s, and it has had a direct impact on state politics. From 1965 to 2006 only one native Vermonter has been elected governor. By 1995 fewer than half of the legislators were native Vermonters.[11]

The state is one of the most liberal in the country. It has relatively high taxes, with a strongly progressive taxation system. Because of the state's size, much of what would otherwise be local functions (for example, county prisons) are state responsibilities, and an unusually high proportion of revenue is collected by the state relative to the local level. Consistent with the Republican tradition of the state, governors try to maintain fiscal discipline, even though the state is not constitutionally required to balance its budgets. Vermont's record on performance budgeting records might be fairly recorded as mixed. In the 1960s the state experimented with PPBS, but to no lasting effect, and the production of performance information has been at the behest of the legislature rather than the governor.[12]

To understand Vermont's current approach to corrections, it is helpful to look at its past, which reflects the state's progressive politics. The DOC boasts of being one of the first states to institute prisons in place of corporal punishment, and Vermont pioneered probations.[13] In the 1960s, the DOC pursued a community approach to corrections, which placed a good deal of emphasis on placing offenders in nonprison settings. These policies continued in the 1970s, when there was strong political consensus "that prisons made criminals worse; that the roots of crime lay in poverty; that rehabilitation of the community went hand-in-hand with rehabilitation of the offender, who was a victim of the ills of society; and that the rehabilitation of both would take place together."[14] By 1973, only one hundred offenders were incarcerated.

A number of factors led to policy changes in corrections. First, new studies raised doubts on the efficacy of rehabilitation. Second, the state population, and especially the number of young males, grew dramatically, increasing the potential criminal population. Thirty-seven violent crimes were reported in 1960, and 914 in 1980.[15] Third, a number of serious crimes—some by parolees—received dramatic media coverage. Finally, crime became a national concern in the 1980s, leading to a trend toward more punitive sentencing. Vermont was not exempt from this trend; the legislature passed twenty crime bills that reflected a more punitive approach. At the same time, the DOC sought to maintain alternatives to incarceration, experimenting with a new form of classification that examined the offenders' propensity to reoffend and providing work camps for offenders, and later, developing reparative boards.

The new restorative justice approach was to some degree an extension of the community approach—it assumed that the community was central in reducing recidivism and that the community should have an even greater say on what happened to the offender. The new approach was also a reaction to the changing political context. The Vermont version of restorative justice acknowledged that some people were violent and likely to reoffend. While prison probably would not rehabilitate those people, it was a suitable solution in the name of offender punishment and community protection. As a result, the DOC came to terms with housing a much larger inmate population. The restorative justice approach therefore married a traditional response with changing political trends, but it did so in the context of a coherent philosophy while adding new policy ideas, such as reparative boards.

Vermont is one of those New England states that elicit images of a democracy enriched by town-hall meetings. The image is not so far from the truth. *Governing* notes: "One thing Vermont does consistently well is solicit public input. Legislators can hardly pick up a six-pack at the grocery store without hearing suggestions from a constituent. But unlike some other small states—which seem to count almost exclusively on this kind of personal contact—Vermont actively solicits citizen opinion."[16] The DOC in the state found a variety of ways to assess opinions, using surveys, focus groups, and directly involving citizens in reparative boards. In this respect, they drew on a tradition of citizen involvement.

Virginia

The comparison between Virginia and Alabama points to the limitations of using general measures of political culture and spending, and the importance of management. Virginia is as conservative as Alabama, and it also spends little on government. But it is regarded as one of the best managed states in the country. The Government Performance Project has consistently ranked Virginia as a top performer.

Like other southern states, Virginia was a post–Civil War Democratic stronghold, with a conservative voting public. Democrats dominated politics until the 1960s, and since 1968 Virginia has voted Republican in presidential elections, and Republicans became the majority of the state's congressional delegation. The first Republican governor of the twentieth century was elected in 1970, and Republicans controlled both the governorship and legislature from 1994 to 2002. Although the last two governors, Mark Warner and Tim Kaine, are Democrats, they have taken moderate policy positions.

Virginia's constitution allows only single-term governors, and its legislature meets for only forty-six to sixty days a year, with the possibility of a thirty-day session extension. As a result, the state has had to build and rely on exceptional administrative capacity, especially in its central agencies. Central agencies were instrumental in promoting performance management in the state of Virginia. The Department of Planning and Budget (DPB) was created in 1976 to combine planning and budget efforts, and it provides exceptional expertise in performance management. In the legislative branch the Joint Legislative Audit and Review Commission (J-LARC) and the Auditor of Public Accounts provide legislators with an effective mechanism for overseeing executive branch performance. In the 1970s and the 1980s there was a strong emphasis on evaluation, and a management by objectives framework had been experimented with, where agencies developed six-year strategic plans. This effort collapsed given the requirements involved and the lack of attention to the information.

In 1991, following a J-LARC report on the budget process, the legislature included language in the Appropriation Act calling for performance measures for new programs and some pilots. In 1992 the DPB, at the behest of the General Assembly, undertook a pilot study of performance measures. The DPB followed up in 1994 with a report: "Strategic Planning and Performance Proposal for the Commonwealth of Virginia," which called for an integrated performance management process. In 1995 Governor Allen's Executive Memorandum 3–95 established goal setting and performance budgeting as part of agencies' budget process. The memo was the forerunner to the current performance budgeting requirements now in statute.

The importance of administrative expertise has cultivated an ethos of prudent and professional management. While Virginia does not spend a great deal of money on government, it seeks to provide good services. The culture of responsible fiscal discipline was demonstrated in recent years. In the late 1990s, Governor Jim Gilmore cut the unpopular car tax on the basis of increased revenues, much of which was made up by a one-off tobacco settlement. As the economy turned sour and revenues dried up, the state faced a fiscal crisis. Members of the Republican legislature showed pragmatism in 2004 when they agreed to balance the state budget through a mixture of budget cuts and tax increases, including a significant increase on the state's relatively low tobacco taxes. The incident demonstrated the state's commitment to fiscal discipline, pragmatism, and a willingness to listen to long-term revenue and expenditure projections that showed the need for new revenue streams. As a result, the state was able to maintain its triple-A bond rating.

The culture of professional management also extends to corrections. Virginia, like most states, passed punitive sentencing laws, and the prison population grew dramatically in the 1980s and 1990s. In the mid-1990s the state adopted truth-in-sentencing policies and abolished parole, with the goal of ensuring that offenders, especially violent felons, served the vast majority of their sentence. However, the state was also willing to build new prison space to house the influx of inmates and has been a net importer of prisoners from states such as New Jersey, Connecticut, and Vermont, which use Virginia to alleviate their overcrowding problems. At the same time, the state has also been willing to adopt policies from states such as Vermont by providing lower-risk offenders with alternative sanctions.

Notes

1. Martin, *Alabama's State & Local Governments,* 3rd ed.
2. Moodey, "Alabama's Dysfunctional State Government."
3. Martin, *Alabama's State & Local Governments.*
4. Moodey, "Alabama's Dysfunctional State Government," 93.
5. Martin, *Alabama's State & Local Governments.*
6. Barrett et al., "The Way We Tax."
7. Thomas and Stewart, *Alabama Government and Politics.*
8. Ibid.
9. Martin, *Alabama's State & Local Governments,* 248.
10. Graff, "Parties and Politics."
11. Ibid.
12. Crisman, "Budgeting and Spending."
13. Perry, "Corrections."
14. Ibid., 278.
15. Ibid.
16. Barrett et al., "The Way We Tax."

Program Assessment Rating Tool

I. Program Purpose and Design

1.1: Is the program purpose clear?

1.2: Does the program address a specific and existing problem, interest, or need?

1.3: Is the program designed so that it is not redundant or duplicative of any other federal, state, local, or private effort?

1.4: Is the program design free of major flaws that would limit the program's effectiveness or efficiency?

1.5: Is the program design effectively targeted so that resources will address the program's purpose directly and will reach intended beneficiaries?

II. Strategic Planning

2.1: Does the program have a limited number of specific long-term performance measures that focus on outcomes and meaningfully reflect the purpose of the program?

2.2: Does the program have ambitious targets and timeframes for its long-term measures?

2.3: Does the program have a limited number of specific annual performance measures that can demonstrate progress toward achieving the program's long-term goals?

2.4: Does the program have baselines and ambitious targets for its annual measures?

2.5: Do all partners (including grantees, subgrantees, contractors, cost-sharing partners, and other government partners) commit to and work toward the annual and/or long-term goals of the program?

2.6: Are independent evaluations of sufficient scope and quality conducted on a regular basis or as needed to support program improvements and evaluate effectiveness and relevance to the problem, interest, or need?

2.7: Are budget requests explicitly tied to accomplishment of the annual and long-term performance goals, and are the resource needs presented in a complete and transparent manner in the program's budget?

2.8: Has the program taken meaningful steps to correct its strategic planning deficiencies?

Specific Strategic Planning Questions by Program Type

2.RG1: Are all regulations issued by the program/agency necessary to meet the stated goals of the program, and do all regulations clearly indicate how the rules contribute to achievement of the goals? (Regulatory)

2.CA1: Has the agency/program conducted a recent, meaningful, credible analysis of alternatives that includes trade-offs between cost, schedule, risk, and performance goals, and has it used the results to guide the resulting activity? (Capital Assets and Service Acquisition)

2.RD1: If applicable, does the program assess and compare the potential benefits of efforts within the program and (if relevant) to other efforts in other programs that have similar goals? (R&D)

2.RD2: Does the program use a prioritization process to guide budget requests and funding decisions? (R&D)

III. Program Management

3.1: Does the agency regularly collect timely and credible performance information, including information from key program partners, and use it to manage the program and improve performance?

3.2: Are federal managers and program partners (including grantees, subgrantees, contractors, cost-sharing partners, and other government partners) held accountable for cost, schedule, and performance results?

3.3: Are funds (federal and partners') obligated in a timely manner, spent for the intended purpose, and accurately reported?

3.4: Does the program have procedures (e.g., competitive sourcing/cost comparisons, IT improvements, appropriate incentives) to measure and achieve efficiencies and cost-effectiveness in program execution?

3.5: Does the program collaborate and coordinate effectively with related programs?

3.6: Does the program use strong financial management practices?

3.7: Has the program taken meaningful steps to address its management deficiencies?

Specific Program Management Questions by Program Type

3.CO1: Are grants awarded based on a clear competitive process that includes a qualified assessment of merit? (Competitive Grants)

3.CO2: Does the program have oversight practices that provide sufficient knowledge of grantee activities? (Competitive Grants)

3.CO3: Does the program collect grantee performance data on an annual basis and make it available to the public in a transparent and meaningful manner? (Competitive Grants)

3.BF1: Does the program have oversight practices that provide sufficient knowledge of grantee activities? (Block/Formula Grant)

3.BF2: Does the program collect grantee performance data on an annual basis and make it available to the public in a transparent and meaningful manner? (Block/Formula Grant)

3.RG1: Did the program seek and take into account the views of all affected parties (e.g., consumers; large and small businesses; state, local, and tribal governments; beneficiaries; and the general public) when developing significant regulations? (Regulatory)

3.RG2: Did the program prepare adequate regulatory impact analyses if required by Executive Order 12866, regulatory flexibility analyses if required by the Regulatory Flexibility Act and SBREFA, and cost–benefit analyses if required under the Unfunded Mandates Reform Act; and did those analyses comply with OMB guidelines? (Regulatory)

3.RG3: Does the program systematically review its current regulations to ensure consistency among all regulations in accomplishing program goals? (Regulatory)

3.RG4: Are the regulations designed to achieve program goals, to the extent practicable, by maximizing the net benefits of its regulatory activity? (Regulatory)

3.CA1: Is the program managed by maintaining clearly defined deliverables, capability/performance characteristics, and appropriate, credible cost and schedule goals? (Capital Assets and Service Acquisition)

3.CR1: Is the program managed on an ongoing basis to ensure credit quality remains sound, collections and disbursements are timely, and reporting requirements are fulfilled? (Credit)

3.CR2: Do the program's credit models adequately provide reliable, consistent, accurate, and transparent estimates of costs and the risk to the government? (Credit)

3.RD1: For R&D programs other than competitive grants programs, does the program allocate funds and use management processes that maintain program quality? (R&D)

IV. Program Results/Accountability

4.1: Has the program demonstrated adequate progress in achieving its long-term performance goals?

4.2: Does the program (including program partners) achieve its annual performance goals?

4.3: Does the program demonstrate improved efficiencies or cost-effectiveness in achieving program goals each year?

4.4: Does the performance of this program compare favorably to other programs, including government, private, etc., with similar purpose and goals?

4.5: Do independent evaluations of sufficient scope and quality indicate that the program is effective and achieving results?

Specific Results Questions by Program Type

4.RG1: Were programmatic goals (and benefits) achieved at the least incremental societal cost, and did the program maximize net benefits? (Regulatory)

4.CA1: Were program goals achieved within budgeted costs and established schedules? (Capital Assets and Service Acquisition)

Questions taken from a 2006 OMB document, *Guide to Assessing the Program Assessment Rating Tool,* available at www.whitehouse.gov/omb/part/fy2006/2006 _guidance_final.pdf.

Bibliography

Ammons, David. "A Proper Mentality for Benchmarking." *Public Administration Review* 59, no. 2 (1999): 105–9.

———. "Raising the Performance Bar Locally." *Public Management* 79, no. 9 (1997): 10–16.

Anders, Kathleen. "Performance Measures as Strategic Management Tools: An Alternative View of the Latest Reform." Paper presented at the annual meeting of the Academy of Management Association, Atlanta, August 11–16, 2006.

Andrews, Matthew, and Donald P. Moynihan. "Why Reforms Don't Always Have to Work to Succeed: A Tale of Two Managed Competition Initiatives." *Public Performance and Management Review* 25, no. 3 (2002): 282–97.

Ansoff, H. Igor, Roger Pierre Declerck, and Robert L. Hayes, eds. *From Strategic Planning to Strategic Management.* London: John Wiley, 1976.

Argyris, Chris. *On Organizational Learning,* 2nd ed. Malden, MA: Blackwell Publishers Ltd., 1999.

Argyris, Chris, and Donald Schön. *Organizational Learning: A Theory of Action Perspective,* 2nd ed. Reading, MA: Addison Wesley, 1996.

Aristigueta, Maria. *Managing for Results in State Government.* Westport, CT: Connecticut, 1999.

Ban, Carolyn. *How Do Public Managers Manage? Bureaucratic Constraints, Organizational Culture, and the Potential for Reform.* San Francisco: Jossey-Bass, 1995.

Barnow, Burt S. "The Effects of Performance Standards on State and Local Programs." In *Evaluating Welfare and Training Programs,* edited by Charles F. Manski and Irwin Garfinkel, 277–309. Cambridge, MA.: Harvard University Press, 1999.

Barrett, Katherine, Richard Green, Michele Mariani, and Anya Sostek, "The Way We Tax: A 50 State Report." *Governing,* February 2003. www.*governing.com/gpp/2003/gp3intro.htm* (accessed July 10, 2006).

Barrett, Katherine, Richard Green, Zach Patton, and J. Michael Keeling, "Grading the States '05: The Year of Living Dangerously," *Governing,* February 2005. Available at www. governing.com/gpp/2005/intro.htm (accessed July 10, 2006).

Barzelay, Michael. "How to Argue about the New Public Management." *International Public Management Journal* 2, no. 2 (1999): 183–217.

———. *The New Public Management: Improving Research and Policy Dialogue.* Berkeley: University of California Press, 2001.

Baumgartner, Frank R., and Byran D. Jones. *Agendas and Instability in American Politics.* Chicago: University of Chicago Press, 1993.

Behn, Bob. "The Varieties of CitiStat," *Public Administration Review* 66, no. 3 (2006): 332–41.

225

Berry, Frances S. "Innovation in Public Management: The Adoption of Strategic Planning." *Public Administration Review* 54, no. 4 (1994): 322–30.

Berry, Frances S., Ralph S. Brower, and Geraldo Flowers. "Implementing Performance Accountability in Florida: What Changed, What Mattered, and What Resulted?" *Public Productivity and Management Review* 23, no. 3 (2000): 338–58.

Blalock, Ann B., and Burt S. Barnow. "Is the New Obsession with Performance Management Masking the Truth about Social Programs?" In *Quicker, Better, Cheaper?: Managing Performance in American Government,* edited by Dall Forsythe, 485–517. Albany, NY: The Rockefeller Institute, 2001.

Bolman, Lee G., and Terrence E. Deal. *Reframing Organizations: Artistry, Choice, and Leadership.* San Francisco, CA: Jossey-Bass, 1991.

Borins, Sanford. *Innovating with Integrity: How Local Heroes Are Transforming American Government.* Washington, DC: Georgetown University Press, 1998.

Bossidy, Larry, and Ram Charan with Charles Burck. *Execution: The Discipline of Getting Things Done.* New York: Crown Business, 2002.

Bouckaert, Geert. "Measurement and Meaningful Management." *Public Productivity and Management Review* 17, no. 1 (1993): 31–43.

Bourdeaux, Carolyn. "Do Legislatures Matter in Budgetary Reform?" *Public Budgeting & Finance* 26, no. 1 (2006): 126–42.

———. *Legislative Influences on Performance-Based Budgeting Reform.* A Fiscal Research Center Report no. 128. Atlanta: Young School, Georgia State University, 2006. Available at http://frc.gsu.edu/frpreports/report128/Rpt128.pdf.

Boyne, George A. "Sources of Public Improvement: A Critical Review and Research Agenda." *Journal of Public Administration Research and Theory* 13, no. 3 (2003): 367–94.

Boyne, George A., and Jay Dahya. "Executive Succession and the Performance of Public Organizations." *Public Administration* 80, no. 1 (2002): 179–200.

Bozeman, Barry, and Patrick Scott. "Laboratory Experiments in Public Policy and Management." *Journal of Public Administration Research and Theory* 2, no. 3 (1992): 293–313.

Brass, Clinton. "The Bush Administration's Program Assessment Rating Tool." Washington, DC: Congressional Research Service, 2004.

Bretschneider, Stu, Jeffery Straussman, and Dan Mullins. "Do Revenue Forecasts Influence Budget Setting? A Small Group Experiment." *Policy Sciences* 21, no. 2 (1988): 305–25.

Brewer, Gene A. "In the Eye of the Storm: Frontline Supervisors and Federal Agency Performance." *Journal of Public Administration Research and Theory* 15, no. 4 (2005): 505–27.

Brewer, Gene A., and Hu Li. "Implementation of Performance Budgeting in the States: The Impact of Management and Organizational Capacity." Paper presented at the 2005 annual meeting of the American Political Science Association, Washington, DC, September 1–4.

Brewer, Gene A., and Sally C. Selden. "Why Elephants Gallop: Assessing and Predicting Organizational Performance in Federal Agencies." *Journal of Public Administration Research and Theory* 10, no. 4 (2000): 685–712.

Bridge, Gavin, and Phil McManus. "Sticks and Stones: Environmental Narratives and Discursive Regulation in the Forestry and Mining Sectors." *Antipode* 31, no. 4 (2000): 10–47.

Bridgman, Todd, and David Barry. "Regulation Is Evil: An Application of Narrative Policy Analysis to Regulatory Debate in New Zealand." *Policy Sciences* 35, no. 2 (2002): 141–61.

Brodkin, Evelyn Z. "Policy Politics: If We Can't Govern, Can We Manage?" *Political Science Quarterly* 102, no. 4 (1987): 571–87.

Brudney, Jeffery L., Brendan Burke, Chung-Lae Cho, and Deil Wright. "Reassessing the Reform Decade: Conceptualizing and Explaining Administrative Reform across American State Agencies in the 1990s." Paper presented at the annual meeting of the American Political Science Association, Marriott, Loews Philadelphia, and the Pennsylvania Convention Center, Philadelphia, PA, August 31–September 3, 2006.

Brudney, Jeffrey L., F. Ted Hebert, and Deil S. Wright. "Reinventing Government in the American States: Measuring and Explaining Administrative Reform." *Public Administration Review* 59, no. 1 (1999): 19–30.

Brunnson, Nils. *The Organization of Hypocrisy: Talk, Decisions, and Action in Organizations.* New York: John Wiley, 1989.

Burke, Brendan, Chun-Lae Cho, Jeffery L. Brudney, and Deil S. Wright. "No 'One Best Way' to Manage Change: Understanding Administrative Reform in Its Managerial, Policy, and Political Contexts across the Fifty American States." Paper presented at the Eighth Public Management Research Conference, University of Southern California, CA, September 29–October 1, 2005.

Callahan, Kathe, Melvin J. Dubnick, and Dorothy Olshfski. "War Narratives: Framing Our Understanding of the War on Terror." *Public Administration Review* 66 (2006): 544–68.

Camp, Robert C. *Benchmarking: The Search for Industry Best Practices That Lead to Superior Performance.* Milwaukee, WI: ASQC Quality Press, 1989.

Carlin, Tyrone M., and James Guthrie. "Accrual Output–Based Budgeting Systems in Australia: The Rhetoric–Reality Gap." *Public Management Review* 5, no. 2 (2003): 145–62.

Chetkovich, Carol A. *The NYPD Takes on Crime in New York City (B): CompStat,* Kennedy School Case Study, 2000.

Chubb, John E., and Terry Moe. *Politics, Markets, and America's Schools.* Washington, DC: Brookings Institution, 1990.

Chun, Young Han, and Hal Rainey. "Goal Ambiguity and Organizational Performance in U.S. Federal Agencies." *Journal of Public Administration Research and Theory* 15, no. 4 (2005): 529–57.

Cothran, Dan A. "Entrepreneurial Budgeting: An Emerging Reform?" *Public Administration Review* 53, no. 5 (1993): 445–54.

Coursey, David H. "Information Credibility and Choosing Policy Alternatives: An Experimental Test of Cognitive-Response Theory." *Journal of Public Administration Research and Theory* 2, no. 3 (1992): 315–31.

Crisman, Ronald. "Budgeting and Spending." In *Vermont State Government Since 1965,* edited by Michael Sherman, 173–86. Burlington: University of Vermont Press, 1999.

Crozier, Michael. *The Bureaucratic Phenomenon.* Chicago: Chicago University Press, 1964.

Daniels, Mitch. *Program Performance Assessments for the FY 2004 Budget, Memorandum for Heads of Executive Departments and Agencies.* Available at www.whitehouse.gov/omb/budintegration/part_guidance_letter_agencies.doc, 2002 (accessed March 13, 2006).

deHaven-Smith, Lance, and Kenneth C. Jenne. "Management by Inquiry: A Discursive Accountability System for Large Organizations." *Public Administration Review* 66 (2006): 64–76.

de Lancer Julnes, Patria, and Marc Holzer. "Promoting the Utilization of Performance Measures in Public Organizations: An Empirical Study of Factors Affecting Adoption and Implementation." *Public Administration Review* 61, no. 6 (2001): 693–708.

deLeon, Peter. "The Missing Link Revisited: Contemporary Implementation Research." *Policy Studies Review* 16, no. 3 (1999): 311–38.

Delli Carpini, Michael. X., and Scott Keeter. *What Americans Know about Politics and Why It Matters.* New Haven, CT: Yale University Press, 1996.

Denhardt, Robert B. "Strategic Planning in State and Local Government." *State and Local Government Review* 17, no. 1 (1985): 174–79.

DeYoung, Karen. "Iraq War's Statistics Prove Fleeting." *Washington Post,* March 19, 2007, A1.

DiIulio, John, Jr. *Governing Prisons.* New York: Free Press, 1987.

———. "Managing a Barbed-Wire Bureaucracy: The Impossible Job of Corrections Commissioner." In *Impossible Jobs in Public Management,* edited by Edwin C. Hargrove and John C. Glidewell, 49–71. Lawrence: University Press of Kansas, 1990.

DiMaggio, Paul J., and Woody W. Powell. "The Iron Cage Revisited: Institutional Isomorphism and Collective Rationality in Organizational Fields." *American Sociological Review* 48, no. 4 (1983): 147–60.

Donahue, Amy K. "The Influence of Management on the Cost of Fire Protection." *Journal of Policy Analysis and Management* 23, no. 1 (2004): 71–92.

Donahue, Amy K., Sally C. Selden, and Patricia W. Ingraham. "Measuring Government Management Capacity: A Comparative Analysis of Human Resources Management Systems." *Journal of Public Administration and Research Theory* 10, no. 2 (2000): 381–411.

Downs, George W., and Patrick D. Larkey. *The Search for Government Efficiency.* New York: Random House, 1986.

Dull, Matthew. *The Politics of Results: Comprehensive Reform and Institutional Choice.* PhD diss., University of Wisconsin–Madison, 2006.

Durant, Robert. "The Political Economy of Results-Oriented Management in the 'Neoadministrative State': Lessons from the MCDHHS Experience." *American Review of Public Administration* 29, no. 4 (1999): 307–31.

Edelman, Murray. *The Symbolic Uses of Politics.* Chicago: University of Illinois Press, 1964.

Edwards, David, and John Clayton Thomas. "Developing a Municipal Performance-Measurement System: Reflections on the Atlanta Dashboard." *Public Administration Review* 65, no. 3 (2005): 369–76.

Elmore, Richard F. "Backward Mapping: Implementation Research and Policy Decisions." *Political Science Quarterly* 94, no. 4 (1979): 601–16.

Feldman, Martha S. *Order Without Design: Information Production and Policy Making.* Palo Alto, CA: Stanford University Press, 1989.

Fiol, Marlene C., and Marjorie A. Lyles. "Organizational Learning." *Academy of Management Review* 10, no. 4 (1985): 803–13.

Firestone, David. "Packed Alabama Jail Draws Ire of Court Again." *New York Times,* May 1, 2006, A1.

Fischer, Frank, and John Forrester, eds. *The Argumentative Turn in Policy Analysis and Planning*. London: University College Press, 1993.

Flood, Christopher. *Political Myth: A Theoretical Introduction*. New York: Routledge, 1996.

Fording, Richard, Sanford Schram, and Joe Soss. "The Bottom-Line, the Business Model, and the Bogey: Performance Management, Sanctions, and the Brave New World of Welfare-to-Work in Florida." Paper prepared for delivery at the Annual Meeting of the American Political Science Association, Philadelphia, PA, August 31–September 3, 2006.

Forrester, John P., and Guy B. Adams. "Budgetary Reform through Organizational Learning: Toward an Organizational Theory of Budgeting." *Administration and Society* 28, no. 4 (1997): 466–88.

Franklin, Aimee L. "An Examination of Bureaucratic Reactions to Institutional Controls." *Public Performance and Management Review* 24, no. 1 (2000): 8–21.

Frederickson, David G., and H. George Frederickson. *Measuring the Performance of the Hollow State*. Washington, DC: Georgetown University Press, 2006.

Gawthrop, Louis C. *Public Sector Management: Systems and Ethics*. Bloomington: Indiana University Press, 1984.

Gilmour, John B. *Implementing OMB's Program Assessment Rating Tool (PART): Meeting the Challenges of Integrating Budget and Performance*. Washington, DC: IBM Center for the Business of Government, 2006.

Gilmour, John B., and David E. Lewis. "Does Performance Budgeting Work? An Examination of OMB's PART Scores." *Public Administration Review* 66, no. 5 (2006): 742–52.

———. "Assessing Performance Budgeting at the OMB: The Influence of Politics, Performance, and Program Size." *Journal of Public Administration Research and Theory* 16, no. 2 (2006): 169–86.

Goodsell, Charles T. *The Case for Bureaucracy: A Public Administration Polemic*. Chatham, NJ: Chatham House, 1994.

Gormley, William T., Jr., and David L. Weimer. *Organizational Report Cards*. Cambridge, MA: Harvard University Press, 1999.

Governmental Accounting Standards Board. *State and Local Government Case Studies and the Effects of Using Performance Measures for Budgeting, Managing, and Reporting*. Available at www.seagov.org/, 2000 (accessed March 12, 2000).

Graff, Christopher. "Parties and Politics." In *Vermont State Government Since 1965*, edited by Michael Sherman, 273–96. Burlington: The University of Vermont Press, 1999.

Grant, David, Cynthia Hardy, Cliff Oswick, and Linda Putnam, eds. *The Sage Handbook of Organizational Discourse*. London: Sage Publications, 2004.

Gregory, Robert, and Zsuzsanna Lonti. "'Never Mind the Quality, Feel the Width': Performance Measurement and Policy Advice in New Zealand Government Departments." Paper presented at A Performing Public Sector: The Second Transatlantic Dialogue, Katholieke Universiteit Leuven, June 1–3, 2006.

Grizzle, Gloria. "Does Budget Format Really Govern the Actions of Budgetmakers?" *Public Budgeting and Finance* 6, no. 1 (1986): 60–70.

———. "Linking Performance to Decisions: What Is the Budgeter's Role?" *Public Productivity and Management Review* 41, no. 1 (1987): 33–44.

Gruber, Ameila. "The Big Squeeze," *Government Executive* 37, no. 2 (February 1, 2005). Available at www.govexec.com/features/0205–01/0205–01s2.htm (accessed August 12, 2006).

Gruening, Genod. "Origin and Theoretical Basis of New Public Management." *International Public Management Journal* 4, no. 1 (2001): 1–25.

Hardy, Cynthia, and Nelson Philips. "Discourse and Power." In *The Sage Handbook of Organizational Discourse,* edited by David Grant, Cynthia Hardy, Cliff Oswick, and Linda Putnam, 299–316. London: Sage Publications, 2004.

Hargrove, Edwin C., and John G. Glidewell, eds. *Impossible Jobs in Public Management.* Lawrence: University Press of Kansas, 1990.

Hatry, Harry. *Performance Measurement: Getting Results.* Washington, DC: Urban Institute, 1999.

———. *Comments of the Members of the Performance Advisory Council,* 2003, 8. Available at www.whitehouse.gov/omb/budintegration/pmac_030303comments.pdf.

Hedberg, Bo. "How Organizations Learn and Unlearn." In *Handbook of Organizational Design,* edited by Paul C. Nystrom and William H. Starbuck, 8–27. London: Oxford University Press, 1981.

Heinrich, Carolyn J. "Do Government Bureaucrats Make Effective Use of Performance Management Information?" *Journal of Public Administration Research and Theory* 9, no. 3 (1999): 363–93.

———. "Organizational Form and Performance: An Empirical Investigation of Nonprofit and For-Profit Job-Training Service Providers." *Journal of Policy Analysis and Management* 19, no. 2 (2000): 233–61.

———. "Measuring Public Sector Performance and Effectiveness." In *Handbook of Public Administration,* edited by B. Guy Peters and Jon Pierre, 25–37. London: Sage Publications, 2003.

Heinrich, Carolyn J., and Elizabeth Fournier. "Dimensions of Publicness and Performance in Substance Abuse Treatment Programs." *Journal of Policy Analysis and Management* 23, no. 1 (2004): 49–70.

Henderson, Lenneal J. "The Baltimore CitiStat Program: Performance and Accountability." In *Managing for Results 2005,* edited by John Kamensky and Albert Morales, 465–98. Lanham, MD: Rowman and Littlefield, 2005.

Hongren, Charles T., Gary Sundem, and William O. Stratton. *Introduction to Management Accounting,* 10th ed. London: Prentice-Hall International, 1996.

Hood, Christopher. "Gaming in Targetworld: The Targets Approach to Managing Public Services." *Public Administration Review* 66 (2006): 515–21.

Hood, Christopher, and Michael Jackson. *Administrative Argument.* Aldershot, Hants, UK: Dartmouth, 1991.

———. "Key for Locks in Administrative Argument." *Administration and Society* 25, no. 4 (1994): 467–88.

Hou, Yilin, Sally C. Selden, Patricia W. Ingraham, and Stuart I. Bretschneider. "Decentralization of Human Resource Management: Driving Forces and Implications." *Review of Public Personnel Administration* 20, no. 4 (2000): 9–23.

Howard, S. Kenneth. "State Budgeting." In *The Book of States 1980–1981*. Lexington, KY: Council of State Governments, 1981.

Hughes, Adam, OMB Watch. *Testimony to the Senate Homeland Security and Government Affairs Subcommittee on Federal Financial Management, Government Information, and International Security*, June 16, 2006.

Ingraham, Patricia W. "Of Pigs in Pokes and Policy Diffusion: Another Look at Pay-for-Performance." *Public Administration Review* 53, no. 4 (1993): 348–56.

Ingraham, Patricia W., ed. *In Pursuit of Performance: Management Systems in State and Local Government*. Baltimore: Johns Hopkins University Press, 2007.

Ingraham, Patricia W., and Donald P. Moynihan. "Evolving Dimensions of Performance from the CSRA to the Present." In *The Future of Merit: Twenty Years after the Civil Service Reform Act*, edited by James P. Pfiffner and Douglas A. Brooks, 103–26. Baltimore, MD: Johns Hopkins University Press, 2000.

————. "Beyond Measurement: Managing for Results in State Government." In *Quicker, Better, Cheaper?: Managing Performance in American Government*, edited by Dall Forsythe, 309–34. Albany, NY: Rockefeller Institute Press, 2001.

Ingraham, Patricia W., Jessica E. Sowa, and Donald P. Moynihan. "Public Sector Integrative Leadership: Linking Leadership to Performance in Public Organizations." In *The Art of Governance: Analyzing Management and Administration*, edited by Patricia W. Ingraham and Laurence E. Lynn Jr., 152–70. Washington, DC: Georgetown University Press, 2005.

Jacobs, Rowena, Maria Goddard, and Peter C. Smith. "Public Services: Are Composite Measures a Robust Reflection of Performance in the Public Sector?" CHE Research Paper 16, Centre for Health Economics: University of York, June 2006.

Jennings, Edward T., Jr., and Meg Patrick Haist. "Putting Performance Measurement in Context." In *The Art of Governance: Analyzing Management and Administration*, edited by Patricia W. Ingraham and Laurence E. Lynn Jr., 173–94. Washington, DC: Georgetown University Press, 2005.

Johnson, Clay. Testimony before the Subcommittee on Government Efficiency and Financial Management of the Committee on Government Reform. *The President's Management Agenda: Are Agencies Getting to Green?* 108th Congress, 2nd session, Feb. 11, 2004, serial no. 108–55. Washington, DC: Government Printing Office, 2004.

Joyce, Philip J. *Linking Performance and Budgeting: Opportunities in the Federal Budgeting Process*. Washington, DC: IBM Center of the Business of Government, 2003.

Joyce, Philip G., and Susan S. Tompkins. "Using Performance Information for Budgeting: Clarifying the Framework and Investigating Recent State Experience." In *Meeting the Challenges of Performance-Oriented Government*, edited by Kathryn Newcomer, Cheryl Broom Jennings, and Allen Lomax, 61–96. Washington, DC: American Society for Public Administration, 2002.

Kaplan, Robert S., and David P. Norton. *The Balanced Scorecard: Translating Strategy into Action*. Boston, MA: Harvard Business School Press, 1996.

Katz, Daniel, and Robert L. Kahn. *The Social Psychology of Organizations*. New York: Wiley, 1966.

Keating, Michael, and Malcolm Holmes. "Australia's Budgetary and Financial Management Reforms." *Governance* 3, no. 2 (1990): 168–85.

Kellough, J. Edward, and Haoran Lu. "The Paradox of Merit Pay in the Public Sector: Persistence of a Problematic Procedure." *Review of Public Personnel Administration* 13, no. 2 (1993): 45–64.

Kellough, Ed, and Sally C. Selden. "The Reinvention of Public Personnel Administration: An Analysis of the Diffusion of Personnel Management Reforms in the States." *Public Administration Review* 63, no. 2 (2003): 165–76.

Key, V. O. "The Lack of a Budgetary Theory." *American Political Science Review* 34, no. 6 (1940): 1137–44.

Kingdon, John. *Agenda, Alternatives, and Public Policies.* Boston: Little, Brown & Company, 1984.

Knott, Jack H., and A. Abigail Payne. "The Impact of State Governance Structures on Management and Performance of Public Organizations: A Study of Higher Education Institutions." *Journal of Policy Analysis and Management* 23, no. 1 (2004): 13–30.

Koteen, Jack. *Strategic Management in Public and Nonprofit Organizations: Thinking and Acting Strategically on Public Concerns.* New York: Praeger, 1989.

Lauth, Thomas P. "Zero-Based Budgeting in Georgia State Government: Myth and Reality." *Public Administration Review* 38, no. 5 (1978): 420–30.

———. "Budgeting and Productivity in State Government: Not Integrated But Friendly." *Public Productivity and Management Review* 41, no. 2 (1987): 21–32.

Lemley, Eileen C. "Designing Restorative Justice Policy: An Analytical Perspective." *Criminal Justice Policy Review* 12, no. 1 (2001): 43–65.

Levitt, Barbara, and James G. March. "Chester I. Barnard and the Intelligence of Learning." In *Organization Theory: From Chester Barnard to the Present and Beyond,* edited by Oliver E. Williamson, 11–37. New York: Oxford University Press, 1988.

Liner, Blaine, Harry Hatry, Elisa Vinson, Ryan Allen, Pat Dusenbery, Scott Byrant, and Ron Snell. *Making Results-Based State Government Work.* Washington, DC: Urban Institute, 2001.

Lipshitz, Raanan, Micha Popper, and Sasson Oz. "Building Learning Organizations: The Design and Implementation of Organizational Learning Mechanisms." *Journal of Applied Behavioral Science* 32, no. 3 (1996): 292–305.

Lynn, Laurence E., Jr. "Public Management." In *Handbook of Public Administration,* edited by Jon Pierre and B. Guy Peters, 14–24. Thousand Oaks, CA: Sage Publications, 2003.

Macintosh, Norman B. *Management Accounting and Control Systems: An Organizational and Behavioral Approach.* Chichester, UK: Wiley, 1994.

Mahler, Julianne. "Influences of Organizational Culture in Learning in Public Agencies." *Journal of Public Administration Research and Theory* 7, no. 4 (1997): 519–40.

Majone, Giandomenico. *Evidence, Argument, and Persuasion in the Policy Process.* New Haven, CT: Yale University Press, 1989.

March, James G. "Ambiguity and Accounting: The Elusive Link between Information and Decision Making." *Accounting, Organizations, and Society* 12, no. 2 (1987): 153–68.

———. *The Pursuit of Organizational Intelligence.* Malden, MA: Blackwell Publishers, 1999.

March, James G., and Johan P. Olsen. *Ambiguity and Choice in Organizations.* Bergen, Norway: Universitetsforlaget, 1976.

———. "Organizing Political Life: What Administrative Reform Tells Us about Government." *American Political Science Review* 77, no. 2 (1983): 281–96.

———. *Rediscovering Institutions.* New York: Free Press, 1989.

Martin, Bernard H., Joseph T. Wholey, and Roy T. Meyers. "The New Equation at the OMB: M+B=RMO." *Public Budgeting and Finance* 15, no. 4 (1995): 86–96.

Martin, David L. *Alabama's State & Local Governments,* 3rd ed. Tuscaloosa: University of Alabama Press, 1994.

Mazmanian, Daniel A., and Paul A. Sabatier. *Implementation and Public Policy.* New York: University Press of America, 1989.

McCubbins, Mathew D., and Thomas Schwartz. "Congressional Oversight Overlooked: Police Patrol versus Fire Alarms." *American Journal of Political Science* 28, no. 1 (1984): 165–79.

Meier, Kenneth J. *Politics and the Bureaucracy: Policymaking in the Fourth Branch of Government,* 4th ed. Fort Worth: Harcourt, 2000.

Meier, Kenneth J., and Laurence J. O'Toole Jr. "Public Management and Organizational Performance: The Impact of Managerial Quality." *Journal of Policy Analysis and Management* 21, no. 4 (2002): 543–629.

Melkers, Julia E., and Katherine G. Willoughby. "The State of the States: Performance-Based Budgeting Requirements in 47 out of 50." *Public Administration Review* 58, no. 1 (1998): 66–73.

———. "Budgeters' Views of State Performance—Budgeting Systems: Distinctions across Branches." *Public Administration Review* 61, no. 1 (2001): 54–64.

———. *Staying the Course: The Use of Performance Measurement in State Government.* Washington, DC: IBM Center for the Business of Government, 2004.

———. "T Models of Performance-Measurement Use in Local Governments: Understanding Budgeting, Communication, and Lasting Effects." *Public Administration Review* 65 (2005): 180–90.

Miller, Gerald J., Jack Rabin, and W. Bartley Hilldreth. "Strategy, Values, and Productivity." *Public Productivity and Management Review* 43, no. 3 (1987): 81–96.

Mintzberg, Henry. *The Nature of Managerial Work.* New York: Harpercollins, 1975.

———. "The Pitfalls of Strategic Planning." *California Management Review* 36, no. 1 (1993): 32–48.

———. "The Fall and Rise of Strategic Planning." *Harvard Business Review* 72, no. 1 (1994): 107–14.

Moe, Terry. "The New Economics of Organization." *American Journal of Political Science* 28 (1984): 739–77.

———. "The Politics of Bureaucratic Structure." In *Can the Government Govern?* edited by John E. Chubb and Paul E. Peterson, 267–329. Washington, DC: Brookings Institution, 1989.

Moodey, Bradley. "Alabama's Dysfunctional State Government." In *A Century of Controversy: Constitutional Reform in Alabama,* edited by Bailey Thompson. Tuscaloosa: University of Alabama Press, 2002.

Mook, Douglas G. "In Defense of External Invalidity." *American Psychologist* 38, no. 4 (1983): 379–87.

Moore, Mark H. *Creating Public Value: Strategic Management in Government.* Cambridge, MA.: Harvard University Press, 1995.

Mosher, Frederick M. *Democracy and the Public Service,* 2nd ed. New York: Oxford University Press, 1982.

Moynihan, Donald P. "Public Management Policy Change in the United States 1993–2001." *International Public Management Journal* 6, no. 3 (2003): 371–94.

———. "Protection versus Flexibility: The Civil Service Reform Act, Competing Administrative Doctrines and the Roots of Contemporary Public Management Debate." *Journal of Policy History* 16, no. 1 (2004): 1–35.

———. "Goal-Based Learning and the Future of Performance Management." *Public Administration Review* 65, no. 2 (2005): 203–16.

———. "Homeland Security and the U.S. Public Management Policy Agenda." *Governance: An International Journal of Policy, Administration, and Institutions* 18, no. 2 (2005): 171–96.

———. "Why and How Do State Governments Adopt and Implement 'Managing for Results' Reforms?" *Journal of Public Administration Research and Theory* 15, no. 2 (2005): 219–43.

———. "Managing for Results in State Government: Evaluating a Decade of Reform." *Public Administration Review* 66, no. 1 (2006): 78–90.

———. "What Do We Talk About When We Talk About Performance?: Dialogue Theory and Performance Budgeting." *Journal of Public Administration Research and Theory* 16, no. 2 (2006): 151–68.

Moynihan, Donald P., and Patricia W. Ingraham. "Integrative Leadership in the Public Sector." *Administration & Society* 36, no. 4 (2004): 427–53.

Moynihan, Donald P., and Sanjay K. Pandey. "Testing How Management Matters in an Era of Government by Performance Management." *Journal of Public Administration Research and Theory* 15, no. 3 (2005): 421–39.

Nathan, Richard. "Presidential Address: '*Complexifying*' Government Oversight in America's Government." *Journal of Policy Analysis and Management* 4, no. 2 (2005): 207–15.

Nickerson, Raymond. "Confirmation Bias: A Ubiquitous Phenomenon in Many Guises." *Review of General Psychology* 2, no. 2 (1998): 175–220.

Nyhan, Ronald C., and Herbert A. Marlowe Jr. "Performance Measurement in the Public Sector: Challenges and Opportunities." *Public Productivity and Management Review* 18, no. 4 (1995): 333–48.

Office of Program Policy Analysis and Government Accountability (State of Florida). *A Report on Performance-Based Program Budgeting in Context: History and Comparison.* Tallahassee, FL: OPPAGA Report Production, 1997.

Osborne, David E., and Ted Gaebler. *Reinventing Government: How the Entrepreneurial Government Is Transforming the Public Sector.* New York: Plume, 1992.

O'Toole, Laurence J., Jr. "Research on Policy Implementation: Assessment and Prospects." *Journal of Public Administration Research and Theory* 10, no. 2 (2000): 263–88.

———. "Treating Networks Seriously: Practical and Research-Based Agendas in Public Administration." *Public Administration Review* 57, no. 1 (1997): 45–52.

Overman, E. Sam, and Kathy J. Boyd. "Best Practice Research and Postbureaucratic Reform." *Journal of Public Administration Research and Theory* 4, no. 1 (1994): 67–83.

Peelo, Moira, and Keith Soothill. "The Place of Public Narratives in Reproducing Social Order." *Theoretical Criminology* 4, no. 2 (2000): 131–48.

Performance Institute. "President's Budget Uses Performance Budgeting to Help Make Tough Decisions." Press release. February 7, 2005.

Perry, John. "Corrections." In *Vermont State Government Since 1965,* edited by Michael Sherman, 273–96. Burlington: University of Vermont Press, 1999.

Phillips, Nelson, Thomas B. Lawrence, and Cynthia Hardy. "Discourse and Institutions." *Academy of Management Review* 29, no. 4 (2004): 635–52.

Poister, Theodore H., and Gregory D. Streib. "Strategic Management in the Public Sector." *Public Productivity and Management* 22, no. 3 (1999): 308–25.

Poister, Theodore H., and Gregory Streib. "Elements of Strategic Planning and Management in Municipal Government: Status after Two Decades." *Public Administration Review* 65, no. 1 (2005): 45–56.

Pressman, Jeffery L., and Aaron A. Wildavksy. *Implementation.* Berkeley: University of California Press, 1973.

Radin, Beryl A. "The Government Performance and Results Act (GPRA): Hydra-Headed Monster or Flexible Management Tool?" *Public Administration Review* 58, no. 4 (1998): 307–17.

———. "The Government Performance and Results Act and the Tradition of Federal Management Reform: Square Pegs in Round Holes." *Journal of Public Administration and Research Theory* 10, no. 1 (2000): 111–35.

———. *Testimony to the Senate Homeland Security and Government Affairs Subcommittee on Federal Financial Management, Government Information, and International Security,* June 14, 2005.

———. *The Accountable Juggler: The Art of Leadership in a Federal Agency.* Washington, DC: CQ Press, 2006.

———. *Challenging the Performance Movement: Accountability, Complexity, and Democratic Values.* Washington, DC: Georgetown University Press, 2006.

Rainey, Hal G., and Paula Steinbauer. "Galloping Elephants: Developing Elements of a Theory of Effective Government Organizations." *Journal of Public Administration Research and Theory* 9, no. 1 (1999): 1–32.

Roe, Emery. *Narrative Policy Analysis: Theory and Practice.* Durham, NC: Duke University Press, 1994.

Romzek, Barbara, and Melvin Dubnick. "Accountability in the Public Sector: Lessons from the Challenger Disaster." *Public Administration Review* 47, no. 3 (1987): 227–38.

Rosenbloom, David H. *Building a Legislative-Centered Public Administration: Congress and the Administrative State 1946–1999.* Tuscaloosa: University of Alabama Press, 2002.

Roy, Calude, and Francine Seguin. "The Institutionalization of Efficiency-Oriented Approaches for Public Service Improvement." *Public Productivity and Management Review* 23, no. 4 (2000): 449–68.

Rubin, Irene S., and Joanne Kelly, "Budget and Accounting Reforms." In *The Oxford Handbook of Public Management,* edited by Ewan Ferlie, Laurence E. Lynn Jr., and Christopher Pollitt, 563–90. Oxford: Oxford University Press, 2005.

Sala, Brian R., John T. Scott, and James F. Spriggs II. "The Cold War on Ice: Constructivism and the Politics of Olympic Figure Skating Judging." *Perspectives on Politics* 5, no. 1 (2007): 17–29.

Schick, Allen. "The Road to PBB: The Stages of Budget Reform." *Public Administration Review* 26, no. 4 (1966): 243–58.

———. *A Contemporary Approach to Public Expenditure Management.* Washington, DC: World Bank, 1998.

———. "Why Most Countries Should Not Try New Zealand's Reforms." *The World Bank Research Observer* 13, no. 1 (1998): 123–31.

———. "Getting Performance Measures to Measure Up." In *Quicker, Better, Cheaper: Managing Performance in American Government,* edited by Dall Forsythe, 39–60. Albany, New York: Rockefeller Institute, 2002.

———. "Opportunity, Strategy, and Tactics in Reforming Public Management." *OECD Journal of Budgeting* 2, no. 3 (2002): 7–35.

———. "The Performing State: Reflections on an Idea Whose Time Has Come, But Whose Implementation Has Not." *OECD Journal of Budgeting* 3, no. 2 (2003): 71–103.

Scott, William G. "Organization Theory: An Overview and an Appraisal." *Academy of Management Journal* 4, no. 1 (1961): 7–26.

Selden, Sally C., Patricia W. Ingraham, and Willow Jacobson. "Human Resources Practices in State Government: Findings from a National Survey." *Public Administration Review* 61, no. 5 (2001): 598–607.

Senge, Peter. *The Fifth Discipline.* New York: Doubleday, 1990.

Seong, Si Kyung. "Adoption of Innovation: Event History Analysis on State Legislation of Performance Budgeting in the 1990s." Paper presented at the annual meeting of the American Political Science Association, Hilton Chicago and the Palmer House Hilton, September 1–4, 2004.

Shtull, Penny. *Assessment of the Vermont Department of Corrections Vision, Mission, and Values, and Principles 1998 Revision.* Report to the Vermont Department of Corrections, 1999.

Siegelman, Don. *ACHIEVE: Achieving Accountability for Alabama.* Montgomery, AL: Government Printing Press, 2000.

Simon, Herbert A. *Administrative Behavior: A Study of Decisionmaking Processes in Administrative Organizations,* 5th ed. New York: Macmillian Company, 1997.

———. "Bounded Rationality and Organizational Learning." *Organization Science* 1, no. 2 (1991): 125–34.

Simons, Robert. *Levers of Control: How Managers Use Innovative Control Systems to Drive Strategic Renewal.* Boston: Harvard Business School Press, 1995.

Snell, Ron, and Jennifer Grooters. *Governing-for-Results: Legislation in the States. A Report to the Urban Institute.* Washington, DC: Urban Institute, 2000.

Stewart, J. D. "The Role of Information in Public Accountability." In *Issues in Public Sector Accounting,* edited by Anthony Hopwood and Cyril Tompkins, 13–34. Oxford: Philip Allan, 1984.

Stone, Deborah. *Policy Paradox: The Art of Political Decisionmaking.* New York: W. W. Norton and Company, 1997.

Talbot, Colin. "Executive Agencies: Have They Improved Management in Government?" *Public Money and Management* 24, no. 2 (2004): 104–12.

———. "Performance Management." In *The Oxford Handbook of Public Management,* edited by Ewan Ferlie, Laurence E. Lynn Jr., and Christopher Pollitt, 491–517. Oxford: Oxford University Press, 2005.

Tat-Kei Ho, Alfred. "Accounting for the Value of Performance Measurement from the Perspective of Midwestern Mayors." *Journal of Public Administration Research and Theory* 16, no. 2 (2006): 217–37.

Thomas, James D., and William H. Stewart, *Alabama Government and Politics.* Lincoln: University of Nebraska Press, 1992.

Thompson, Fred. "Mission-Driven, Results-Oriented Budgeting: Fiscal Administration and the New Public Management." *Public Budgeting and Finance* 14, no. 3 (1994): 90–105.

Thurmaier, Kurt, and Katherine Willoughby. *Policy and Politics in State Budgeting.* New York: ME Sharpe, 2001.

Toft, Graham S. "Synoptic (One Best Way) Approaches to Strategic Management." In *Handbook of Strategic Management,* edited by Jack Rabin, Gerald J. Miller, and W. Bartley Hildreth, 3–34. New York: Marcel Dekker Inc., 1989.

Toulmin, Stephen. *The Uses of Argument.* London: Cambridge University Press, 1958.

U.S Congress. *Departments of Labor, Health, and Human Services, and Education, and Related Agencies Appropriation Bill,* 2004, Report 108–88. Available at http://frwebgate .access.gpo.gov/cgi-in/getdoc.cgi?dbname=108_cong_reports&docid=f:hr188.108.pdf.

U.S. Congress. *The Program Assessment and Results Act,* H.R. 105, 2005. Available at http:// frwebgate.access.gpo.gov/cgi-bin/getdoc.cgi?dbname=109_cong_bills&docid=f:h185ih.txt .pdf.

U.S. Congress. House. Subcommittee on Government Efficiency and Financial Management. *Should We PART Ways with GPRA: A Look at Performance Budgeting and Program Review* (February 4, 2004. Serial No. 108–144). Washington, DC: Government Printing Office, 2004.

U.S. General Accounting Office. *NPR's Savings: Claimed Agency Savings Cannot Be All Attributed to the NPR.* Washington, DC: GAO, 1999.

———. *Observations on the Use of OMB's Program Assessment Rating Tool for the Fiscal Year 2004 Budget.* Washington, DC: GAO, 2004.

———. *Performance Budgeting: OMB's Program Assessment Rating Tool Presents Opportunities and Challenges for Budget and Performance Integration.* Washington, DC: GAO, 2004.

U.S. Government Accountability Office. *Performance Budgeting: Efforts to Restructure Budgets to Better Align Resources with Performance.* Washington, DC: GAO, 2005.

———. *Performance Budgeting: States' Experiences Can Inform Federal Efforts.* Washington, DC: GAO, 2005.

———. *Performance Budgeting: PART Focuses Attention on Program Performance, but More Can Be Done to Engage Congress.* Washington, DC: GAO, 2005.

———. *Program Evaluation: OMB's PART Reviews Increased Agencies' Attention to Improving Evidence of Program Results.* Washington, DC: GAO, 2005.

U.S. Office of Management and Budget. *The President's Management Agenda.* Washington, DC: Government Printing Office, 2001.

———. *Analytical Perspectives, Budget of the United States Government.* Washington, DC: Government Printing Office, 2002.

———. "Budget Procedures Memorandum No. 861." Washington, DC: Office of Management and Budget, 2003. Available at www.whitehouse.gov/omb/budget/fy2005/pdf/bpm861.pdf.

———. *Major Savings and Reforms in the President's 2006 Budget.* Washington, DC: Government Printing Office, 2005.

———. *Guide to Assessing the Program Assessment Rating Tool.* Available at www.whitehouse.gov/omb/part/fy2006/2006_guidance_final.pdf.

VanLandingham, Gary, Martha Wellman, and Matthew Andrews. "Useful, But Not a Panacea: Performance-Based Program Budgeting in Florida." *International Journal of Public Administration* 28, no. 3 (2005): 233–54.

van Thiel, Sandra, and Frances Leeuw. "The Performance Paradox in the Public Sector." *Public Performance and Management Review* 25, no. 3 (2002): 267–81.

Vermont Department of Corrections. *Corrections in Vermont: A Five-Year Plan—Making Vermont Safe for the Twenty-first Century.* Montpelier: Vermont Department of Corrections, 2000.

———. *Facts and Figures FY1999.* Montpelier: Vermont Department of Corrections, 2000.

Virginia Department of Corrections, *Strategy Performance Budgeting Plan 2000–2002.* Richmond, VA: Virginia Department of Corrections, 1999.

Virginia Department of Planning and Budgeting. *Virginia's Handbook on Planning and Performance for State Agencies and Institutions.* Richmond: Virginia Department of Planning and Budgeting, 1998.

Wang, Xiaohu. "Performance Measurement in Budgeting: A Study of County Governments." *Public Budgeting and Finance* 20 (2000): 102–18.

Walton, Douglas. *Plausible Reasoning in Everyday Conversation.* Albany: SUNY Press, 1992.

———. *One-Sided Arguments: A Dialectal Analysis of Bias.* Albany: SUNY Press, 1999.

Weaver, R. Kent, and Bert A. Rockman, eds. *Do Institutions Matter? Government Capabilities in the United States and Abroad.* Washington, DC: Brookings Institution, 1993.

Weick, Karl. *Making Sense of the Organization.* Oxford: Blackwell, 2001.

White, Barry. "Examining Budgets for Chief Executives." In *Handbook of Government Budgeting,* edited by Roy Meyers, 462–84. San Francisco: Jossey-Bass, 1999.

Wildavsky, Aaron A. "The Political Economy of Efficiency: Cost–Benefit Analysis, System Analysis, and Program Budgeting." *Public Administration Review* 26 (1968): 292–310.

———. "If Planning Is Everything, Maybe It's Nothing." *Policy Sciences* 26, no. 4 (1973): 127–53.

———. *Budgeting: A Comparative Theory of Budgeting Processes.* Boston: Little Brown and Company, 1975.

———. *Speaking Truth to Power: The Art and Craft of Policy Analysis.* Boston: Little Brown, and Company, 1979.

Wildavsky, Aaron A., and Naomi Caiden. *The New Politics of the Budgetary Process,* 5th ed. New York: Longman, 2003.

Williams, Daniel W. "Measuring Government in the Early Twentieth Century." *Public Administration Review* 60, no. 6 (2000): 522–34.

Wilson, James Q. *Bureaucracy: What Government Agencies Do and Why They Do It,* 2nd ed. New York: Basic Books, 2000.

Wittmer, Dennis. "Ethical Sensitivity and Managerial Decisionmaking: An Experiment." *Journal of Public Administration Research and Theory* 2, no. 4 (1992): 443–62.

Wolf, Patrick J. "A Case Survey of Bureaucratic Effectiveness in U.S. Cabinet Agencies: Preliminary Results." *Journal of Public Administration Research and Theory* 3, no. 2 (1993): 161–81.

———. "Why Must We Reinvent the Federal Government? Putting Historical Developmental Claims to the Test." *Journal of Public Administration Research and Theory* 7, no. 3 (1997): 353–88.

Wye, Chris. "Performance Management for Career Executives: A 'Start Where You Are, Use What You Have Guide.'" In *Managing for Results 2005,* edited by John Kamensky and Albert Morales, 17–82. Lanham, MD: Rowman and Littlefield, 2005.

Yin, Robert K. *Case Study Research: Design and Methods,* 2nd ed. Thousand Oaks, CA: Sage Publications, 1994.

Index

Note: Page numbers followed by box, t, or f indicate boxes, tables, or figures in the text. Page numbers followed by n indicate notes.

abandonment of performance management planning, 55, 75
academic critique, of performance movement, 8–9, 11–12
accountability
changed via performance management doctrine, 11, 35–37
and defensiveness, 180–84
enabled by results-based reform, 7, 63–67, 224
external (government to public), 35, 36t, 54
by Vermont DOC, 63–64, 85, 171–72, 175, 176
in Virginia, 51, 63–64
hampered by managers' lack of authority, 47–48, 146
internal (bureaucrats to elected officials), 35–36, 36t, 54, 64
of managers, 26, 32, 146
political, as instrumental benefit, 64–67
public, as instrumental benefit, 63–64
public demand for questioned, 63, 69
responsibility, 37, 54, 87–89
See also efficiency
Achieve: Achieving Accountability for Alabama (strategic plan), 49–50
achievement of goals, 29, 88–89, 133, 140, 146
debated, 153–55
adoption of performance management reforms, 14–15
Alabama, 49–50, 59–60, 62, 66, 68–69
partial, in state governments, 39–56, 58–72
study and theory, 9, 21–22, 59
U.S.-specific issues, 10, 11, 15
Vermont, 51–52, 59–60, 62, 63–65, 68
Virginia, 50–51, 60, 62, 63–64, 69–70
agencies
beneficiaries of reforms, 12, 15–16, 76, 84–85, 196–201
budget submission, 18, 101, 118, 120–22, 124

burden of proof upon, in PART, 18, 140, 183
central, 14, 15, 43, 109, 198–99
budget officials, 97, 101, 197
defining policy, 59–62
goal planning, 54
in Virginia, 50–51, 87, 106, 219
characteristics, 164
clientele, 202
leadership motivation, 78–79, 83–84, 87, 169, 171, 199
main users of performance information, 197–98
performance dialogue, 19, 114, 195
performance management implementation variation, 75–76, 109–10, 164
policy change by, 17, 80–81, 173–75, 200–201
(*see also* double-loop learning)
relationship with OMB, 114, 119–21, 124, 145–46, 156, 183, 198
resources issues, 17, 42, 43box, 86, 89
structure, 204
agency-centered approach, to performance management, 198–200
Alabama, performance management efforts, 22, 99
adoption, 49–50, 59–60, 62, 66, 68–69
comments by participants, 89, 91, 92
Department of Corrections (DOC), 66, 80, 86, 89–92, 184
example set by leadership, 78, 79
Strategic Plan and Performance Measurement System, 30, 50
strategic planning, 49–50, 88, 90–91
Alabama, state background, 214–16
constitutional and tax reform, 68, 214–16
governors, 49–50, 68, 86, 94n10, 214, 216
Alaska, performance management efforts, 55
allocation. *See* resources
allocative efficiency, 35, 36t, 97, 118

241

ambiguity
  in organizations/organizational life, 103–5
  of PART, 114, 142–43, 154–55
  of performance information, 2, 9, 16–17, 18–
    19, 95–96, 104, 112–13, 142, 193–94
  and interactive dialogue model, 102, 105
  potential for increase in political settings, 106–
    10
  See also interactive dialogue model, of
    performance information use; subjectivity
American Correctional Association, 85, 86
Angelone, Ron, 83, 84
appropriations, in U.S. Congress, 121t, 122,
  123box, 133
  appropriators' roles and preferences, 124–25,
    131
argument, 59, 86–87, 100–101, 102–3, 111–12
  administrative/doctrines, 26–27
  construction, 96, 115n6, 179
  within PART, 143
  See also persuasion
Argyris, Chris, 165, 186n4
Arkansas, performance management efforts, 55
authority, managerial, 31–35, 44t, 71, 86–89
  limited, 44–49, 58, 61, 146
autonomy, 14, 43, 202–4, 205

balanced scorecard approach, 49–50, 62
benchmark organizations, 33
benefits of reforms, 35–37, 36t, 93
  agency-level, 12, 15–16, 76, 84–85, 196–201
  instrumental, 73n13, 80–81, 81t, 83
    political accountability, 64–67
    public accountability, 63–64
  local level, 10
  managerial level, 48
  promised, 52–54, 53t
  symbolic, 59, 62, 68–70, 73n13, 77, 84–85,
    93
best-practice examples, 60, 201
Biddle, Jack, III, 89
Brunnson, Nils, 106, 116n41
budget accounts, 121
budget process. *See* performance budgeting
bureaucracy, 14, 32, 33f, 65, 199, 200
bureaucrats
  accountability, 35–36, 36t, 54, 64–67, 71, 88
  goal attainment, 165–66
  providing or altering data, 5, 15, 65, 110
Bush, George W., 126, 134
Bush (George W.) administration
  on Government Performance and Results Act,
    17–18, 119
  HR reform, 47

performance management under, 22, 113–14,
  118–36, 149
contrasted with Clinton administration, 140,
  147
use of Office of Management and Budget, 17–
  19, 109, 113–14, 119–36
  OMB evaluations against Bush ideology, 141
Bush School of Government and Public Service
  (Texas A&M), 149, 151–52
business, as metaphor, 173, 187n22

Carter, Jimmy, 100
case studies. *See specific states*
causality, 87, 103, 131
central agencies, 14, 15, 43, 109, 198–99
  budget officials, 97, 101, 197
  defining policy, 59–62
  goal planning, 54
  Virginia, 50–51, 87, 106, 219
Challenging the Performance Movement (Radin),
  8
CitiStat, 74n16, 181–82
citizen involvement, in governing, 174, 218
CJs. *See* congressional justifications
Clinton administration, 46–47, 140, 147
codes, on state performance management, 40t
college students. *See* graduate students
communication, as goal of performance
  management, 98
compliance, passive, 12, 15, 52, 80, 146, 207
comprehensive measures, 105
CompStat, 181–82
confirmation bias, 109
Congress, U.S.
  appropriations examples, 121t, 122, 123box,
    131, 133
  attitude toward PART, 134–35, 148–49, 158
  Congressional Record, 28box
  performance dialogue, 130–34
  relationship with OMB, and performance data,
    18, 119–36, 123box, 130–34, 148–49, 158
  reluctance to use performance information,
    113, 124, 132, 194
congressional justifications, 119–22
consultants, 59–62, 200
controls, 5
  financial, 42–43, 43box, 131, 156
    tie-in with personnel controls, 29, 48, 61,
      66–67, 168
  human resource management, 43–45, 44t
  legislative, 67
  public vs. private sector, 33, 167–68
  systems, 29, 33, 60–61, 66–67
  traditional, 10, 66–67, 89

corrections systems. *See* Department(s) of Corrections (DOC)
costs, of performance management, 70–71, 85–86
cross-functional teams, 180
cross-institutional dialogue, 4, 9, 111–12, 163–64
culture
    of learning, 166–68, 195
    role of, 169t, 183–85

Daniels, Mitch, 125, 127, 134
data, performance. *See* performance information
data collection
    of performance information, 72, 107–8, 122
    for text, 20–21
data sources, 21t
decentralization
    effects of political (U.S.), 10, 11, 64
    in human resources, 43
    in NPM benchmark countries, 31
decision making
    altered by changed information formats, 130–31
    as alternative of dialogue, 95
    confirmation bias, 109, 112
    informed by performance management/information, 5–7, 20, 48, 167, 194–96
    role of ambiguity, 105, 112–13
    and interactive dialogue model, 111–13
    past influencing present in, 98, 100, 112
defensiveness, and accountability, 180–84
Democrats in Congress, and PART, 134–35
Department of Finance and Management (Vermont), 52, 65
Department of Housing and Development (HUD), 123box
Department of Planning and Budget (Virginia), 51, 60, 82, 219
Department of Transportation (DOT), 123box
Department(s) of Corrections (DOC)
    Alabama, 66, 80, 86, 89–92, 184
    budgets and budgeting, 88, 89, 91–92, 100–102
    interview questions, regarding performance management, 211–13
    Vermont, 80–81, 85, 170–78, 184
        sentencing alternatives and innovations, 172–78, 217–18
    Virginia, 81–83, 101, 168–69
dialogue
    cross-institutional, 4, 9, 111–12, 163–64
    evidence-based, 113–14, 139–42
    interactive, 18, 95–96, 111, 164–65, 178, 195
    intra-institutional, 4, 9, 164

in learning forums, 178–84, 179box
performance, 19, 114, 130–34, 159
and policy process, 9, 17–18, 19, 103
problem-solving, 111, 180–82
public, 109
routines, 110–11, 114, 159, 163–86
    and learning types, 165–66
See also interactive dialogue model, of performance information use
discourse, 103–4, 110–11, 144, 182
DOC. *See* Department(s) of Corrections (DOC)
doctrine of performance management, 10–11, 164
    claims and assumptions, 26, 27–37, 87, 205
    interpreted by state governments, 13–14, 47
    partial adoption by state governments, 45–47, 59, 61
    predicted benefits, 11, 35–37, 36t, 53t
    shortcomings, 20, 76, 207
doctrines, 26
double-loop learning, 81, 165–66
    and policy shaping, 80–81, 170–78, 200
dramatic events, effects on budgets, 108–9
duplicated programs, 158, 183–84

education
    performance measures demanded for, 132
    programs rated, 128, 133, 154, 156
efficiency
    allocative, 35, 36t, 97, 118
    technical, 33f, 36t, 37, 118, 196
elected officials
    accountability, 35–36, 36t, 63–67, 89
    campaigning and reform rhetoric, 14, 94n10, 192
    frustration with performance management, 12, 113
    motivation, 62–64
    power and oversight, 11, 64, 66, 197
    reform promotion and use, 69–70, 78
    social interaction, 115n3
    using performance information, 18, 78
        budget decisions, 97
        challenges/skepticism, 89, 98, 193–94
        ordering, not using, 67
    See also Congress, U.S.
election process, 14, 94n10
executive branch, of U.S. government
    highest status assumed, for reforms, 11, 42
    program assessment dialogue, 18
    providing performance information, 189–90
    See also Bush (George W.) administration
expectmore.gov, 126–27

experimental test, by public affairs school
  programs, 149–59
expert opinion, 155

failure, and budgeting support, 7–8, 18–19, 85–
  86, 104–5, 129–30, 155–56
fair play, 156, 196
Federal Aviation Administration (FAA), 123box
federal management reforms
  under George W. Bush, 118–36
  post–September 11, 47
federal programs. *See* programs
federal/state level parallels, 9, 12, 17
financial controls, 29, 42–43, 43box, 48, 61, 66–
  67, 156
Florida, performance management efforts, 74n30,
  99, 100
  PowerTrac, 181–82
  welfare-to-work programs, 112
foreign (non-U.S.) countries' performance
  management, 10, 31, 105
formal reforms, 77–78
future of performance management, 5, 118

GAO. *See* Government Accountability Office
  (GAO)
general interview protocol, for states, 211–13
Georgia
  budget history, 100
  performance management efforts, 55, 56n13
goals
  achievement of, 29, 88–89, 133, 140, 146
  debated, 153–55
  and dialogue/learning routines, 163, 165–66,
    180
  equity, 8, 144
  missed/overlooked, in performance
    measurement, 153–54
  multiple, 66, 105, 107
  performance, 36, 39, 121, 122, 144
    linked to results, 30, 185, 224
    not linked to results, 54, 88–89
  political, 128
goal-setting
  aligning with resources, 121
  with GPRA, 147
  and implementation (steering vs. rowing), 34
  as primary purpose of strategic planning,
    178
  using performance information, 5, 11, 30,
    36
    achievability, 98
Gorczyk, John, 170, 172, 178
government, assumptions about, 27

Government Accountability Office (GAO)
  opinion on performance budgeting, 7–8, 98–
    99, 124, 183
  reports on performance management and
    budgeting, 53, 99, 119, 123box, 147–48,
    152
Government Performance and Results Act
  (GPRA), 118
  assumptions about, 27–28
  Bush (George W.) administration on, 17–18,
    119
  federal compliance, 39, 114n1
  Findings and Purposes section, 27, 28box
  OMB on, 147
  potential for learning, 188n49
  states' versions, 9, 39
  See also Program Assessment and Results Act
    (PARA); Program Assessment Rating Tool
    (PART)
Government Performance Project (GPP)
  content analysis, 21, 41t
  grades, 12–13, 13t
  states' reports to, 30–31, 40–41, 41t, 45
  surveys, 12–13, 21–22, 55
government programs. *See* programs
government reform, 14, 27, 70, 94n10, 192
governors. *See* state governors
GPP. *See* Government Performance Project (GPP)
GPRA. *See* Government Performance and Results
  Act (GPRA)
graduate students
  analyzing PART assessments, 19, 149–59,
    161n36
  political attitudes, 151–52

hierarchy. *See* top-down performance expectations
House Appropriations Committee, 123box, 133
human resources (HR)
  managerial authority over, 31, 43–45, 44t, 45–
    46
  reform, 47

Illinois, performance management efforts, 55
implementation of performance management
  reforms, 53, 78, 185
  explained, 75–93
  failure, 12, 20, 55, 78
implementation theory, 76, 92–93, 200
incrementalism, 98, 100, 111, 128
information asymmetry, 64–65, 151, 155, 182
information overload, 11, 17, 48, 65, 98, 139
inputs
  constraints on, 67
  vs. outcomes/results, 6, 29, 31–34, 33f

institutional roles. *See* roles' influence on performance information use
instrumental (concrete) benefits, of performance management, 73n13, 80–81, 81t, 83, 93
 political accountability, 64–67
 public accountability, 63–64
 See also symbolic benefits, of performance management
interactive dialogue model, of performance information use, 4, 9, 14, 16, 95–114
 assessment, 113–14
 basic assumptions, 102–13, 142, 143, 163
 and decision making, 111–13
 experimental test of, 149–59
 in management, 163–65
 and PART, 139–59
 political nature, 96
interpretation conflicts, data, 143, 144, 152–55, 153box
interview examples
 correctional employees
  Alabama, 89, 91, 92
  Vermont, 100, 185
  Virginia, 79, 83
 OMB members, 22–23, 25n36
 state officials, 12, 22
  Vermont, 80, 100–101, 108–9
  Virginia, 69–70, 83–84, 98, 106
interview protocol, for states, 211–13
intra-institutional dialogues, 4, 9, 164

Kansas, performance management efforts, 55

La Follette School of Public Affairs (University of Wisconsin–Madison), 149, 152
language
 accountability rhetoric, 4, 63
 ambiguity of, in PART, 114, 142–43, 154–55
 "coding" to clarify information, 6
 and naming of management systems, 3–4
 of performance, 183–85
 performance information as a unique, 6–7
 in public policy, 96
leadership, 204
 motivation in agencies, 78–79, 83–84, 87, 169, 171, 199
learning
 double-loop, 81, 165–66
  Vermont, 80–81, 170–78, 200
 goal-based, 163, 169t, 179box, 185, 195
 metaphors, 172–73
 organizational, 164–86
 single-loop, 165–66, 180
  CitiStat, 181–82

Virginia, 168–70
 structural and cultural routes to, 166–68, 178, 184
learning forums, 19, 163–86, 179box
legislation
 federal, 46–47
 state, 40t, 51, 71, 177, 214–15, 219
 See also Government Performance and Results Act (GPRA)
line-item budgets, 42, 131
literature
 critiquing performance management, 8–9, 11–12
 empirical, on performance, 190, 202, 205
 on organizational discourse and learning, 103, 109, 144, 164–66, 178–79, 180–81, 186n4
 on policymaking and adoption, 14, 58, 59
logic of appropriateness, 93, 184, 185
logic of consequentiality, 93
logic of fair play, 156, 196
Louisiana, performance management efforts, 30

managerial authority, 31–35, 44t, 71, 86–89
 limited, 44–49, 58, 61, 146
managers
 autonomy, 14, 43, 205
 dialogue with, 179
 discretion, 45, 47
 in reform use, 77–78
 focus on results, 6, 11, 33f, 61, 169
 freedom/flexibility, 5, 11, 42–43, 71
 human resources role, 26, 31, 43, 44t
 improving productivity, 37
 training, 62, 170, 185
 using performance information, 19, 87, 95, 163–65, 167, 179–80, 195
 See also managerial authority
Maryland, performance management efforts, 55, 74n16, 181–82
measurement of performance. *See* performance measurement
Measuring the Performance of the Hollow State (Frederickson and Frederickson), 8–9
mechanisms
 organizational learning, 166–67, 178, 185
 reporting, 15, 153–54, 184
metaphors, use in learning, 172–73, 187n22
Mosher, Frederick, 3
multiple goals, 66, 105, 107

NASA budget requests, 121t, 124, 125
National Academy of Public Administration, 60, 127, 148

National Performance Review, 73n16–74n16, 119, 147
New Public Management (NPM)
  benchmark countries, 31
  ideas, 31–34, 76
  reform adoption, 10
  states' diversion from ideals of, 47
New York, CompStat program, 181–82
North Carolina, performance management efforts, 181
NPM. See New Public Management (NPM)
numbers
  objectivity and subjectivity, 9, 95, 107
  unreflected by policy subtleties, 105

objectivity
  implied as inherent in numbers, 9, 95, 107
  lack of, in performance information, 193–94
    ambiguous performance information, 9, 16–17, 18–19, 95–96, 102, 104, 105, 142
Office of Management and Budget (OMB)
  budget examiners, 124, 126–30, 141–43, 147–48, 197–98
  Circular A-11, 114n1, 120
  critique of GPRA, 147
  Directors' Review, 141–42
  Performance Evaluation Team, 125–26
  relationship with agencies, 114, 119–21, 124, 145–46, 156, 183, 198
  relationship with Congress, and performance information, 18, 119–36, 123box, 130–34, 148–49, 158
  role during George W. Bush administration, 17–19, 109, 113–14, 119–36
  evaluations against Bush ideology, 141
  use of PART, 18, 19, 114, 119–20, 125–30, 139–59
    experimental re-creation, 149–59
OLM. See under organizational learning
OMB. See Office of Management and Budget (OMB)
OMB Watch (watchdog group), 145–46
organizational culture, 19, 82–84, 164, 166–68, 184–85, 203, 205
  interview questions regarding, 213
  NYPD, 182
  Vermont DOC, 172
  Virginia DOC, 168–70
organizational environment, 175–78, 197, 204
organizational factors, 202box, 205–6
organizational learning, 164–86
  literature, 103, 109, 144, 164–66, 178–79, 180–81, 186n4
  mechanisms (OLM), 166–67, 178, 185

organizational life, 103–5, 106
outcomes, 77, 101
  measures, 146, 154
  results vs. inputs, 6, 29, 31–34, 33f
  of Vermont and Virginia efforts, 169t
overlapping programs, 158, 183–84

Paperwork Reduction Act, 146
PAR Act. See Program Assessment and Results Act (PARA)
PART. See Program Assessment Rating Tool (PART)
partial adoption, of state performance management reforms, 39–56, 58–72
performance appraisals, 43
performance budgeting
  agencies' submission requirements, 18, 118, 120, 124
  alternative approaches, 98–99
  budget formats, 130–31
  cycle/routine, 111
  information collection/interpretation, 9, 11, 17, 19, 108, 120–22, 130–31, 196
  lack of theory for, 96–99
  past reorganization systems, 11
  political influence on, 7, 11, 17, 108–10, 118, 123box, 128, 183, 196
  redefined ("in practice"), 8
  strict model, 7, 97–98, 100, 119–20, 127, 130
  synonymous with performance management, 97, 128
  as unrealistic, 7–8, 11, 53, 89, 98–99
  See also Program Assessment Rating Tool (PART); zero-based budgeting (ZBB)
performance information
  ambiguity of, 2, 9, 16–17, 18–19, 95–96, 102, 104–7, 112–13, 142, 193–94
  available to public, 51, 63, 181
  cities' use of, 181–82
  communication paths, 7, 51, 110
  data collection, 72, 107–8, 122
  desire for increasing amounts of, 67, 132, 148, 191
  driving process improvement, 87
  encouragement of use, 194–95
  government neglect of, 67, 191
    federal, 113, 124, 132
    state, 49, 53, 78, 92
  inconsistency of use, 67, 95, 102, 132, 197–98
  influence on budgets, 53, 97, 99, 111
    federal, 119–20, 127–30, 183–84
  informing decision making, 5–7, 20, 48, 105, 112–13, 167, 194–96

interactive/social component of, 95–96
as language entity, 4, 6–7
managers managing, 19, 87, 95, 163–65, 167,
    179–80
overload, 11, 17, 48, 65, 98, 139
resource allocation and, 5, 7, 8, 18, 48, 51, 97–
    98
    for DOC efforts, 85–86, 89–92, 100–102
state use/management of, 13–14, 41t, 44–46,
    51–53, 99
    DOC-specific, 101–2, 168–72, 176–77
systems, 48, 167
    agency-centered, 59–62, 198–200
    building, 29–31, 39–42
    do not equal performance management,
        190–91
    popularity, 98
    unreliability of, 153–54
uses for, 5, 16–20
See also interactive dialogue model, of
    performance information use; performance
    budgeting; performance measurement
Performance Institute, 62, 73n11, 129
performance management
    defined, 5, 189
    doctrine (see doctrine of performance
        management)
    history, 3, 11
    model, 6f
    reforms (see reforms, in performance
        management)
    rethinking, 8–12, 189–207
    See also performance budgeting; performance
        information
performance measurement
    absence of, 7, 49
    databases, 53, 63, 125
    desire for, documented in 2004 budget texts,
        131–34
    illustrated, 6f
    immeasurable programs, 126, 128–29, 152–54
        (see also "results not demonstrated" rating)
    interview questions regarding, 211–13
    problems reported in, 110, 125
    program ratings categories, 126, 129
    program ratings questions, 143, 221–24
    public indifference, 63
    in sports, 1–2
    See also performance information; Program
        Assessment Rating Tool (PART); reporting
        mechanisms
personnel
    classifications, 43
    federal legislation regarding, 46–47

lack of, as barrier to performance management
    success, 39
    management, 61, 71 (see also human resources
        (HR))
perspectives. See roles' influence on performance
    information use
persuasion, 108, 110, 112, 115n6, 159
    of PART, 143, 151
    by Vermont DOC, 172
    See also argument
Platts, Todd Russell, 135
PMA. See President's Management Agenda (PMA)
policy change by agencies, 17, 80–81, 173–75,
    200–201
    See also double-loop learning
political appointments, 10, 66, 88
"political context," 128, 203, 206
political influence on budgets, 7, 11, 17, 108–10,
    118, 123box, 128, 183, 196
political leanings
    in Alabama, 214
    of graduate students, 151–52
    of PART, 134–35
    in Vermont, 217
    in Virginia, 218
pork projects, 128, 215
PowerTrac, 181–82
premanagement governance era, 3
President's Management Agenda (PMA), 118–19,
    134–35
private sector
    control system in organizations, 33–34
    learning philosophy, 200
    as source of reforms, 11
probity, 29, 48, 61, 89, 147
problem-solving, 104, 111, 180–82
process improvement, 87
productivity, 37, 98
professional organizations, 60, 85
Program Assessment and Results Act (PARA), 135
Program Assessment Rating Tool (PART), 221–24
    assessing federal programs, 18–19, 114, 119–
        20, 125–35, 139–41
        experimental re-creation, 149–59
    development of, 125–27
    impact limited, 128
    influence on budget, 18, 127–30
    and interactive dialogue model, 139–59
    partisan nature debated, 134–35, 144
    persuasiveness of, 143, 151
    prompting evidence-based dialogue, 139–41
    questions list, 143, 221–24
    reactions to assessments by, 18, 19, 128, 142,
        146, 149–59, 153box

recommendations, 130, 140–42, 147–48, 155
subjectivity of tool, 125, 127, 135, 143–49 (*see also under* ambiguity)
values of, 198
See also Government Performance and Results Act (GPRA)
programs
analysis of 2004 budgets, 131–34
assessed via PART program, 18–19, 114, 119–20, 125–35, 139–41
experimental re-creation of assessments, 149–59
and policy decisions, 126, 141–42, 144–45
questions about management, 222–24
definition and categorization, 146–47
"full costs" of, 121, 122
"one-size-fits-all" reforms on, 9
overlapping, 158, 183–84
performance-based funding of, 7–8, 85–86, 104–5, 118–25, 128–30, 155–56
ratings verbiage, 126, 129, 161n38
social, 154, 155
public administration field, nature of, 26
public affairs school programs, experimental test, 149–59
public discourse. *See* discourse
public–government relations
assumed traits of public, 63, 69
enabled by accountability, 11, 35, 63–64
examples of good communication, 51, 85, 181
marked by distrust, 4
public programs. *See* programs
public sector
claims about traditional organizations within, 28–29, 166
control systems in, 33–34, 61, 167–68
leadership, 78–79
not understood by management consultants, 62
public service unions, 15, 71, 192

Radin, Beryl, 4, 8, 9, 108, 144
redundant programs, 158, 183–84
reforms, in performance management
adoption, 9, 14–15
partial, in state governments, 39–56, 58–72
cultural, 167
episodic treatment, 55
expectations, 196–97
formal, 77–78
implementation, 53, 78, 185 (*see also* implementation theory)
explained, 75–93
failure, 12, 20, 55, 78

importance of, in government, 4–5, 9–10
leadership influence, 78–79
manager accountability, 146
organizational factors affecting, 205–6
promised benefits, 52–54, 53t
reducing costs, 70–71, 85–86
results-based, 7, 75–76, 94n19
symbolic nature of, 11–12, 14, 94n19, 192
systems changes as, 3
theory and assumptions, 5, 16, 26
usage, 15–16
See also benefits of reforms
Reinventing Government (Osborne and Gaebler), 34
reparative boards, 174–75
reporting mechanisms, 15, 153–54, 184
resources, 203
allocation, and performance information, 5, 7, 8, 18, 48, 51, 97–98
for DOC efforts, 85–86, 89–92, 100–102, 175
at federal level, 118–25, 127–30, 183–84
discretion in allocation, 7, 29, 42–43, 43box, 46, 97
reduced without PART assessment, 129
responsibility accountability, 37, 54, 87–89
restorative justice, 171, 174–77, 201, 218
results
-based reforms, 7, 75–76, 94n19
focus on, 6f, 33f, 46, 47–49, 169
lack of focus on, 29, 32, 33f, 54, 88–89
PART questions about, 224
"results not demonstrated" rating, 126, 128–29, 140, 142–43, 148
agency staff interpretation, 161n38
debated/rejected, 152–54, 156, 157, 161n38
Riley, Bob, 50, 55, 68, 216
Roadmap for Virginia's Future (strategic plan), 51
Roche, James, 133
roles' influence on performance information use, 2, 105–10, 151
routines. *See under* dialogue

safety, as value and goal, 66, 79, 90, 101, 170–71, 176
Schick, Allen, 31–32, 137n27
Schön, Donald, 165
science, as metaphor, 173, 174
self-censorship, 141
self-reporting, 40, 48, 139
sentencing alternatives and innovations, 172–78, 217–18
Siegelman, Don, 49–50, 94n10, 99, 216
single-loop learning, 165–66, 180

CitiStat, 181–82
Virginia, 168–70
social constructionist view, 2, 9, 103–4
social interaction, 95, 111, 114n3
social programs, 154, 155
stability, in organizations, 204
stakeholders
  convincing, 85
  dealing with PART, 145, 158
  responsibilities and input, 6, 67, 119, 128,
    147, 171
"stat" approach to performance management and
    programs, 181–82
state backgrounds
  Alabama, 214–16
  Vermont, 216–18
  Virginia, 218–20
state case studies. See specific states
state codes, on performance management, 40t
state/federal level parallels, 9, 12, 17
state governments
  adoption of performance management reforms,
    21–22, 39–56, 58–72
  agency performance information management,
    13–14, 44–46, 51–53, 99, 167, 197–98
  DOC examples, 100–102
  diversion from NPM ideals, 47, 76
  documented performance data, and variances,
    40–42, 41t
  GPRA compliance, 9, 39
  histories: Alabama, Vermont, Virginia, 214–20
  mirroring federal-level performance
    management, 9, 12, 17
  performance budgeting examples/evidence, 99–
    102
  performance information neglect, 49, 53, 78,
    92
  reports to GPP, 30–31, 40–41, 41t
  See also under surveys and studies
state governors
  Alabama, 49–50, 68, 86, 94n10, 214, 216
    noncollaboration between, 55, 99
  budgeting communication processes, 42, 110
  Vermont, 52, 217
  Virginia, 51, 60, 82, 218–19
state interview protocol, 211–13
states' report cards, Government Performance
    Project (GPP), 12–13, 13t
strategic planning, 178
  absence/impossibility of, 7, 49, 90–91
  Alabama, 49–50, 89, 90–91
  dialogue, 80, 178
  by federal-level agencies (GPRA-required), 39,
    118

link to performance measurement, 6f, 7, 29–30
policymaking aspect of, 165–66
questions regarding
  for interviews, 211
  in PART, 221–22
Vermont, 51–52, 81, 81t, 170–72, 173
Virginia, 51, 81–84, 81t, 101, 168–69
structural routes to learning, 166–68, 178, 183
studies/critiques of performance management, 8–
    9, 11–12
subjectivity
  of numbers when interpreted/processed, 9, 95,
    107
  of PART, as tool, 125, 127, 135, 143–49
surveys and studies
  federal government, 21t, 22–23, 25n36, 47
  GPP, 12–13, 21–22, 55
  about performance information use, 23, 39,
    195
  public, about state corrections systems, 171–
    72, 175, 176
  self-reported, 40, 48, 139
  state government, 21t, 39, 44–45
symbolic benefits, of performance management,
    59, 62, 68–70, 73n13, 77, 84–85, 93
  See also instrumental (concrete) benefits, of
    performance management
symbolic motivations, for performance
    management, 192–93
symbolic nature of reforms, 11–12, 14, 94n19, 192
systems
  bureaucratic and prebureaucratic, 32, 33f
  control, 29, 33, 60–61, 66–67
  performance information, 48, 167
    building, 29–31, 39–42
    do not equal performance management,
      190–91
    popularity, 98
  performance management, 6, 33f, 37, 39–42,
    167, 178
    agency-centered, 59–62, 198–200

technical efficiency, 33f, 36t, 37, 118, 196
Texas, performance management efforts, 30,
    56n13, 100
third parties
  program review, 18, 139, 145, 193
    use of outside evidence, 155
  service providers, 9, 146, 197
top-down performance expectations, 8–9, 36–37,
    61, 147, 181–82
Total Quality Management, 184
traditional public management organizations,
    assumptions about, 28–29, 31, 34

unions, public service, 15, 71, 192
United Kingdom, comprehensive measures, 105
use of performance information, 5, 16–20
    agency-level majority, 197–98
    vital to management success, 194–95

values
    legislative, 67
    organizational, 106–7, 170
    of PART, 198
    political, 98
    role in program management, 105, 110–11
venues, decision, 6f, 7, 30–31, 48
Vermont, performance management efforts, 22,
    169t
    adoption, 51–52, 59–60, 62, 63–65, 68
    comments by participants, 80, 100–101, 107–
        8, 108–9, 185
    Department of Corrections (DOC), 80–81,
        85, 170–78, 184
        sentencing alternatives and innovations,
            172–78, 217–18
    Department of Finance and Management, 52,
        65
    double-loop learning, 170–78, 200
    example set by leadership, 79, 170–71, 172, 178
    strategic planning, 51–52, 81, 81t, 170–72,
        173

Vermont, state background, 216–18
    governors, 52, 217
Veterans Administration, performance budgeting,
    123box
Virginia, performance management efforts, 22,
    99, 169t, 184
    adoption, 50–51, 60, 62, 63–64, 69–70
    comments by participants, 69–70, 79, 83–84,
        98, 106
    Department of Corrections (DOC), 81–83,
        101, 168–69
    Department of Planning and Budget, 51, 60,
        82, 219
    example set by leadership, 79, 168–70
    Performance Management System, 30
    single-loop learning, 168–70
    strategic planning, 51, 81–84, 81t, 101, 168–
        69
Virginia, state background, 218–20
    governors, 51, 60, 82, 218–19

Washington, performance management efforts,
    30–31
Wildavsky, Aaron A., 95, 104, 114–15nn3–n4
wording, role in performance evaluation, 143
Wyoming, performance management efforts, 55

zero-based budgeting (ZBB), 100